School Libraries and the Electronic Community

The Internet Connection

Laurel A. Clyde

The Scarecrow Press, Inc.
Lanham, Md., & London
1997

SCARECROW PRESS, INC.

Published in the United States of America
by Scarecrow Press, Inc.
4720 Boston Way
Lanham, Maryland 20706

4 Pleydell Gardens, Folkestone
Kent CT20 2DN, England

British Library Cataloguing in Publication Information Available

Library of Congress Cataloging-in-Publication Data

Clyde, Laurel A.
School libraries and the electronic community : the internet connection.
p. cm.
Includes bibliographical references and index.
ISBN 0-8108-3193-7 (pbk.: alk. paper)
1. Computer-assisted instruction—United States. I. Title.
LB 1028.43.035 1996
371.3'34—dc20 96-1438
CIP

ISBN 0–8108–3193-7 (pbk. : alk. paper)

™ The paper used in this publication meets the minimum requirements of American National Standard for Information Sciences—Permanence of Paper for Printed Library Materials, ANSI Z39.48–1984.
Manufactured in the United States of America.

CONTENTS

LIST OF TABLES

LIST OF FIGURES

LIST OF ILLUSTRATIONS

ACKNOWLEDGMENTS

The research for this book was carried out at the University of Iceland, Reykjavík, with funds from the Faculty of Social Science. A university grant provided for the purchase of the new computer equipment that was used for much of the work.

The research project, and the book, had the support of the founders and "owners" of the LM_NET listserv for "school library media people" on the Internet, and this is gratefully acknowledged. Professor Michael Eisenberg and Peter Milbury provided information throughout the project, including drafts of their own work, photographs, and advice. They also gave permission to quote from their own articles and communications.

Members of LM_NET and readers of the LM_NET discussions (105 of them in all) responded to the online questionnaire on which part of the book is based, and some provided additional information, either as attachments to their questionnaire responses or in response to follow-up messages. Direct or indirect quotations from the questionnaire responses of the following people are included in the book: Debbie Abilock; Katie Bailey; Ronald J. Bettencourt; Joseph Brockington; Margaret C. Cargo; carolan@ids.net; Melissa Davis; Diane Durbin; Lynn Evarts; Bena Fancher; Tamar Fox; Nancy Fralic; Bonnie Fulmer; Carrie Gardner; D. Gibbons; Betty Hamilton; Judith F. Harrington; Frances F. Jacobson; Rita Kaikow; Jacqueline A. C. Keith; Kathleen

M. Kentner; Diana Kisselburg; Marsha Korobkin; Bill McGee; Jane Merryman; Diane Midness; Maria Elena Ovalle; Victoria Pennell; Joni Rathbun; Mel Roseman; Kay S. Salling; Phil Shapiro; Hope Shastri; Dr. Carol Simpson; Sandal Stephenson; Stephen Titchenal; J. J. Towler; David Waters; Allison Williams; Barbara Winans.

In addition, short direct or indirect quotations from LM_NET postings by the following people are included in the book: Debbie Abilock; Dan Barron; Linda S. Bennett; Margaret C. Cargo; carolan@ids.net; Donna Carroll; Gerry Clare; Irene Clise; Stephen E. Collins; Melissa Davis; Professor Michael Eisenberg; Olga Erbe; Cynthia Foley; Bonnie Fulmer; Evie Funk; Kathy Geronzin; Patricia Gosda; Steve K. Grant; Marybeth Green; Eugene Hainer; Betty Hamilton; Tom Hart; Professor Ken Haycock; Karen Hollenshead; Doug Johnson; Rita Kaikow; Michael Kankiewicz; Amanda Carey Lucas; Beth Luikart; Bernie Lukenbill; Gloria McClanahan; Diana L. Medvitz; Jane Merryman; Donna Poole Miller; Carolyn Mitchell; Maria Elena Ovalle; Ronnie Pastecki; Linda Ramsey; Nancy Reed; Jane Rhodus; William Russell; Bill Sears; Betsy Sywetz; Gail M. Szeliga; Pamela J. Tinker; Theresa Toy; Monique Turcotte; Jan Wee; Charline Wilkins; Nancy Wissman; Jan Ziglin. All extended direct quotations (those of a sentence or more) have been acknowledged in the references at the end of each chapter.

Photographs came from a range of sources. Personal photographs were provided by LM_NET members Betty Hamilton, Director of Library Media, Brownfield High School, Brownfield, Texas, USA, and Linda C. Joseph, Library Media Specialist, Columbus Public Schools, Columbus, Ohio, USA. Edee Miller, of Bemidji Middle School, Minnesota, USA, arranged for a series of photographs to be taken at her school, to demonstrate the use of the Internet by teachers and students. Lára Stefánsdóttir (the Icelandic Education Network, Reykjavík, Iceland) arranged for photographs taken in Iceland of a 1993

KIDLINK project to be made available. The photograph of the KIDLINK activity in the north of Iceland was taken by Robyn Redman (DAGUR) and supplied by Tryggvi R. Jónsson. Malcolm Beazley AM, Founder and International President of Computer Pals Across the World, provided the Computer Pals photographs and gave permission for publication. Sue Sherif, of Fairbanks North Star Borough Public Library, Fairbanks, Alaska, USA, gave permission for her photographs, which were taken at an international seminar held at the University of Iceland in 1993, to be used.

Students in the library and information science program at the University of Iceland trialled the research questionnaire. In addition, four students (Gu›run Pálsdóttir, Ingibjörg Árnadóttir, Ingibjörg Sverrisdóttir, Ragnhildur Blöndal) in a postgraduate course on "Research in Library and Information Science" trialled the questionnaire online and provided comments on it.

Information or documents were provided for the project by a number of people, sometimes informally, and sometimes through very comprehensive reports. Particular thanks go to the following people. Jane Klobas (Graduate School of Management, University of Western Australia, Perth) provided documents electronically, particularly material related to industry developments and research methodology, and she also forwarded material from Internet listservs that she was monitoring. Henry Legedza (Angle Park Computing Centre, South Australian Department of Education, Adelaide) provided information about the Australian NEXUS online service for schools. Linda C. Joseph sent print and electronic copies of her Internet newsletter *World Link,* and information about her own Internet guide for teachers. Margaret Butterworth (Senior Lecturer in the School of Applied Science at Nanyang Technological University, Singapore) provided information about developments in Singapore schools. Malcolm Beazley sent copies of the Computer Pals Across the World newsletter, *Global Ed,* via electronic mail, and also provided copies of papers presented at international conferences. Colleen Dibley (Preolenna, Tasmania, Australia) forwarded a copy of the "Computers and High Technology" section from each Tuesday's issue of the national newspaper *The Australian*.

The following people or organizations gave permission to quote from their work or publications: Associate Professor Joyce Kirk, Head of the School of Information Studies at the University of Technology Sydney, Australia; Bill McGee, Coordinator, Hildalgo County Library System, McAllen, Texas, USA (for his electronic signature); Karen G. Schneider, Internet Trainer, Blue Highways Internet Services, New Jersey, USA; Brendan Kehoe (for the Cygnus Support Christmas tree); Debbie Abilock, Librarian/ Information Specialist, The Nueva School, Hillsborough, California, USA (for the NuevaNet Acceptable Use Policy and related documentation); Jennifer Sellers, NASA K-12 Internet Initiative, Sterling Software, Washington, DC, USA; Dana C. Rooks, Assistant Director for Administration, University of Houston Libraries, Texas, USA; and Bill Linklater, 1994 President, Australian Library and Information Association.

The following people or organizations gave permission to reproduce their World Wide Web home pages: Tim Lauer, Buckman School, Portland, Oregon, USA; Christine Collins, Hillside Elementary School, Cottage Grove, Minnesota, USA; and Stewart Noble of ERIN (for the ERIN—Australian Environmental Resources Information Network—home page).

Finally, special thanks to "my Icelandic penfriend" Patricia Hand (Vogar, Iceland), who undertook the proofreading of the final draft of the book, in return (as it turned out) for new Christmas curtains for her kitchen.

INTRODUCTION

Can we get a current list of animal species that are in danger of extinction? What scientific experiments were carried out on the last American space mission? How can I get a copy of a free software package for making big signs and notices? Can we get examples of resource-based curriculum units on water pollution for year seven classes? What was the annual average wage in Latvia just before independence, and what is it now? How can I get my class involved in an international email project in which they work with students in another country to produce a newspaper? Can I get the lyrics for the tracks on this U2 album? I need to find out what the American Bill of Rights actually says about the right to bear arms. What was the lowest temperature recorded in Antarctica last year? Worldwide, what disease or medical condition was the greatest cause of deaths in 1993? Are there any guidelines available for schools that want to link to international networks? All these questions, and many others, can be answered by using free information services available on the Internet.

Computer links can also provide the basis for professional development activities for school staff, resources for school management and curriculum implementation, and a means for communication between people in the school and their colleagues and other students around the world. From the computer on his or her desk, the school librarian can read mail and messages; check bulletin boards and newsgroups for new material of interest to members of the school community; collect information about new resources; download bibliographies, lesson plans, curriculum documents, photographs, and educational software from remote computers (computers on the other side of the city or the other side of the world); discuss school library problems and issues with other colleagues "on the net"; carry out online searches of remote databases; and plan cooperative projects with schools in other places, among other things.

The Internet, a global network of linked local, regional, and national computer networks, makes this electronic "globe-trotting" and information gathering possible. The resources, services, databases, discussion groups, conferences, news magazines, electronic reference works, and contacts on the Internet are almost infinitely varied. Amongst all this, there is much that will be of interest to school librarians and the people who use school libraries, including schoolchildren (of all ages), teachers (of all subjects), school administrators, and parent groups. There is material related to the curriculum, to current events, and to leisure interests.

It is only since around 1990 that articles about the Internet have been appearing in education journals and newsletters. At first there was just the occasional article or notice, but since the latter part of 1992, the number has increased a great deal. This is reflected in the information stored in the major online information services about publications dealing with the Internet in elementary and secondary schools. Online searches of ERIC (the Educational Resources Information Center database), LISA (Library and Information Science Abstracts), and Microcomputer Abstracts (shown as MA in the Figure I.1) on DIALOG, carried out in June 1994, revealed the following numbers of references related to the search terms "internet and school". The publications covered by the references

Figure I.1: References Related to the Internet in Schools, Found in Online Information Services

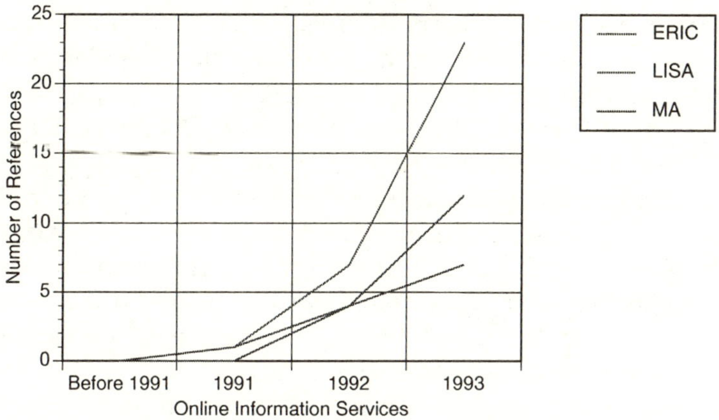

included books, periodical articles, reports, and university theses or dissertations.

Of course, some of the publications that were identified through these searches mention the Internet only briefly, while others provide detailed information. However, the number of references demonstrates a growing recognition of the idea that the Internet is something that teachers and school librarians should know about.

In addition, there is evidence of increasing interest in using the Internet. Conferences in the field of librarianship, education, and school librarianship have incorporated sessions related to the Internet. Short courses on "getting to know the Internet" are being advertised in professional newsletters. Further, the publishing of "guides to the Internet" has become a growth industry.

The Internet has become one of the hottest topics at conferences and in professional journals in a wide range of subject areas. For example, at the Tel*Ed 93 conference in Dallas, Texas, USA, in November 1993, no fewer than sixteen sessions (including preconference sessions) dealt with topics related to the Internet, while the 1993 "Databases in Schools" conference (also in November) had several sessions that covered aspects of the Internet. There have been conferences and seminars devoted solely to consideration of the Internet and its use. For example, Mecklermedia began sponsoring an annual conference in London, England, in 1993, called "Internet World and Document Delivery World", at which research or discussion papers are presented on many different aspects of the Internet and its use (including school use). For elementary and secondary school personnel, TIES (Technology and Information Education Services) in Minnesota, USA, sponsored a three-day symposium in January 1994 on "The Internet Connection: Issues and Applications in K-12 Education". A two-day conference was held in Sydney, Australia, in July 1994, on "The Information Highway and Australian Schools".

Many Internet-related books have been published, including the well-known *Zen and the Art of the Internet* by Brendan Kehoe (the third edition is now available), *The Internet Guide for New Users* by Daniel Dern, and Ed Krol's *The Whole Internet*. There are specialist journals, such as *Internet World* and *Online Access*, to keep people up to date with what is happening on the Internet. In addition, journals in professional fields, including education and librarianship, have been publishing articles about the Internet and its resources. An example is the journal *The Computing Teacher*, which has been publishing a series of articles by Judi Harris under the title "Mining the Internet".

There is also evidence on the net itself of increasing interest in the Internet. More countries are being connected to the Internet and this is apparent from the increased participation of people from developing countries in international projects based on the Internet as well as from the evidence in lists of new Internet host computers. The number of information providers on the network is increasing. Membership of discussion groups, listservs, and bulletin boards on the Internet is growing (both in terms of membership numbers and in terms of representation from a wider range of countries and groups).

"Eight years ago, cyberspace was science fiction, a word in a best-selling novel about the distant future"; today, it is "a territory where people spend large parts of their lives, working and playing" (Scott, 1992, p.D10). In 1992, the Internet was "discovered" by the mainstream news media, with, for instance, a series of articles with the theme "on the line" by Michael Scott appearing in the *Vancouver Sun*. United States vice president Al Gore has worked to promote public interest in "information superhighways" and a National Information Infrastructure. United States president Bill Clinton, Queen Elizabeth II of the United Kingdom, and the President of Spain, are well-publicised users of electronic mail. By 1993, the Internet was considered sufficiently well-established in the public mind to be the subject of cartoons: both *New Yorker* and *Time* magazine printed Internet-related cartoons in 1993, and the *Doonesbury* cartoon strip characters joined the Internet users. "The Internet global network is leading the way down the information superhighway" said the *Financial Times* on 30 November (Kehoe, 1993, p.11). With twenty million users and a million more joining them each month, "the Internet is suddenly the place to be" said *Time* on 6 December (Elmer-Dewitt 1993, p.62).

However, there is another side to the "information superhighway". One aspect of this has been described most succinctly by Louise Kehoe: "Access to vast amounts of information is not the whole answer. The power to discover the right information quickly and easily, to separate 'nice to know' from 'need to know' information is essential if information superhighway users do not drown in electronic 'junk info'" (1993, p.11). An information flood does not necessarily mean that people become informed. Information skills will be more and more important in a future where there will be more and more information to be assimilated.

Another cause for concern is that the "information superhighway" will be a one-way street to what the Toronto newspaper *The Globe and Mail,* in a cartoon in the 15 January 1994 issue, called "the lowest common denominator". This cartoon shows vehicles labeled "Home Carnage Network", "Bobbit Trial", "Geraldo", "Phone Fantasies", and "The Roadkill Channel" heading (at great speed) down the track towards the future. Already, the Internet equivalent of junk mail is something that worries many people. It would be a step backwards if this developing global communications medium simply made it easier for people to lock in to the present media programming and formats without resulting in a wider range of choices for more people.

There is no doubt that the Internet, or something like it, will be an important part of the future. However, issues of information access, equality of access, freedom of information, information quality, information skills, and the increasing gap between the "information rich" and the "information poor" (both within a society and internationally) need to be examined.

With all the books, articles, and reports that have been appearing about the Internet, why was there a need for this particular book? There are plenty of guides to the Internet and this book does not seek to replace them. Rather, it aims to meet the needs of school librarians and others responsible for library and information services in schools for a discussion of the Internet as it relates to school libraries. The need for such a book has been mentioned by several people in communications posted to the LM_NET discussion list for "school library media people" on the Internet. It is also demonstrated in the number of messages posted to the same discussion list requesting information on how school libraries are making use of the Internet.

The information in this book is based on the results of a research project carried out in 1993 from the University of

Iceland, a project that investigated school library use of the Internet and Internet resources and services for school libraries. The project had several aspects, including

- a review of the literature (material published electronically and available via the Internet, as well as printed material and other documents),
- an analysis of policy documents (from different countries and at a range of levels),
- a questionnaire survey of members of the LM_NET discussion list (a questionnaire distributed by electronic mail),
- quantitative and content analyses of Internet traffic on services related to school librarianship,
- interviews (by telephone and via electronic mail) with people who are providing or using services via the Internet, and
- the identification of Internet resources that could be useful in the school library setting.

While the strategies outlined above provided much relevant information, a great deal of time was spent online—locating potentially useful sources and services, exploring them, and describing them in relation to the information and resource needs of the school community.

The scope of the project was international (in as much as the Internet is international), and that is evident in this book. This raised a problem of terminology, particularly in relation to the English-speaking countries. In English, many different terms are used to describe the school library and the school librarian. These terms are often associated with deeply felt, and sometimes contradictory, views about the function of the school library and the role of the school librarian. This has been reflected in the many discussions on LM_NET about "what we are called". In the United States, many different terms are in current use, including "school library media specialist", "library media generalist", "school librarian", "school library media teacher", "library media consultant", "resource teacher", and just simply "librarian". In English-speaking Canada, the term "teacher librarian" has become widely accepted, but other terms are also current. In the United Kingdom, "school librarian" has usually been used to describe a chartered librarian working in a school library (or a person with minimal qualifications working in a school library), while the term "teacher librarian" has usually been used to describe a teacher without librarianship qualifications who is responsible for the school library (though there are many exceptions to this and other terms are also used). In most parts of Australia, the term "teacher librarian" is used to describe a person with dual qualifications in education and librarianship (or teacher librarianship), but the term "school librarian" is also used, along with other terms, including "resource teacher". The sources on which this project was partly based used a wide range of terminology, and it did not seem appropriate to reduce them all to the one set of terms, especially when it was clear that different people sometimes used the terms to mean different things. Consequently, the terminology used throughout the book is not consistent and reflects the sources, except that, when the discussion is general, the terms "school library" and "school librarian" have normally been used, since they are the terms that are most generally understood in the international context, and the terms that most closely reflect the usage in other European languages (from which some of the material used for the book was translated).

REFERENCES

Elmer-Dewitt, Philip (1993), "First nation in cyberspace", *Time*, 6 December, pp.62-64.

"Information superhighway", (cartoon) (1994), *The Globe and Mail*, 15 January.

Kehoe, Louise (1993), "Casting the net worldwide", *Financial Times*, 30 November, p.11.

Scott, Michael (1992), "Countdown to cyberspace blast-off", *Vancouver Sun*, 4 December, p.D10.

CHAPTER ONE

THE INTERNET

Computer networks have been in existence for more than 25 years, but it is only in the last five years that they have moved from being the province of a small number of research scientists and academics to being a resource that is used by millions of people around the world each day. The Internet has been the most publicized aspect of wide-scale networking. Discussion of it, as well as use of it, has increased in recent years, to the point where most educated people have heard of the Internet, even if they do not understand what it is. Discussion of the National Information Infrastructure in the United States has been partly responsible for the politicization of the Internet in recent times. Its increasing use in education has resulted in discussion of the Internet in educational journals and in the popular press.

What is being referred to (with little definition and sometimes with little understanding) as the "information superhighway" will be a vital link for all people who want to keep abreast of developments in the 1990s and into the next century. The Internet will be important for professionals, business people, and politicians, and it will also be increasingly important as a means of providing entertainment. Regardless of whether people are interested in current world news, want to collect the latest financial information, are looking for books in library collections, need access to local or national political information, are tracing their genealogy, want to discuss professional issues with people in other countries, are trying to find backgammon partners online, want to promote a particular point of view, or are just interested in establishing contact with people who have similar ideas or concerns, the Internet can provide the way and the means—as long as those people have access to a computer that is linked to the Internet.

WHAT IS THE INTERNET?

The Internet has become a phenomenon of the 1990s, but its beginnings date from the late 1960s, when the United States Defense Department created a national distributed network of linked computers to enable the transmission of data between researchers who were working on projects related to defense. A product of the Cold War, the network was designed by RAND Corporation expert Paul Baran to operate without a central authority, thus reducing its susceptibility to nuclear attack. It was also designed, from the beginning, to "operate while in tatters", so that in the event of an attack that disabled part of the network, it would still function effectively (Sterling, 1992). The principles that governed the design of the early network are still evident in the decentralised (some say "chaotic" or "anarchic") nature of the Internet that grew out of its successors.

During the 1970s the network grew, both in terms of the numbers of computers that were linked and in terms of the type of organizations represented. Computers in the major United States government agencies, research centers, and universities began to be linked to the existing network and to each other by dedicated data lines, so that information could be shared. The result of this was a national defense research and education network called ARPANET (Advanced Research Projects Agency Network) (since decommissioned, though many of the links remain). Through this network, communications protocols (standard ways of sending and receiving messages and files and of communicating between computers) were developed.

The success of this electronic networking, and the more widespread use of computers of all kinds in the 1980s, led first to network congestion, and then to the development of more powerful and wider high-speed networks. Five supercomputer centers were established in the United States by the National Science Foundation in 1985. Through the five computers that formed this "backbone network", local, state, and regional computer networks were linked. As time went on, more and more computers were linked to this network. Further, since most of these computers were linked in turn to other computers, the complexity of the network increased. National and international networks in Europe, Australia, Canada, the Nordic countries, and elsewhere, were linked to this growing network. By mid-1993 some 12,349 separate national and regional computer networks in more than 56 countries were linked to what has become the Internet (Bocher, 1993), and many more were linked through electronic mail gateways. In 1993, estimates of the number of users linked through the networks were in the range of ten million (Sellers and Marine, 1993); by mid-1994, it was 25 million. The spectacular growth of recent years shows no signs of slowing down.

The Internet is popularly described as a "network of networks". This is true; it is a series of more than 12 thousand interconnected computer networks around the world. The networks are owned by educational, research, government, commercial and other organizations, as well as individuals. However, the Internet is also just one of many such networks. Others have grown up, many of them linked to the Internet through "gateways", that is, computers that not only provide a physical link between the networks but also a protocol translator that enables each network to send information and files to and through the other.

Among the many networks linked to the Internet are

- USENET (begun in 1979 to link computers in North Carolina, and now a world-wide net that focuses on research and discussion),
- BITNET (begun in 1981 with the aim of linking IBM computers at the major universities in the eastern part of the United States, and now largely an academic and electronic mail network in the United States),
- EARN (a European academic network that had a similar history to BITNET),
- FidoNet (a private network of electronic bulletin boards and electronic mail systems based on MS-DOS computers, a network that relies on modems to provide direct links through the telephone lines from computer to computer), and
- FrEdMail (an international consortium of schools, universities, and colleges, that links students and their teachers around the world).

While the networks that form part of the Internet may have some form of network governance of their own, the Internet as a whole is a concept rather than an institution as such. There is no real central organization at the international level, though technical coordination has always been managed cooperatively by such organizations as Advanced Network Services Inc. and others, and the development and improvement of the TCP/IP protocols on which many Internet services are based is approved by the Internet Society. Nevertheless, it is generally true that such standards as presently exist are those that have grown up over time and come to be more or less generally accepted. The Internet came into being because technology made it possible, and before there was a general realization of what had happened. It transcends any national boundaries and any set of rules or regulations. It provides enormous possibilities for cheap electronic mail and access to information worldwide, because it is not dependent on the public telephone lines (though many users access host computers on the Internet through those lines).

Both the Internet and the proposed National Research and Education Network (NREN) in the United States are often referred to as the "information superhighway". The Internet is generally seen as the precursor to the "information superhighway". Provisions for establishing the NREN were included in the High Performance Computing Act of 1991; it is part of a broader United States government program on High Performance Computing and Communications. The NREN has always been seen as evolving from the United States Internet structure, with assistance in various forms from federal agencies and interested parties (including state agencies and telecommunications agencies). As a senator, the present vice president of the United States, Al Gore, was the NREN's major sponsor. Discussion about the NREN, and work on legislation to facilitate it, is continuing.

Although the number of Internet users outside the United States is currently growing faster than the number of United States users ("Internet grabs big share...", 1994), the Internet is still heavily based in United States computers, and this is likely to continue for the next few years. This means that policies of the United States government will influence the development of the net in the near future, just as they have done in the past. Since both President Bill Clinton and Vice President Al Gore are interested in the Internet and the development of "information superhighways", and since bills related to telecommunications and the "National Information Infrastructure" have been coming before Congress and the Senate in the last two years, it is likely that we will see many discussion papers, policy documents, and research papers related to these topics circulating in the United States and elsewhere. A gopher and a listserv have been established on the Internet for the purpose of disseminating documents and discussing issues related to the "National Information Infrastructure", and there have been statements released on the Internet from the White House. Some of the discussion has focused on the need to ensure that schools and their requirements are considered when policy is being decided. The extent to which United States decisions and policies will influence network users outside the United States is as yet unclear, and to a certain extent it may depend on the growth of the Internet outside the United States.

Contrary to popular belief, the Internet is not "free". Some networks that are part of the Internet are funded by government agencies for the use of scholars and researchers. The academic networks, such as AARNet in Australia, are mainly funded through the government budget allocations for universities and colleges. Other networks are partially funded by government agencies (such as the National Science Foundation in the United States) to provide support for research and tertiary education. However, each institution, organization, company/corporation, or individual person who has access to the Internet has either paid for that access through an information service provider, or had it paid for on their behalf. Because many organizations do not pass the charges on to end users in their organizations, and because some agreements prohibit the passing on of Internet charges to libraries within organizations, a perception has grown up that Internet access is "free". Directly or indirectly everyone pays somehow. However, once a user is connected to the Internet, much of the information available on the net, and the services, software, and files accessible through the net, are free.

Despite the relatively free-form structure of the Internet, there are some tools, resources, and services that help people to "navigate", to get electronic mail to its intended destination, to establish contact with groups and organisations that share their interests, to link with remote computers, and to find documents and files on the hundreds of thousands of computers. These tools, resources, and services are described in Chapter Two; they include telnet, gopher, ftp (file transfer protocol), listservs, and World Wide Web.

However, people still face enormous problems when coming to terms with the Internet. Not the least of these is finding out what to do and where to look for information. In relation to this, Internet pioneer Brendan Kehoe noted in his 1992 book, *Zen and the Art of the Internet*, that "the largest problem people face when first using a network is grasping all that's available. Even seasoned users find themselves surprised when they discover a new service or feature that they've never known even existed" (p.5). It does not help new users to be told that "all the help you need is available on the net" when they have not yet learned the basics of network navigation. Unfortunately, by the time people have discovered the "help" tools on the Internet, they have often passed beyond the stage when those tools would have been of most help. This explains the enormous popularity of printed guides to the Internet, despite the fact that they are likely to be more outdated than most tools available on the net.

THE GROWTH OF THE INTERNET

Regardless of how they are presented, Internet growth figures sound wonderfully impressive. While it is obvious that growth in the number of computers linked to the net, the number of users, and the amount of information transmitted has been enormous, many of the figures quoted give little idea of what is actually being measured or counted, by whom, and for what purpose. This makes it difficult to make comparisons over time, since figures published at different dates by different authorities (or even by the same authority) may be based on counts of different things.

However, some of the analyses of growth do carry more authority than others, because the people involved were experts, the methodology is known, and the information has been widely accepted and quoted. Information collected by Mark Lottor for the Network Systems Information Center, SRI International, in California, showed that in 1981, there were 213 host computers registered as being linked to the Internet. Host computers are the large computers through which organizations or other users (such as those in schools) gain access to the Internet. By 1989, the number was 80,000; in October 1990 there were 313,000; only three months later, in January 1991, there were 376,000; and by January 1992 there were 727,000 registered computers on the Internet (Lottor, 1992). In March 1993, Thomas F. Mandel, a futurist with SRI International, noted that "the Internet is now doubling in size each year. The entire global electronic matrix, which includes the Internet, will probably reach more than 500 million users by the end of this century" (Mandel, 1993).

For much of the last decade, Lottor has executed a program every three months that is designed to reach a host computer at every possible Internet address and to make a count. However, even this method does not result in a complete record, because some of the host computers that are connected to the Internet are "hidden" from the net and thus not reachable by Lottor's program. His count is therefore described as being of "hosts reachable". By the northern autumn of 1993, the number of "hosts reachable" on the Internet exceeded two million. The growth rate of "hosts reachable" was 5 percent per month. This figure has remained steady over the last few years, though it should be noted that a steady percentage increase will result in a greater numerical increase each month ("Internet grabs big share...", 1994).

Table 1.1 shows Internet growth (that is, the growth in the number of host computers linked to the Internet) from 1969 (the beginnings of the Internet) to October 1993. The Table is based on numbers cited by Robert H. Zakon in his "Internet Timeline" (1994) with additions (Rutkowski,

Table 1.1
Host Computers Linked to the Internet

DATE	NUMBER OF HOSTS
1969	4
April 1971	23
June 1974	62
March 1977	111
August 1981	213
May 1982	235
August 1983	562
October 1984	1024
October 1985	1961
February 1986	2038
November 1986	5089
December 1987	28,174
July 1988	33,000
October 1988	56,000
January 1989	80,000
July 1989	130,000
October 1989	159,000
October 1990	313,000
January 1991	376,000
July 1991	535,000
October 1991	617,000
January 1992	727,000
April 1992	890,000
July 1992	992,000
October 1992	1,136,000
January 1993	1,313,000
April 1993	1,486,000
July 1993	1,776,000
October 1993	2,056,000
January 1994	2,217,000
July 1994	3,225,177
October 1994	3,898,233

1994). Although no one specific source is given by Zakon for this particular information, the numbers appear to agree with those given by Lottor and NSFNet.

These figures, which represent international totals, give a picture of the growth of the Internet as a whole, but they hide the massive growth of the Internet outside the United States in the last two years. While growth within the United States has slowed a little (to 80 percent in 1992), growth elsewhere in the world has been increasing. The rate of growth has been greatest in Australia, which at the end of 1993 was the fourth largest user of the Internet, measured in terms of Australian traffic over the North American backbone network (NSFNET Backbone Service..., 1994). However, in the United Kingdom, the number of hosts increased by 200 percent in 1992 (to around 58,000 by the end of the year), and the rate of increase in the number of hosts in Japan in the same year was 170 percent (to nearly 24,000 by the end of the year) (Mandel, 1993). Other countries where there was very significant growth include Canada, Iceland, Finland, and New Zealand.

While overall, the rate of growth in the United States may have slowed a little in 1992/93, statistics released in April 1994 by the Internet Society showed that in just the preceding month, usage of the Internet's NSF (National Science Foundation) North American backbone increased by 20.7 percent, the "largest single jump in the history of the Internet", ("Internet statistics, 1994") while international gopher use grew by 17.6 percent during March and World Wide Web use increased by 32.9 percent in that month.

In December 1993, Win Treese made "The Internet Index" available on the net. This presented figures for Internet growth, collected from various sources; some of these figures were serious, and some, not-so-serious. The average time between new networks connecting to the Internet was ten minutes by the end of 1993. By December 1993, approximately 137 countries were reachable by electronic mail. Among the less-than-serious figures given by Treese (which nevertheless present an image of the changing Internet) were the number of online coffee shops in San Francisco (that is, coffee shops where patrons can drink coffee and use computers to access the Internet for a fee) (18); the cost for four minutes of Internet time at those coffee shops ($0.25); and the length of the round-the-Internet trip from Digital's American headquarters to the electronic mail address `mcmvax.mcmurdo.gov` in McMurdo, Antarctica (640 milliseconds, with 16 "hops" from computer to computer).

In 1993 and 1994 many analysts and commentators produced statistics or comparisons to show various aspects of Internet growth. The following are examples:

- The electronic journal EDUPAGE, early in 1994, cited a report in *Boardwatch*, a magazine that covers issues associated with electronic bulletin boards and online information services, as showing that the number of electronic bulletin boards in the United States doubled to 60,000 in the eighteen months from August 1992 to February 1994. At that time, an average of more than 12 million Americans called into a bulletin board every day. Not all these bulletin boards were connected to the Internet, of course, but many were.
- A basic analysis of gopher connections showed that, by February 1994, more than one hundred publicly accessible gophers were provided by the United States government or its agencies (Boyer, 1994).
- When Ed Krol wrote the 1992 edition of his book *The Whole Internet*, he mentioned that there were about one hundred gophers in existence. On 28 November 1993, Dick St. Peters wrote that "as of a few minutes ago, there have been 902 new gophers listed just since the beginning of October!"
- Between January and December 1993, use of the World Wide Web (measured in bytes of traffic across the NSF North American backbone) increased by a factor of 187;

in December 1993, the Web ranked 11th among Internet services in terms of bytes of traffic, whereas a year before, it had ranked 127th (How Popular is the Web?, 1994).

- The commercial online service, America Online, which is linked to the Internet, has experienced such rapid growth that there were even reports of "traffic jams on the information highway", though if this was the case, it does not seem to have bothered the many new users. America Online's user population was reported, on 1 March 1994, as having "doubled from 300,000 since last summer" ("Traffic jams...", 1994).

As the networks have grown, so has the amount of "traffic" passing through them. In December 1993, ten terabytes of data, that is, "the equivalent of 5 billion pages", passed over the central backbone of the Internet in the United States, the National Science Foundation network (NSFNet), according to statistics collated by NSFNet. This included electronic mail, USENET newsgroups, file transfers, the use of Internet browsers such as gopher, and World Wide Web. ("Internet grabs big share...", 1994). The traffic in December 1991 was just over 2.5 terabytes, and in December 1992, nearly 5.5 terabytes.

The growth in network usage that is apparent from these figures is reflected in the usage statistics that are available for particular services. In fact, the uptake in usage of a new information source can be very rapid. For example, on 25 January 1994, it was announced that the California Legislative Information files were available online through the InfoSlug, the gopher of the University of California, Santa Cruz. Included in the files were the State Constitution, Senate and Assembly Bills, the California Code and Statutes, and various directories and guides to the legislative process. By Tuesday 22 February, after only 26 days (there were two days of system downtime early in February), the following accesses had been recorded (Watkins, 1994):

Guide to Government	12,148
California Code	9,219
California Bills	2,873
California Dailyfile	815
California Statutes	148

It should be noted that, though these figures are impressive for a new service (and one that, it was claimed by those who opposed the California Bill AB1624 that made the provision of electronic access to legislative information a requirement, would never be used by "anyone except a few elite computer nerds"), they by no means reflect the likely total online usage of California Legislative Information. InfoSlug is just one of several gophers that carries this information (information that is made available in electronic form by the California Legislative Data Center).

In 1993, the Internet recorded several notable "firsts", events that demonstrate its increasing importance as a medium of information transfer and communication. In the United States, the White House came online. On 2 March, United States president Bill Clinton became the first president to send an electronic mail message, though the first known public electronic mail message to be sent by a head of state was sent some years earlier by Queen Elizabeth II of the United Kingdom. On 21 May, the first National Public Radio program was broadcast simultaneously on the Internet. In early 1994 United States vice president Al Gore became the first vice president (or holder of one of the leading offices of the country) to "meet the general public" through a computer conference or "electronic town meeting", when he answered questions live online via keyboard on 13 January in a session hosted by US News Online and CompuServe; the conference was also carried on live television by C-SPAN, and transcripts were posted to the Internet by the White House. New York Governor Mario Cuomo also chalked up a first in January 1994 when his "State of the State" address to the New York legislature was available to Internet users through the New York State Library gopher the same day.

THE INTERNET AND LIBRARIES

In an interview that was posted to the Internet in November 1993, Barry Shein commented that "The Internet is all about information. So are librarians and libraries.... Having enormous amounts of information online is not much use if you can't figure out how to get to it. Librarians are trained professionals in the art and science of connecting people with the right information. I would say that ... the Internet is almost a birthright of the librarians". Yet while some librarians have accepted this idea, in part or totally, others have not yet taken note of it. Even where the idea has been accepted, the use of the Internet ranges from simply searching for information in response to reference questions, to making the library's catalog available online, to providing Internet access for library patrons, to embracing the concept of the "virtual library".

It is in terms of the use of the Internet to answer reference questions and to provide information services that its acceptance has been greatest in libraries of all kinds. To illustrate the potential of the Internet as a source of information, Karen G. Schneider carried out a survey in 1993 through the PUBLIB listserv for public librarians on the Internet, the LIBREF-L listserv for reference librarians, and GAYLIB-N. She asked readers to send in their Internet success stories—descriptions of cases where a librarian had used the Internet to answer a reference question from a patron. She compiled the results into a document, "Twenty-two Internet Reference Success Stories", which was posted to PUBLIB and other listservs in September 1993. While some of the respondents were working in large libraries that might have been expected to be making use of the Internet, others were working in small libraries. One response indicated that the library would never have the space to print copies of some of the sources they used on the Internet, including hard copies of United States federal laws and regulations. The reference success stories covered a wide range of topics and involved the use of an equally wide range of Internet sources. Among them were searches for copyright information, a request for a copy of the text of Clinton's health care plan, a request to verify the lyrics of a Guns 'n' Roses song, the regular provision of census information to patrons, a request for the proceedings of a particular conference, a question about HIV testing for a child born to an at-risk mother, a high school project that required the geographical coordinates of a United States city, an anthropologist's need for information about women in pastoral systems in Africa, and a request for information about creating a ceremonial mace at university commencement and its use.

A Seattle Public Library staff member was one of the respondents to the Schneider survey, reporting a "success story" involving an Internet search for agricultural information. However, the Seattle Public Library is one of those libraries that has taken the idea of Internet applications further (Taylor, 1993). This library provides Internet access for library patrons (as reported in September 1993), through the menus of its online public access catalog. The Dynix library automation system, which is used at Seattle, enables libraries to provide access to a wide range of services and databases through the public access catalog, including Internet access; this is an option that has, at this stage, been implemented by only a small proportion of the libraries that are using Dynix. The option appears on the two hundred terminals in the Seattle library system, as well as on the menu that is seen by patrons who dial in from home using a modem. At the time of writing, users were offered an initial choice of eight or nine Internet gophers, but through those gophers or "destinations" they had access to an enormous range of other services worldwide. An idea of the extent of public interest in the Internet access option can be gleaned from the library's usage statistics: in August 1993, "about one-fifth" of the 260,000 selections from the online public access catalog menu was from the Internet connection. Neither public electronic mail nor file transfer facilities were offered, nor were there plans to do so, since this would involve considerable staff time in training and education. However, the library was looking at mounting its own gopher to provide public information, as the Cleveland Public Library had already done.

Meanwhile, in December 1993, the New York State Librarian, Joseph F. Shubert, made a public announcement (via a media release posted to the Internet) that took the idea of the Internet and its relationship to libraries a step further, to the idea of "electronic doorway libraries" for New York State. A report that had been prepared for the library service defined an electronic doorway library as one that

> uses computer telecommunications technology, a full range of library resources and the services of skilled librarians to meet the library and information needs of business, government, and people of all ages, background and interest and abilities, extending services into people's homes, work places, and other locations, going beyond the library's walls to obtain information and resources, facilitating access by people with disabilities, and providing powerful new ways of assembling, evaluating and using information.

The assumptions on which the report was based include the assumption that "the library and information environment in the nation is being radically transformed by computers and telecommunications"; the assumption that "electronic information resources are becoming primary sources of information, along with books, journals and other printed information"; and the assumption that "computer-literate New Yorkers of all ages demand access to electronic information".

The concept of the "virtual library" takes these ideas

still further, though it is important to note that, at this stage, the virtual library remains a "vision of the library of the future" (Rooks, 1993, p.22) rather than an established and workable basis for library service today. While the term "virtual library" has come to mean different things to different people, a definition that has gained some currency is that of Rooks, for whom the basis of the virtual library is the "universal application of advanced high-speed computing and telecommunications capabilities" to provide access to information resources and to deliver information. "Carried to its ultimate end", says Rooks, the virtual library "offers a universe of information to any user, anywhere in the world, at any time of the day or night through the power of a personal computer with telecommunication capabilities".

However, there are currently barriers to the full implementation of this concept, some of which are identified by Rooks. These include problems associated with actually locating specific information on the Internet (and the lack of easy-to-use and precise search tools); the willingness and capability of libraries to contribute to the shared resources and services; cost factors and funding; the willingness of library staff to develop new skills; and the general lack of appreciation, within the community as a whole, of information as a resource. In addition, there are people who, while acknowledging that libraries will change, feel that the virtual library is not necessarily the best model for the library of the future.

THE INTERNET AND EDUCATION

Communications technology can serve many purposes in education. It can be a key factor in creating new and stimulating learning environments for students. It can also be important in creating a new professional development culture for teachers, and in providing both impetus and support for school reform and restructuring and the development of the school as a "community of learners". Where the Internet is already a part of the educational process, its influence can be seen in teacher attitudes, teaching methods, classroom practice and activities, information provision and use, student involvement in learning, and inservice education of teachers. These aspects will be discussed further in later chapters of this book.

In the United States, Canada, the United Kingdom, Australia, and other countries, the idea of school reform has been discussed. In some places, it has become an essential part of educational policy. While the terms "school reform" and "school restructuring" have different meanings in different places, they illustrate a widespread concern that today's school education is failing both students (who are seen as emerging from an educational process that is not equipping them with the skills they will need in tomorrow's world) and the community (whose expectations are so often not being met by the processes of formal education). In May 1993, in sponsoring the United States Technology for Education Act, Senator Edward Kennedy alluded to some aspects of these issues. He noted that:

> Our children are trying to learn in the 1990s with classroom techniques of the 1950s. If we genuinely want to prepare them for the workforce of the future, the schools of today cannot teach with yesterday's technology. In Massachusetts, a number of model schools are already in the forefront, using technology in the classroom in creative and innovative ways that expand the curriculum of its students. But in most schools, high-tech classrooms are rare. In few other important institutions in our society do professionals have such limited access to modern technology as teachers in our schools today. Last month teachers from Williamstown, Massachusetts told me they don't even have access to telephones, let alone fax machines or computers for students to use information networks. If we are to meet the National Education Goals we have established for the year 2000 and regain our competitive edge in the workplace, we must enable our students in classrooms to tap the immense potential of contemporary technology.

Because the Internet can help to shift the focus of classroom education away from the teacher-as-expert model towards one of shared responsibility for learning, it can become a vital part of school reform. Other technologies have been seen in this role in the past, of course. However, the Internet presents a situation in which no one can sustain the role of expert, simply because it provides ready access to such a wide range of resources and expertise, and its use virtually requires that people be ready to explore and to discover new techniques, new information, and new ideas. Much of the current trend of school reform relates to attempts to move away from teacher isolation to teacher collaboration, both in the classroom and within the school, and also outside the school. It also attempts to change ideas about education and learning, in several ways. While many good teachers everywhere have long held these ideas, for others accustomed to structured and formal educational organizations and structured management, they are new. Ideas about learning are moving away from the idea that it is an activity that occurs just within the context of the school, and towards the idea of learning in a life context. They are also moving away from a focus on subject content and towards a focus on concepts and skills, away from an emphasis on knowing the answers to a small range of questions, and towards a focus on the ability to find out and to use sources of information to answer new questions as they arise. The skills of a lifelong learner include the skills of locating information, assessing the value of information, and working collaboratively with others whose expertise complements that of the learner. The Internet can be used within the educational setting to help to achieve these shifts, and its use in the educational setting will provide students with skills that will be directly related to their needs in the future.

The following quotation, from a 1993 draft document on "Elementary and Secondary School Internet User Frequently Asked Questions" (Sellers and Marine, 1993), will give some idea of the ways in which the use of the Internet is shaping today's educational ideas and practice.

> The Internet expands classroom resources dramatically by making many resources from all over the world available to students, teachers, and media specialists, including original source materials. It brings information, data, images, and even computer software into the classroom from places otherwise impossible to reach, and it does this almost instantly. Access to these resources can yield individual and group projects, collaboration, curriculum materials, and idea sharing not found in schools without Internet access. Internet access also makes possible contact with people all over the world, bringing into the classroom experts in every content area, new and old friends, and colleagues in education. With an Internet connection, your site can become a valuable source of information as well. The isolation inherent in the teaching profession is well known among educators. By having access to colleagues in other parts of the world, as well as to those who work outside of classrooms, educators able to reach the Internet are not as isolated. A hands-on classroom tool, the use of networks can be a motivator for students in and of itself, and their use encourages the kind of independence and autonomy that many educators agree is important for students to achieve in their learning process. Because the Internet is blind to class, race, ability, and disability, it is a natural for addressing the needs of all students; exactly how this is done will vary from school to school as the school empowers the individual.

Although this document has since been re-issued in new versions, this particular passage remains valid as an indication of what was possible at the time that the survey of LM_NET members (described in later chapters) was being carried out.

The Texas Education Network (TENET) has had a great impact on educational administration and educational practice in that state, and in 1993, more than 15,000 educators in that American state were linked to the Internet through TENET. This is reflected in the fact that the largest group of members of LM_NET, the discussion group for school library personnel on the Internet, come from TENET. Patsy Lanclos, a TENET trainer, is quoted (LaQuey and Ryer, 1992, p.15) as saying that

> I think that one of the greatest things I have seen regarding TENET and the Internet is the enthusiasm it has put back into teachers. Teachers who were tired and worn have suddenly been retread and are ready to roll! They are out there creating new and innovative lessons incorporating telecommunications of all kinds. They are taking risks. They are asking for the unthinkable—telephone lines in the classrooms and computers! They want to belong. It has created a wonderful network of support.

Further, these teachers have come to expect that current information will be available to them and their classes almost immediately. From the dismantling of the Berlin Wall to the California earthquakes, they have come to anticipate immediate involvement. They have also come to expect that they will be able to use electronic reference works, archives of lesson plans, research documents, government press releases, and other sources of information available through the Internet, as well as electronic mail communications.

The number of resources on the Internet that are directed specifically at elementary and secondary schools are increasing. There are gophers that have been established with the specific purpose of providing education and curriculum information to teachers and school administrators. Some of these provide lesson plans, computer software, and other classroom resources, as well as information. Among these gophers are Canada's SchoolNet, the CICNet K-12 gopher in Michigan, and the Empire Schoolhouse gopher of NYSERNet in New York State. In addition, gophers established for the benefit of the whole education community, such as the AskERIC gopher in Syracuse, New York, and the Education Gopher at Florida Tech, provide a wide range of resources for schools. Gophers established to make resources available in particular subject fields are usually designed to cater to the needs of a wide range of users, only some of whom may be school users, but, nevertheless, these gophers often contain a great deal of useful information at a range of levels. Examples are the Australian Environmental Information Network (ERIN) gopher, the Israel Information Service gopher, and the Smithsonian Institution's Natural History gopher. There are listservs (Internet discussion groups) that cater to the needs of teachers, school administrators, careers advisers, and other school personnel (including, for instance, one for school janitors). There are listservs related to many different aspects of the school curriculum or school activities—including listservs for the discussion of children's literature, educational technology, children with disabilities, or the use of electronic mail in education. Other Internet resources that provide information that can be used in classroom activities include electronic bulletin boards, community freenets, electronic journals and magazines, and World Wide Web services (which usually incorporate graphics and other media as well as text).

There are tools available that will help new users in schools to explore the Internet and its resources. These include Internet guides and directories (available online through the Internet itself), and Internet services such as gopher and World Wide Web. Information search tools include WAIS, gopher, VERONICA, and whois. Chapter Two of this book provides information that will help school librarians to locate resources and to identify tools that will help them to make better use of the Internet.

ACCESS TO THE INTERNET

Access to the Internet is normally through a local area network (LAN) of microcomputers (within a school or other organization) linked to a host computer on the Internet. The host computer might be a large computer in a university or college, a computer that supports a statewide network, a computer accessed through a commercial Internet access provider, a community freenet, or any one of a number of other options. Schools in different geographic locations will have very different options. At the most basic level, access to the Internet requires a microcomputer (any kind), a modem, communications and/or networking software, and either a telephone line (to access a host computer on the Internet) or a link to a host computer that is linked to the Internet. Within a school, a LAN of microcomputers might be linked to the Internet by various means, particularly in a situation where a school district or library authority provides an Internet connection for the school. The costs for schools will include hardware costs, software costs, costs of maintaining hardware and software, plus any subscription fee for Internet access (set by the access provider, whether a university or college, commercial organization, or educational or library network), plus any telephone charges. Clearly, the closer a school is to the host computer or network through which it has access to the Internet, the lower the telephone charges will be.

Many Internet users have access through a host computer in a university or college, or through a regional or educational network (such as TENET or VA PEN in the United States or NEXUS in Australia or Íslenska menntaneti› in Iceland). Users who do not have the benefit of an institutional or network link get their access in a variety of ways. This may be through a commercial provider (such as Delphi or America Online in the United States or Mindlink in Canada), through a community freenet (such as the Victoria Free-Net in British Columbia, Canada, or Freenet Finland), or public library or other public access site (Seattle Public Library is one of several American public libraries that provides Internet access for patrons through its online public access catalog menu), or through a professional association.

The costs of Internet access can vary. Library networks or education networks may provide unlimited access either free or for a monthly fee. Some universities provide accounts for graduates, or for members of local professional associations, or for local schools, for a monthly fee. Some commercial providers charge as little as US$15 a month for Internet electronic mail access. However, Internet access is not always readily available, or available at reasonable prices, particularly in developing countries, or in the more remote areas of developed countries. Even in large cities in developed countries, such as the United States, access to telephone services in schools may be so poor that Internet access is effectively impossible. This issue needs to be addressed in different ways in different places, but it does not negate the basic idea that access to the Internet can provide information and services that are available in no other way.

When a school's Internet connection has been established, the access provider (whether a university or college, an education authority, a community freenet, a commercial access provider, or other provider) will supply a copy of their "Acceptable Use Policy" or a set of rules or guidelines that perform a similar function. This document will explain what the school is and is not allowed to do with their Internet connection. It will usually contain a statement that the school cannot use the connection for illegal purposes, and may state that the connection cannot be used for commercial purposes. In addition, there may be restrictions on what kinds of information can be provided to different groups of people, including minors, and there may be copyright restrictions on the uses of some kinds of information. There may be a requirement that users under the age of 18 are supervised. To support this, the school will need to develop a school-wide policy on Internet access and use. This will be particularly important where parents are worried that their children will be unwittingly exposed, through Internet use, to materials of which the parents disapprove, or that access to the Internet will not be available equally to all members of the school community.

The information provided in this book is, of necessity, general. Given the nature of the Internet, it is impossible to provide directions for Internet access and use that meet every case. Software and hardware used locally will affect the ways in which things are done and the type of access that a user has. In addition, the rules established by the access provider, and the procedures required, will affect access and use. This explains a recurring comment on Internet listservs or discussion groups: "I did what you said, but it didn't work for me". What works in one place may not work in another, simply because the systems have been set up differently, or because the access software is different.

Difficult as it can be in some circumstances, physical access to the Internet (the hardware, the telephone lines, the links to a host computer) is only one part of the process—and sometimes the easiest part. More complex is the area of intellectual access—developing an appreciation of the value of the Internet and online sources, and developing the skills necessary to access those sources and to use them in the context of the school's educational program. Ultimately, the difficulties involved in intellectual access may be a greater barrier to Internet use than the problems of physical access. There are solutions to both, of course, and this book will discuss these in several chapters. However, it can be more difficult to change people and their ideas than to acquire the necessary hardware and links in the school.

Nevertheless, any plan for introducing the use of the Internet in schools, and for its ongoing use, should cover the aspect of staff development, as well as such aspects as hardware, software, and an ongoing budget. This will include training for the school librarians and any school library staff. Bill Linklater, the 1994 president of the Australian Library and Information Association, has commented that

> There is an urgent and pressing need for professional development for those librarians who currently lack both access to the networks, and an awareness of the value of the data on these networks to their professional roles. Those librarians working in public and school

> libraries are two particularly important groups in this context. The appropriate use of networks and the library's role in using the facilitating use of the networks is probably the best opportunity that we have had in the last ten years to re-assert or re-establish our professional roles in the management of information access.

However, all potential users of the Internet will need some kind of training, whether they are teachers, school librarians, students, school administrators, volunteers, or others who have a role within the school. In addition, parents will need some familiarization with the Internet and its resources, if they are to be supportive of the efforts of the school in introducing access to communications technology.

Depending on the hardware involved, and the technological commitment to Internet access within the school, there may also be the need for technical support. Some education authorities, school districts, or local authorities, are beginning to provide this at the district or local level. Some schools rely on volunteers from business or industry. And some support is available over the net itself, through listservs, USENET newsgroups, documents available through gophers, and even through formal courses conducted by electronic mail through the Internet. However, where it is not provided by a central authority, finding this support can be very difficult, simply because few people yet have high level skills in this field, and some people who need the support lack the skills to find it. Yet many schools have found that using the Internet is in itself an educational experience that leads to the development of these skills within the school community. And many school librarians around the world have discovered that they have built a reputation as Internet experts (and information technology experts) on the basis of what were initially extremely low-level skills, but skills coupled with a willingness to learn and to learn with others.

Even for those who use the Internet on a regular basis, there is another factor to be considered in making use of its resources in the educational setting. The Internet is always growing, and the facilities and services available are in a state of constant change. Any information provided about Internet tools and services is, by its nature, out-of-date before it is published. New services are being made available each day. New tools provide new ways of doing things, and new ways of accessing information. For those who thrive on change, the Internet is fascinating and exciting. For those who like to have things documented and explained, the Internet is constantly frustrating. This is the "digital frontier", and it is not for nothing that Internet users are often referred to as "explorers" or even "Internauts". The Internet foreshadows a world in which the skills required for coping with change may be more important than any other skill.

THE FUTURE

In his testimony to the United States House of Representatives Subcommittee on Science Hearing on the High Performance Computing and High Speed Networking Act of 1993, Professor Edward D. Lazowska said that

> Advances in high performance computing and communications have been phenomenal ... [but] As phenomenal as these advances have been, "you ain't seen nothin' yet"... It's incredibly difficult to accurately predict this kind of progress. I recently ran across a chart from 1972 that synthesized a number of "expert predictions" concerning progress in "large scale" computing. The experts' predictions for 1990—which undoubtedly seemed wild back in 1972—turned out to be low by a factor of about 25 both for memory capacity and for processing speed! And the experts' predictions for the year 2000 are a factor of 1000 below current estimates for where we will be by then. But as difficult as it is to predict this kind of progress, it's even more difficult to forecast the changes that will be brought about by such progress.

Yet we continue to try, partly because it helps us to plan for a future that we know will be very different from the past.

Many commentators see the Internet, or a more advanced version of it, as the centerpiece in a worldwide network of technologies. We will see the increasing convergence of familiar technologies, along with the development of new technologies, all linked through communications networks. The distinctions between telephone, television, cable television, the VCR, audio technologies, the microcomputer, CD-ROM, photocopying, fax, electronic mail will become more and more blurred. On 24 January 1994, *Business Week* reported (Ziegler, p.37) that the American company AT&T was working on a "souped-up phone" which would form the center of a "home-information network", linking the home to the "information superhighway", and supporting a television set, a video recorder, a microcomputer, and other devices. Companies are known to be working on telephones that will have memories and be capable of sending and receiving messages in formats other than voice. On the other hand, the AV Macintosh computers, released in late 1993, have the capability for voice mail, electronic mail, answering machine, speaker phone, video conferencing, fax, and television, as well as producing multimedia presentations and responding to voice commands ("All-media marvel...", 1993, pp.1–2). Other companies are working on computers with equally wide-ranging capabilities. Electronic mail will soon be able to handle the transmission of voice, television, faxes, and radio programming; already, most of this is possible.

What all this means is that the information flood will become a deluge, and this may not necessarily be to the advantage of everyone. It will not be a deluge of information that is immediately useful to the people who receive it; rather, the Internet has already taught us that it will be a deluge of miscellaneous material, some of it of marginal value, and much of it just "noise", that is, information of so little value that it is a nuisance rather than a help. This "noise" may even be dangerous, in that it will prevent many people from getting to the information that is worthwhile and useful in their settings. At the same time, while many people are even now aware that there is an enormous amount of information available online, this awareness is not of much value if those people cannot get to the information that they actually need. For people without appropriate knowledge and skills for this new information age, the information flood might just as well be an information drought. People who are unable to use the information will be severely disadvantaged against those who have developed the skills to take advantage of what the new developments in technology are offering.

In this world, information skills will be at a premium, but they will not necessarily be the skills that are currently taught as information skills in schools. At present, information skills instruction tends to be based on the idea of inquiry learning, a process of formulating questions, and locating, evaluating, and using information to answer those questions. In a situation where, regardless of the questions, people are faced with a mass of information that may or may not be relevant, new skills will be required, including skills for information access, evaluation, and use, but also skills of exploration, organization, assimilation. These information skills will become more and more important if people are to be able to cope with, and use, the information that will be coming at them in many different forms.

REFERENCES

ALA Proposes Plan to FCC to Connect Schools and Libraries to NII 1994, ALAWON (ALA Washington Office Newsletter) 3, no. 36, 20 July.

"All-media marvel—the new AV Macintosh" (1993), *Apple Australia Education News*, Spring, pp.1–2.

Bocher, Robert (1993), The Internet, NREN and Current Networking

Issues, Paper written for distribution in the Internet Room at the American Library Association Conference, 1993, and subsequently posted to the PUBLIB listserv on the Internet, 26 July.

Boyer, Calvin (1994), US Government Gopher Servers, Message posted to the Net-Happenings listserv on the Internet, 15 February.

"Burgeoning bulletin boards" (1994), EDUPAGE (an electronic journal on the Internet), 17 February.

Calcari, Susan (1994), "A snapshot of the Internet", *Internet World*, September, pp.54–58.

Carey, John, et al. (1994), "Yield signs on the info interstate", *Business Week*, 24 January, pp.88–90.

Carroll, Jim (1994), The Information Highway is a Bunch of Hooey, Article posted to the Net-Happenings listserv on the Internet, 21 July.

Ciuffetti, Peter (1993), "The future of electronic libraries: beyond file server technology", paper delivered at the Information Online and On Disc Conference, Sydney, January. (Copy of the conference proceedings provided on CD-ROM at the conference).

How Popular is the Web? (1994), Document made available on the World Wide Web, May.

"Internet grabs big share of global market" (1994), *The Internet Letter*, 1, 5, 1 February, pp.1, 3.

"Internet statistics: the new keeps growing and growing" (1994), EDUPAGE, 28 April.

Kehoe, Brendan (1992), *Zen and the Art of the Internet*, Copy downloaded via ftp from the Internet, February. (Document subsequently conventionally published in an amended version).

Kennedy, Edward M. Senator (1993), Statement on the Introduction of Technology for Education Act of 1993, Document posted to the EDTECH listserv on the Internet, 8 June.

Krol, Ed (1992), *The Whole Internet: User's Guide and catalog*, O'Reilly and Associates, Sebastopal, Cal.

LaQuey, Tracy and Ryer, Jeanne C. (1992), The Internet Companion: A Beginner's Guide to Global Networking, The Online Bookstore Edition, Addison-Wesley, and subsequently available in printed editions.

Lazowska, Edward D. (1993), Statement of Edward D. Lazowska, Professor of Computer Science and Engineering at the University of Washington and Member of the Board of Directors, Computing Research Association to the US House of Representatives Subcommittee on Science Hearing on the High Performance Computing and High Speed Networking Act of 1993, HR 1757, Document posted to the LM_NET listserv on the Internet, 3 June.

Linklater, Bill (1994), "Front line", *InCite*, 4 March, p.4.

Lottor, Mark (1992), Internet Growth (1981–1991), Network Working Group Request for Comments, RFC 1296, Network Information Systems Center, SRI International, Menlo Park, California, January.

Mandel, Thomas F. (1993), Surfing the Wild Internet, Document created for SRI International, and available on the gopher of the Ontario Institute for Studies in Education (OISE), March 1994.

NSFNET Backbone Service Traffic Distribution by Country, February (1994), available via ftp from NIC.MERIT.EDU in the path nsfnet/statistics/1994/nsf-9402.country

NSFNET Traffic Distribution Highlights, March (1994), available via ftp from NIC.MERIT.EDU in the path /nsfnet/statistics/1994/nsf-9403.highlights

Rooks, Dana (1993), "The virtual library: pitfalls, promises, and potential", *The Public-Access Computer Systems Review,* 4, no. 5, pp.22–29. (Copy downloaded via electronic mail from LISTSERV@UHUPVM1.UH.EDU on the Internet, 16 November).

Rutkowski, Tony (1994), Press Release: Internet Survey Reaches 3.8 Million Internet Host Level, 3rd Quarter 1994 Growth is 21 Percent, Message posted to the Net-Happenings listserv on the Internet, 6 November.

St. Peters, Dick (1993), "Wired" Gopher and Infobot, Message posted to the Net-Happenings listserv on the Internet, 28 November.

Schneider, Karen G. (1993), Twenty-two Internet Reference Success Stories, Document posted to the PUBLIB listserv on the Internet, 24 September. In the first half of 1994, Schneider carried out a second electronic survey, and posted the results as "Internet Reference Success Stories, Part Deux".

Shubert, Joseph F. (1993), State Report Depicts Plan for Electronic Doorway Libraries, Public announcement posted to the PUBLIB listserv on the Internet, 4 December.

Sellers, Jennifer and Marine, April (1993), Elementary and Secondary School Internet User Frequently Asked Questions (FAQ), Draft, Documents posted to the EDTECH listserv on the Internet, 12 June.

Shein, Barry (1993), PUBLIB Interview, Transcript of an interview with Barry Shein, Posted to the PUBLIB listserv on the Internet, 12 November.

Sterling, Bruce (1992), "Internet", *The Magazine of Fantasy and Science Fiction,* February; copy available on the gopher of the Ontario Institute for Studies in Education (OISE), March 1994.

Stott, Kay (1993), An overview of the Internet, presentation for the Australian Library and Information Association, Perth, Western Australia, December, and reported by Margaret Watson.

Strangelove, Michael (1994), The Geography of Consciousness:

Cyberspace and the Changing Landscape of Self, Essay posted to the Net-Happenings listserv on the Internet, 20 July.

Taylor, Jim (1993), Internet Access at Seattle Public Library, Message posted to the PUBLIB listserv on the Internet, 24 September.

"Traffic jams on the information highway?" (1994), *Bits and Bytes Online* 2, no. 2, 28 February.

Treese, Win (1993), The Internet Index, Document posted on the Net-Happenings listserv on the Internet, 21 December. (Document revised 16 December 1993).

Watkins, Steve (1994), California Leginfo Usage Stats—Just from *One* External Gopher, Message posted to the Net-Happenings listserv on the Internet, 7 March.

Zakon, Robert H'obbes' (1994), Internet Timeline v1.0, Document posted to the Net-Happenings listserv on the Internet, 23 January.

Ziegler, Bart (1994), "Future phone?", *Business Week*, 24 January, p.37.

CHAPTER TWO

INTERNET RESOURCES AND SERVICES

All members of the school community have information needs, many of which can be met through the school library and through the use of resources and services on the Internet. School students need information related to their school courses; their hobbies and special interests; the school clubs to which they belong; their sporting, cultural, and recreational activities; vocational preparation; and personal development. They also need access to a range of recreational materials and resources, including books, magazines, games, and discussion forums. Teachers need information related to new developments in education and teaching generally and to their particular teaching areas and academic interests, as well as information about current research and important projects in these fields. They also need information and resources to support their teaching, classroom activities, and any extra-curricular activities that they organize within the school's program. School administrators need information on significant developments in education elsewhere; information for planning initiatives in courses, buildings, or other special programs; important documents and research reports which may assist with planning; information about new techniques and tools (for instance, new computer packages for administration); and information about programs and projects that have been trialled in other schools. Parent groups and school councils need information that will help them to make appropriate decisions in relation to the school. While comparatively little research has been done about the information needs of the different members of the school community, we do know that many of the school information needs that have been identified, and which could not be met through the collection of the school library itself, could be met through the use of computer-based communications and Internet resources. In addition, school library staff, while having a responsibility to provide information to meet the needs of members of the school community, have information needs of their own (related to education, curriculum, resources, library management, information technology, professional development), most of which can be met in part through the use of Internet resources and services.

Internet resources and services can be categorized by subject, and there are many subject guides to the Internet, covering areas such as education, librarianship, law, medicine, business, science, environmental science, government, and current affairs. Internet resources can also be categorized by the type of user for which they were developed, and so there are guides for teachers, young people, scientists, journalists, researchers, government employees, and librarians, among others. Finally, Internet resources and services can be categorized on the basis of the tools and equipment that are needed for their use or available to the particular user, and the type of access to the Internet that the user has. If the user has access only to electronic mail, telnet, and gopher, then Internet resources and services that depend on other tools, such as file transfer protocol (ftp) or World Wide Web with Mosaic, will not be of immediate interest, no matter how relevant they may seem to be in terms of subject coverage or intended audience.

In this chapter Internet resources and services are described by type, that is, by the Internet tools with which they were created, and the tools that are needed to make use of them. A section on "Internet Guides" is followed by sections describing tools and services such as electronic mail, telnet, listservs, gopher, World Wide Web, freenets, and a range of other resources and services. Each requires that the user have access to appropriate software, as well as access to the Internet itself.

However, it is important, at this stage, to stress the fact that it is possible to use the Internet, and even to use it well, without necessarily having a full understanding of how it works—or even without having ANY understanding of how it works. It is also possible to use it well without using more than one or two tools, and so new users should not be put off by the list of tools and services in this chapter. It is possible to approach the Internet gradually, to creep up on it, learning a little at each step, mastering new tools and techniques over a period of time. Nevertheless, as in other fields, the more a user knows, the more doors will be open to that user.

It is also important to stress that the Internet is changing, and changing rapidly. The information given in this section was current when this book was being prepared; however, Internet services may disappear (and reappear) without notice, their location may change, the content may change, and instructions for their use may become outdated. In addition, instructions that work for one Internet user in one location, using a particular type of software and having a particular type of Internet account, may not work for another Internet user. With all this in mind, the information in this chapter has been kept as general as possible.

INTERNET GUIDES

Once people are "online", the best sources of information about the Internet, and certainly the cheapest and most up to date, are to be found on the Internet itself. It is one of the ironies of Internet life that the best sources of current information about the Internet or guides to the use of Internet facilities and services, are available mainly to those who can use Internet tools and services sufficiently well to be able to locate those sources or guides.

The guides are available via a variety of Internet services or tools, including anonymous file transfer protocol (ftp), ftpmail, gopher, World Wide Web, electronic mail—or sometimes by all these methods, or some of them, or others. Those who are unfamiliar with the services or tools mentioned should consult one of the published Internet guides listed in the Bibliography at the end of this book for detailed instructions. Meanwhile, information about Internet resources, services, and tools provided below will give some general guidance.

ELECTRONIC MAIL

Electronic mail is the foundation for Internet interactions, and any computer that provides access to the Internet will support at least this feature. Electronic mail can be one-to-one (a correspondence between just two people), or one-to-many (one person sending the same message to many people, perhaps even hundreds or thousands of people), and can form the basis of electronic conferences and discussion groups. Some electronic journals are delivered to the subscriber by electronic mail. In addition, documents on the Internet located using other tools, such as gopher, may be delivered to the user via electronic mail. Correspondence chess (and other games) can be played by electronic mail. Many people who use the Internet use only the electronic mail facility, and a surprising amount can be done with access only to this tool.

At its most basic level, the use of electronic mail requires electronic mail software on the user's own computer, along with a modem and a telephone line, and access to an Internet node (through a host computer on the Internet, or through a network such as FidoNet, or through an electronic bulletin board). Alternatively, the user needs access, through a local area network in the school or other institution, or through a modem and telephone line, to a computer that provides Internet electronic mail facilities.

Each person who has an electronic mail account will have an **email address**, a unique combination of letters, numbers, symbols, and punctuation, that will ensure that mail arrives from anywhere in the world. Each address consists of several "domains" and "sub-domains" that identify the user, the host computer or organization where the person has an account, the organization, sometimes the type of organization, and the place and country. While most electronic mail accounts belong to human beings, an electronic mail address doesn't necessarily have to refer to a person. The address could be the address of a computer, a listserver, an electronic bulletin board, a computer-based information service, or even someone's pocket pager.

The first part of the address is the "user ID" of the person (or the list or the bulletin board). This may incorporate "router" instructions, using the symbol % or other symbols, when the mail goes through a secondary system. The user ID will be followed by the symbol @ (for "at"). Some user IDs are very simple; for example, in the University of Iceland system, the user ID is commonly the person's given name or initials. However, in very large organizations, more complex user IDs may be used. Here are some examples of electronic mail addresses (incorporating user IDs):

`anne@rhi.hi.is` (this is the electronic mail address of the author at the University of Iceland)
`Ronald.Jobe@mtsg.ubc.edu.ca`
`jklobas@ecel.uwa.edu.au`
`ts645@CLEVELAND.FREENET.EDU`
`johnsmith@AOL.COM`
`12467htp%sutp@hatton.umrl.edu.us`
`LM_NET@SUVM.BITNET`

After the @ symbol, there will be a series of domains or sub-domains, which identify such things as the computer (mtsg, hatton), the organization (ubc, uwa, SUVM, hi, AOL), the type of organization (edu, com), the network (BITNET), the country (ca, au, us, is). In the United States, until recently, there was no country (or "top level") domain used at the end of the email address, but now some American email addresses are ending in "us", to fit in with the international pattern. However, American addresses, and those of some other countries, such as Australia, almost invariably incorporate an abbreviation for the type of organization—for instance, edu for an educational institution such as a university or college, gov for a government department or agency, com for a commercial organization, org for a nonprofit organization such as a community organization.

It is important that electronic mail addresses be typed exactly as given. Even a misplaced space or punctuation mark, or in some cases, the substitution of a capital letter for a lower case letter, may result in "returned mail", mail that is undeliverable.

The format of **electronic mail messages** varies a little depending on the computer where the user's account is based, the software that is being used for the email system, and the way in which the software has been "configured" or set up. However, electronic mail messages do have some standard features.

- The Header. The header at the top of a message identifies the sender (with email address), the recipient (with email address), the pathway by which the message was sent (sometimes through several computers or networks), the subject or topic of the message, and the date, and indicates whether the message is a copy, whether it has been forwarded from someone else, and sometimes the length of the message. Some of the information in the header is inserted automatically by the computer system when the message is created or sent. The amount of information in a message header, and the sequence in which the information is presented, will vary from system to system. Figure 2.1 provides an example of an email header from a printout of a message received on the University of Iceland system from Curtin University of Technology in Australia. Some electronic mail software can be set up in such a way that it strips off all or part of the header, to save space on the system. This can be a mixed blessing, because many people forget to put their name or the date in the body of the message, or leave this information out deliberately, on the assumption that it will appear in the header.

```
Date: Mon, 10 Jan 1994 09:24:03 +0800
Date-Warning: Date header was inserted by
   cc.curtin.edu.au
From: AVKW@cc.curtin.edu.au (Vicki Williamson)
Subject: HAPPY NEW YEAR
To: anne@rhi.hi.is (Anne Clyde)
Content-Transfer-Encoding: 7BIT
```

Figure 2.1: Electronic Mail Message Header

- The Body of the Message. This section will contain the text of the email message. The message may also have attachments, such as computer files, or copies of the text of articles, or lists, or even picture or sound files, that have been loaded into the email system from the sender's computer. Any attachments will not appear as part of the message on the receiver's screen; they will be delivered as a separate file, with its own filename.
- The Signature. Most electronic mail software will allow the user to create a "signature", which is then stored on the system and added automatically to all mail sent by that user. It will not show on the user's own screen, but it will show on the screen of the person who receives the message. My "signature" is reproduced as Figure 2.2, and a creative "signature" from Bill McGee is reproduced as Figure 2.3. The purpose of the "signature" is to provide an easy means for adding the

sender's name, address, email address, and any other essential information, to the bottom of a message. It also identifies the message as coming from that particular person—in fact, it takes the place of a handwritten signature on a letter.

```
*********************************************************
* Dr Anne Clyde,                    Email: anne@rhi.hi.is *
* Faculty of Social Science,           Fax: 354-1-26806 *
* University of Iceland,             Voice: 354-1-69 4522 *
* 101 Reykjavik, Iceland.                                 *
*********************************************************
```

Figure 2.2: The Author's Electronic Mail Signature

```
Bill McGee, Coordinator                            \\//|||\\//
Hidalgo County Library System            _________ //  .  .  \\
4305 N.10th Street, Suite E             /           |||  *  |||
McAllen, Texas 78504-3095             _|--_    _--_|///=\\\|
210-682-6397 - FAX 210-682-6398       ||   -__      \ //|||\\_____
INTERNET bmcgee@tenet.edu             ||_____\       \___\  ______\
                                      |---***
Utinam logica falsa philosophiam tuam totam suffodiant!
```

Figure 2.3: Bill McGee's Electronic Mail Signature

Anyone creating a "signature" should be careful about using a lot of space (some people have only limited storage in their email account, and some have to pay for storage space used for their messages, so they will not welcome long "signatures"). Some people include cute quotes and sayings in their signatures—and this practice has had a mixed reception from network users. For one thing, there is a possibility that people from other cultures will be offended by a quotation that seems profound or sparkling to the person who uses it. It is always tempting to assume that one's own cultural context and values are universal, but on the Internet such illusions may be seen as either naive or crass, depending on the context. In addition, a quote that seems fresh and charming on first reading, quickly palls when it appears on message after message from the sender.

Over the years, users of electronic mail (and online "chat" groups) have developed pictographs or **smileys** to embellish their messages, to make their meaning clearer, and to convey the emotions that are sometimes hidden by the typed words on the screen. Smileys can help to avoid misunderstandings, tone down messages that seem too blunt, and indicate irony or humor. Well chosen, they can cross cultural boundaries in a way that words sometimes do not. Smileys are created from the ordinary keyboard characters used in combination. Many hundreds have been developed, but some of the more common are as follows:

`:-)`	the basic smiley
`;-)`	a winking smiley, often used to tone down a sarcastic remark
`:-(`	a frowning smiley, indicating unhappiness, or used to indicate that a comment was uncalled for
`:)`	an abbreviated smiley
`8-` or `B-)`	user is wearing glasses
`%-(`	user after eight hours straight at the computer
`:-@`	user is screaming

There are even dictionaries of smileys, at least two of which are available on the Internet. Printed guides to smileys are Seth Godin's *The Smiley Dictionary,* and *Smileys* by David W. Sanderson and Dale Dougherty. On the Internet, the smiley catalog is available as an experimental telnet-based service; it can be queried for the meaning of a smiley, or on a verbal description of a smiley

Directories of email addresses are also available on the Internet itself, through some gophers. In addition, Internet tools like NetFind and whois are designed to help people to locate email addresses. There are also some published directories, though these, by their nature, are not very current.

TELNET

Telnet is, like electronic mail and file transfer protocol (ftp), one of the older Internet tools. It can be used alone or in conjunction with other tools, such as gopher or World Wide Web, as a means of touring the Internet. Telnet provides users with the facility to log on to remote computers (a computer in another building or another town or another country), and to use databases and software on those computers, even if the computers are of different types. Telnet can be used to reach many gophers, freenets, commercial online information services, library catalogs, and other Internet services. In the real sense of the word, telnet is a "tool"—information is not stored in telnet, but rather telnet is used as a means of getting to the computers and to the information services on those computers.

To use telnet, users need to have telnet software, or have access to a host computer that has telnet. It is also necessary to know the telnet address of the remote computer that is to be used.

Telnet addresses for Internet services such as gophers or electronic bulletin boards or freenets are often provided in two forms: an alphabetical address (the domain name address), and a numeric address (the IP or "Internet protocol" address). For example, the telnet addresses of the Nanaimo SchoolsNET in British Columbia, Canada, are given as `telnet crc.sd68.nanaimo.bc.ca` or `telnet 134.87.120.1` Both types of address have their advantages. The alphabetic address is easier to remember and type; the numeric address can provide faster access. If the service is moved to a new computer (something that may well happen as a service grows), the alphabetic address will usually remain the same, but the numeric address will change.

When telnet is used to link to a remote computer, the user will normally be required to log in with a password or user ID or "login". The password or user ID, or login, will usually be given after the telnet address in directories of Internet resources. For the Library of Congress LC MARVEL service, for instance, the login is `marvel`, while for the Victoria Free-Net it is `guest`.

LISTSERVS

Listservs are Internet resources that are based on electronic mail. They are, in effect, electronic mail discussion groups or "electronic conferences" to which Internet users can "subscribe" by sending an email message to the email address of the computer on which the listserv is based. The term "listserv" originally referred to a particular piece of list server software; it has now become the generally accepted term for almost any electronic mail-based discussion group. Although you join a listserv by "subscribing", most are free, and so a "subscription", in this context, is seldom related to paying money.

Those who are members of a listserv send email to the listserv address (the address of a computer), and this mail is then distributed by the listserv computer to the email addresses of all the members of that particular listserv. Members can read all the mail sent to the listserv, and respond to it, either through an open message to the listserv, or through a private message to the person who sent the mail. Some people join listservs just to read (or "listen to") the messages sent by others; they have no intention of participating. In Internet jargon, these people are known as "lurkers" (no derogatory connotation is intended). Over time, many lurkers are enticed out of their burrows to become fully participating citizens (or "denizens") of the Internet.

Some listservs are "open groups", that is, anyone can join who has an interest in the subject area covered by the listserv. Other listservs are "closed groups", and those who wish to join have to apply for membership (usually by email), and wait until their application to join has been approved, before they can take part. Some listservs are "moderated", that is, the person (or people) who set up the listserv checks messages to make sure that they are suitable and actually intended for the list, before posting them to all members. This process screens out electronic junk mail, mail sent to the wrong email address, and mail intended for the listserv moderator or the computer that supports the listserv. In some cases the moderator also facilitates discussion, welcomes new members, and maintains special features on the listserv.

Listservs provide a forum for discussion of current issues and dissemination of information. Through them, people can ask questions and seek advice. Information is traded about new products, new services, new resources. Some listservs are friendly groups where individuals are recognized and lasting contacts are formed. Others exist purely for the purpose of solving a particular problem or disseminating information on a particular topic, and they may not continue after their immediate purpose is served.

Some listservs are very active, and subscribers may receive up to 50 or so messages a day; others are relatively inactive, and there may be as few as one or two messages a week. When a list is very active, various strategies may be introduced to help subscribers to cope with the amount of mail, while attempting to maintain quality of discussion.

When the discussions on a listserv, and the messages posted to it, are perceived to have more than short-term value, then an archive may be formed, either on the listserv computer or elsewhere, where interested people can search for, read, and download past messages. The archives of many listservs in the field of education or librarianship may contain book and software reviews, extended discussions of issues of continuing professional concern, case studies of the implementation of a new system or a new idea, and other material of ongoing interest. The archives may be made available via a gopher, or through an ftp site, or by other means. Where the archives are on a gopher, special software such as LISTGopher will help the user to locate relevant messages and retrieve them.

There are several thousand listservs on the Internet and its interconnected networks. These cover an enormous range of topics, including topics that are covered in the school curriculum, and topics that are related to the recreational interests of school students and their teachers. There are listservs for people interested in German history, archaeology, languages, consumer studies, insects, environmental topics. There are listservs for people interested in horror movies, chess, breeding cats, playing the guitar, reading murder mysteries (that list is called DOROTHYL), long distance running, genealogy, travel, collecting stamps. Many listservs are related to the needs of members of a particular profession—including teachers, librarians, and others.

There are listservs for librarians in school libraries, public libraries, college and research libraries, art libraries, law libraries; there are listservs for librarians interested in reference services, cataloging, rare books, CD-ROMs, services to people with disabilities, government documents, interlibrary loans; there are listservs for librarians who are using or interested in particular automated systems (such as Geac, CDS/ISIS, NOTIS, VTLS). There are listservs for library schools and for library school students. Within the field of education, there is an equally wide range of listservs. There are listservs for teachers of particular ages groups or subjects, for preschool educators, for school administrators, for people interested in educational research or assessment or curriculum development or the education of children with disabilities.

There are directories and lists of listservs, which can be used to locate the names and Internet addresses of appropriate listservs. Some of these are in print form; some are available on the Internet itself (for example, on LC MARVEL, the Library of Congress gopher, which has a special section related to Internet guides and manuals). Charles W. Bailey provides a list of listservs of interest to librarians in the document "Library-Oriented Lists and Electronic Serials", available by electronic mail through LC MARVEL, through the Clearinghouse of Subject-Oriented Internet Resource Guides (on the University of Michigan gopher), and through other Internet sites.

For people who are involved in school librarianship, useful listservs include LM_NET (the "electronic community" for "school library media people" on the Internet); PUBLIB (a discussion group for people interested in public libraries, which often carries discussions on topics of interest to school library personnel, such as censorship); and KIDLIT-L (for people interested in children's literature).

ELECTRONIC JOURNALS

Electronic journals are journals that are delivered to subscribers via electronic mail, or that can be located and read using other Internet tools such as gopher. There are some very attractive journals and newsletters, complete with graphics and photographs, that are distributed through World Wide Web. Some electronic journals are electronic versions of printed journals; others exist only in electronic form. Many electronic journals are available through the Internet, on all kinds of topics. Some are free; some require a paid subscription. As with printed journals, they vary in the level and quality of their coverage, in the types of articles that they print, in their reliability and readability, and in their attractiveness and audience appeal. There are chatty newsletters, current awareness bulletins, refereed academic or research journals, and magazines carrying practical articles and reviews.

Among all of this variety, there are three main types of electronic journals. The first group consists of journals or newsletters for which the full text is delivered to the subscriber's email box. These journals may contain articles, news items, indexes, even advertisements. All the subscriber has to do is to read the text on the screen, or print it out for later reading. The second group consists of journals or newsletters the full text of which is available on a gopher or on World Wide Web, where it can be read and from which it can be downloaded if desired. Since there is seldom a reminder that a new issue is due out, the user has to remember to log on regularly to the appropriate service to read the journal or newsletter. However, the journals or newsletters that are made available in this way are often very attractive, with illustrations and other graphic material. The third group comprises those journals that are supplied, normally by electronic mail, as a table of contents list, often with an abstract for each article, and with "pointers" to enable subscribers to get the articles in which they are interested. The text for these articles may be stored on different computers, and the subscriber sends an email message to the relevant computer, requesting an email copy of the article or articles. A cumulative index for the journal may be available on a computer, and instructions are provided for obtaining an up-to-date copy of the index by email. Sometimes the articles and the index might be provided by ftp rather than email, and, once again, instructions will be provided. This is a convenient method for delivering larger journals that would take up a great deal of space in electronic mailboxes if they were delivered as one whole unit. It is most often used for research journals and the more serious professional journals which usually carry very long articles.

As with printed journals or magazines, there are directories of electronic journals, which provide information about content, subject coverage, editors, cost (if any), and email address for subscriptions. Among them is the very comprehensive *On Internet: An International Title and Subject Guide to Electronic Journals, Newsletters, Books, and Discussion Lists on the Internet*. There are also guides available on the Internet itself, such as the previously mentioned guide by Charles W. Bailey jnr, "Library-Oriented Lists and Electronic Serials", which can be found on LC MARVEL (the Library of Congress gopher) and at other Internet sites.

For people who are involved in school librarianship, useful electronic journals include *Current Cites* (a monthly current awareness bulletin that provides bibliographic references and annotations for articles and books about topics such as CD-ROM, online searching, and computer networks); *EDUPAGE* (a twice-weekly newsletter with short notices about new developments in technology); and *Bits and Bytes* (a weekly newsletter with information on topics like virtual reality, artificial intelligence, computers in education, the politics of information, and computer games). All three are free.

In addition to the professional and subject journals and newsletters that are available on the Internet, there are also "e-zines", electronic versions of the popular "zines", that is, magazines or "fanzines". There are zines dealing with all aspects of pop culture, music, sports, lifestyles. Zines are usually produced by one person or a small group of people, often as a recreational interest, usually to promote an idea or point of view, and they range from the messianic to the bizarre. An "e-zine" is a zine that is distributed electronically. Some are sent via electronic mail in plain ASCII text format, which can be read on virtually any computer that is connected to the Internet; a few are available in PostScript format for printing on a laser printer; others are in formats like Macintosh HyperCard format. During 1994, more and more zines were made available on World Wide Web, usually with illustrations and graphics. Examples are the *Computer Wave E-Zine* and *CyberZine*, both distributed on World Wide Web. John Labovitz maintains an "E-Zine List" which is updated regularly and available on the World Wide Web at the URL `http://www.ora.com:8080/johnl/e-zine-list/`.

GOPHER

Many organizations, institutions, and community groups provide information services that are linked to the Internet. Universities, colleges, and institutions like the Library of Congress have set up information services based on gopher software. Gopher is a tool that was developed at the University of Minnesota in late 1991, to help people to "navigate" the Internet; there are now more than 7,000 gophers around the world. The name "gopher" suggests two meanings: a gopher is a small burrowing animal, but, in another context, a gopher is a person who "goes for" things that are needed, for instance on a film set. Either way, the idea of the Internet gopher as software that burrows through the mass of information on the net, collecting that which is useful for the person at the computer keyboard, is an attractive one. Gopher has made the Internet more accessible for large numbers of users, particularly for those who do not have the skills to make use of other Internet tools. However, in many ways, it is already, only a few years after its introduction, outmoded; the information retrieval tools embedded in it are not precise enough to cope with the huge amounts of information now available through gopher. Nevertheless, it does provide an interface to the Internet that is easy to use.

To use gopher, access is needed (via telnet or through a network) to a host computer that supports a gopher. Alternatively, users of a network can run a gopher "client", such as TurboGopher for the Macintosh or WSGopher for the IBM PC, on their own microcomputer (with an Internet link), and use it to search for information on gophers around the world.

A gopher provides a series of menus that lead the user to information held on computers worldwide. The information may take the form of library catalogs, databases in various formats, directories, search services, the full text of documents, or links to other gophers or information services. It appears to the user that the information is located in one place, but in fact the gopher collects and brings together information from many different computers. Gopher keeps a record (in the form of bookmarks or pathways) of where things are on the many different computers that are part of the Internet, and collects them only as requested. Thus, in any one search session, a user may look at menus or documents collected from computers in several different places.

In addition, most gophers incorporate the facility to provide the user with a copy of any document that is located through the system. The selected documents are delivered to the user via electronic mail, usually almost immediately, or, alternatively, the user may be able to request that a copy of the document be sent as a file. So the full text of the constitution of Estonia, a bibliography for teenage girls about women in professional occupations, bibliographic records for new textbooks, current employment statistics for Canada, a list of endangered plant species in Australia, or a newsletter compiled by elementary school children in Finland about celebrations this month around the world, can be available within minutes anywhere in the world to people who are connected to the Internet.

Most gophers provide information designed to meet the needs of the people at the institution where they are located, as well as information that will be of interest to users outside the institution. So a gopher set up on a university computer will usually provide information of interest to the students, professors, and staff who make up its community, such as information about courses, university events, the opening hours of the library and other facilities, bus or train schedules, meetings, or the university telephone directory. A gopher set up by a public library might provide local history information, information about community groups and organizations, information about library programs and services, bibliographies, lists of new books. The few gophers that have been set up by schools usually provide information for parents and others as well as teachers and students.

Some gophers are set up as specialist services, designed to provide information, or lead people to information, on specific subjects, such as environmental information or government information. The AskERIC gopher provides access to educational information for people in schools and universities. The KIDLINK gopher provides information about the various KIDLINK projects worldwide (projects that involve schoolchildren aged ten to fifteen).

```
        AskERIC (Educational Resources
              Information Center)
 1. News and Information about ERIC and AskERIC/
 2. Map of the Library/
 3. Search AskERIC Menu Items <?>
 4. AskERIC Toolbox (under construction)/
 5. Frequently Asked Questions (FAQ's)/
 6. AskERIC InfoGuides/
 7. Lesson Plans/
 8. Education Listservs Archives/
 9. ERIC Clearinghouses/Components/
10. ERIC Digests File/
11. ERIC Bibliographic Database (RIE and CIJE)/
12. Bibliographies/
13. News & Announcements: Professional and Commercial
    Organizations/
14. Other Education Resources/
15. Education Conferences (Calendars and Announcements)/
16. Electronic Journals, Books, and Reference Tools/
17. Internet Guides and Directories/
18. Gophers and Library Catalogs/
```

Figure 2.4: The Main Menu of the AskERIC Gopher

```
KIDLINK: Global Network for Youth 10-15
 1. About the KIDLINK Gopher.
 2. About the KIDLINK Projects/
 3. Finding and Using KIDLINK Services/
 4. Special Language KIDLINK Documents and Lists/
 5. KIDLINK in the Classrooms/
 6. KIDLINK People/
 7. KIDLINK Help Wanted/
 8. KIDART Computer Art Gallery/
 9. Research, Reports, Papers, and Newsletters/
10. KIDSHOW and other multimedia programs about KIDLINK/
11. Directly Access the KIDLINK Archive LOG Files/
12. Other Resources About Kids/
13. Search all "Menu Titles" on This Server (fast) <?>
14. FULL TEXT Search of "All Files" on This Server (slow)
    <?>
15. Experimental KIDLINK WWW Home Page [KIDLINK GENERAL
    HTML].
```

Figure 2.5: The Main Menu of the KIDLINK Gopher

Many different information sources and services are available through gophers. These include:

- other gophers;
- community freenets;
- electronic bulletin boards;
- electronic journals;
- electronic books;
- reference works such as encyclopedias, dictionaries, directories, atlases;
- telephone directories and electronic mail directories;
- the full text of documents of many different kinds, including guides to the Internet and its resources;
- the archives of listservs and discussion groups;
- library catalogs;
- computer software for downloading;
- files of artwork or still images;
- sound files;
- commercial online information services;
- electronic shopping services;
- Internet search facilities such as WAIS and Hytelnet.

Gopher menus can lead users to information in many different forms. The way in which each item is presented on the menu will indicate what type of information is behind that menu item. Some menu items lead to the full text of documents (newsletters, articles, books, reports, summaries, bibliographies). Some lead to other menus. Others lead to a search screen where there will be search instructions, space to type search terms, and then the results of the search. Still others lead to an automatic link to another computer, and the user will have to follow new instructions provided for the new computer system.

With so much information available through gophers, tools are needed to help people to find their way. While the menus provide basic guidance, negotiating them can be both cumbersome and time consuming. One of the tools that has been developed to help people to find information related to particular subjects on the gophers of the Internet is VERONICA. The developers have claimed that VERONICA is an acronym for "Very Easy Rodent-Oriented Net-Wide Index to Computerized Archives". VERONICA allows the user to search the whole of "gopherspace", that is, the menus of all gophers, using simple search terms, coupled with the "and", "or", and "not" operators. In response to a search, it creates a "custom-made" menu of all of the items on all of the menus of "gopherspace" that match the search terms. By selecting items from this custom-made menu, the user is connected automatically to the gopher on which the relevant information is located. In librarianship terms, VERONICA is not a very precise search tool: it returns a lot of false "hits"; and it searches only menu items that contain the search terms—it does not search the documents or services behind the menus.

Other search tools associated with gopher include Jughead (which is similar to VERONICA, but searches only the gopher on which the user initiates the search, rather than all gopher servers on the Internet), WAIS, Hytelnet, and whois. Like VERONICA, these tools are accessible through the gopher menus.

The best-known guide to gophers on the Internet is "Gopher Jewels", a catalog of gopher sites by category or subject, maintained by David Riggins, and updated approximately monthly. It is available on the Internet through the University of Southern California gopher and other locations.

For people who are involved in school librarianship, there are many useful gophers worldwide in the fields of librarianship and education, or related to the subjects studied in the school curriculum. Gophers worth investigating in the field of education include AskERIC, Canada's SchoolNet, the Empire Schoolhouse (from NYSERNet), and the CICNet K-12 gopher (which, like AskERIC, has a range of curriculum materials and lesson plans, as well as information related to education in general, schools, and public policy). In the field of librarianship, the Library of Congress's LC MARVEL provides access to information about library science, the Internet, copyright, and publishing, as well as to government information and electronic journals. Other gophers on the Internet provide access to resources and information that can meet curriculum and teaching needs in schools. These include Australia's ERIN environmental information gopher, KIDLINK, the Smithsonian Institution's Natural History Gopher, Healthline, and Armadillo (the Texas Studies gopher).

WORLD WIDE WEB (WWW)

Like gopher, World Wide Web (WWW) enables users to locate Internet resources and services, and to bring "pages" or screens of information from remote computers to their own computer. A World Wide Web "page", normally presented in color, might incorporate text, pictures, graphics, sound, and links to other documents and services. By using a mouse to click on highlighted words anwhere on the "page", users can move to related information, wherever that information might be, and have it presented on their computer screens. Users do not have to request specific information, as one normally does in online searching; rather, users can follow likely leads through the Web until they find something that meets their needs. However, specific subject searches are also possible, for example through services like Yahoo or WebCrawler.

World Wide Web is easy to use and to learn to use. It was developed through a project of CERN (the European Laboratory for Particle Physics) in Switzerland, which aimed to create a distributed hypermedia system for navigating the Internet. World Wide Web has experienced dramatic growth since its first release in 1992, as noted in a special feature in *The Internet Letter* early in 1994 („Internet grabs big share ..." p.7).

Many different information sources and services are accessible through World Wide Web. These include:

- World Wide Web sites worldwide;
- information and resources available through gophers;
- electronic journals;
- electronic books;
- reference works such as encyclopedias, dictionaries, directories, atlases;
- telephone directories and electronic mail directories;
- hypertext documents containing links to other documents and resources;
- the full text of documents of many different kinds, including guides to the Internet and its resources;
- the archives of listservs and discussion groups;
- library catalogs;
- computer software for downloading;
- collections of data in computer-readable form;
- files of artwork or still images;
- sound files;

- animation sequences and moving images;
- commercial online information services;
- electronic shopping services;
- Internet search facilities.

Browsing the World Wide Web can be a pleasant experience, simply because many of services are well designed, and some of the pages are beautiful. For example, the Library of Congress pages related to the Vatican Library exhibition contain well-written text, carefully spaced, with well-defined links to other pages, and color photographs of medieval and Renaissance manuscripts and furniture from the exhibition. Each page incorporates the exhibition logo, and the use of symbols and graphics is very effective throughout. The Australian Environmental Resources Information Network (ERIN) server is also well presented, with an attractive multicolor logo, maps, photographs, and a range of other features.

However, at present, World Wide Web does have some disadvantages. First, servers may be expensive to set up, not least because the services of a wide range of professionals, including designers and writers, are usually needed—though some schools have mounted successful Web servers based on the work of the children. Secondly, even with a powerful microcomputer with lots of internal memory, using the Web through browser software such as Netscape or Mosaic may be almost painfully SLOW. Though it is possible to use much faster software such as the Lynx text-only browser, this means that the graphics and other features that make the Web so attractive and useful are lost to the user.

To access World Wide Web, a browser program is needed. This can be a browser on a UNIX machine to which the user telnets, or it can be a browser on the user's own machine. The browser reads documents and can collect documents from other locations on the Web. Information providers on the Web set up hypermedia servers from which the browsers get the documents. In addition, browsers can access a range of other files using ftp, gopher, and other methods, while presenting the user with a consistent interface to the network. If the server has search capabilities, then the browsers will enable the user to search documents, directories, and databases.

Browsers are available for many different types of computers, including the main microcomputers, and even for dumb terminals. Among the browsers for MS-DOS machines with Windows are Netscape, Mosaic for Windows, and Cello (which require that the user's microcomputer is linked to a SLIP or TCP/IP network). For Apple Macintosh machines, there are Mosaic for Macintosh, Netscape, and Samba (again, both require that the user's microcomputer is linked to a SLIP or TCP/IP network). All these browsers are available on the Internet through anonymous ftp.

The Uniform Resource Locator (URL) is an important concept associated with World Wide Web, though it is designed to apply to other services as well. It is a draft standard for specifying or describing a specific "object" on the Internet. That object might be a document, a picture, a computer, a file, a gopher, a USENET newsgroup, or other resource or service. The URL specifies the access method, path, machine, and other necessary information. Examples of URLs are:

- `http://kaos.erin.gov.au/erin.html` (the URL for the Australian ERIN environmental information service)
- `http://wired.com/` (the URL for Wired Magazine, a popular magazine devoted to online and networking issues, which is available in print and electronic form)
- `http://www.exploratorium.edu/` (the URL for the San Francisco Exploratorium, a museum with an Internet service)

World Wide Web addresses will normally be given in the form of a URL.

Although World Wide Web has been widely available

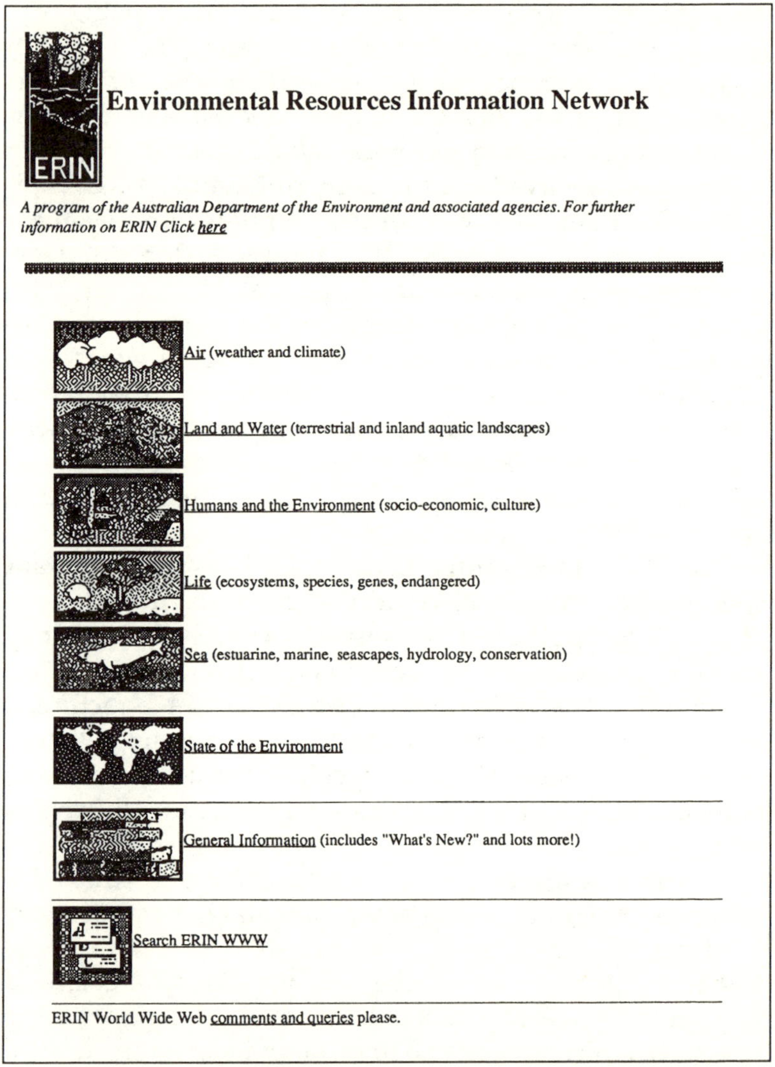

Environmental Resources Information Network

ERIN

A program of the Australian Department of the Environment and associated agencies. For further information on ERIN Click here

Air (weather and climate)

Land and Water (terrestrial and inland aquatic landscapes)

Humans and the Environment (socio-economic, culture)

Life (ecosystems, species, genes, endangered)

Sea (estuarine, marine, seascapes, hydrology, conservation)

State of the Environment

General Information (includes "What's New?" and lots more!)

Search ERIN WWW

ERIN World Wide Web comments and queries please.

2.6 The World Wide Web home page of the Australian ERIN environmental information server.

only since the beginning of 1993, already there are many resources and services on the Web that will be of interest to schools and school libraries—in addition to the gopher, listserv, and other resources that World Wide Web can be used to access. Information services in the field of education include the Scholastic Internet Center, the Educational Online Sources service, and the World Wide Web servers of local education authorities or organizations (such as the ACTEIN server in the Australian Capital Territory). In addition, Web users will be able to find the full text of electronic books, reference works, and electronic journals. In terms of curriculum information resources, there are World Wide Web servers covering most broad areas of the school curriculum, some of which were created specifically for schools, while others contain information or resources that match the needs of schools. Examples include the National Aeronautics and Space Administration (NASA) server, the Australian ERIN environmental information service, the World Wide Web server of Alflingi (the parliament of Iceland), and the Mt. Wilson Observatory Home Page (which has a section devoted to astronomy in education).

ELECTRONIC BULLETIN BOARDS AND INFORMATION SERVICES

While gopher software has become popular over the last two years as a means of setting up information services, campus-wide information systems, and computer networks, and while World Wide Web has gained increasing acceptance since its release in 1992, there are many electronic bulletin boards and information services that are based on other types of software. These may be accessible via gopher (a nice source of confusion), via telnet, or through dial-up access using a modem and the telephone lines.

The information services or electronic bulletin boards may be free, or they may require a subscription fee (on a monthly or annual basis), or they may be free but make charges for particular types of information (such as current news or financial information). If the latter is the case, users will be warned when they are about to enter a section of the system where charges apply, and access to these sections may be password controlled.

Electronic bulletin boards have been set up by government departments (for example, the Economic Bulletin Board of the United States Department of Commerce), libraries (for example, the Redcliff Public Library in Brisbane, Australia), universities and colleges (for example, the ECHIDNA bulletin board or "virtual campus" set up for distance education students by Edith Cowan University in Perth, Western Australia), school districts or education authorities (for example, ED-NET in Vancouver, Canada), schools (for example, Shore School bulletin board in Sydney, Australia, in the 1980s, and the Hong Kong International School Dragon BBS), computer clubs (for example, the Apple User Groups), community groups (for example, the precursors to some of the present community freenets), and individuals (for example, Deep Cove BBS in White Rock, British Columbia, Canada).

Electronic bulletin boards that offer educational information for teachers, school librarians, and school administrators include Big Sky Telegraph and Georgia College EduNet in the United States and Nanaimo SchoolsNET in Canada. Bulletin boards that have curriculum information and resources that could be used in the classroom include the Geographic Name Server at the University of Michigan, WorldClassroom, and the Air Pollution BBS. The quality and quantity of the information on the boards varies a great deal, as does the quality of the software and hardware on which the systems run.

COMMUNITY FREENETS

The freenet concept was developed by Dr. Tom Grundner, who is still associated with the United States National Public Telecomputing Network, an organization that promotes the development of community freenets. Freenets "depend on the generosity of the community" (Broadhead, 1993); it is expected that operating costs will be covered by corporate and government grants, private grants, and donations. In 1986, the first community freenet, the Cleveland Freenet, came on line in Ohio, with the support of local organizations and institutions, including the Cleveland Public Library and Case Western Reserve University. Freenets offer free public access to electronic mail and to a variety of information services, both local and from further afield. Through an Internet gateway, freenets are able to provide access to gophers and library collections worldwide. They are usually established by local committees of interested people, with the support of organizations such as libraries, colleges, local councils, and local businesses. By the end of 1993, there were community freenets in Canada, New Zealand, and Finland, as well as in the United States, and committees were working in several countries to create new freenets.

Most freenets are based on the Freeport commercial software package for UNIX computers; this software was developed at Case Western Reserve University, where the Cleveland Freenet is located. This is easy-to-use, menu-driven software that allows the system operator of each freenet to "customize" it to the local setting. The usual configuration of menus is one that is intended to reflect the city environment—with the library, the school, the community center, the churches, local government, the coffee shop ("chatting"), the post office (electronic mail), and so forth, featured on the main menu.

In communities where a local freenet exists, access may be provided through computers in schools, the public library, the community center, and other places. In addition, people with a microcomputer, modem, and telecommunications software are able to dial in from home, often for the cost of a local call. For people outside the area, Internet access is possible.

These freenets contain an enormous amount of free information that is potentially very useful in schools. For example, the Victoria Free-Net in British Columbia, Canada, has environmental information and environmental reports from the Canadian government (including monthly reports on ozone levels), Canadian statistics, and bibliographies (created by the Greater Victoria Public Library). CapAccess, the National Capital Area Public Access Network in Washington, DC, has information about Washington, local government, and education, and there are "forums" that discuss current issues. Free-Net Finland has the WYN World's Youth News service, through which young people and professional journalists work together to create and disseminate news stories.

FTP SITES

File transfer protocol or ftp is an Internet facility that allows users to log on to remote computers almost anywhere in the world, locate files or programs, and transfer copies of those files or programs to their own computer, via the host computer through which they access the Internet. Thus for many users, ftp will be a two-step process: copying files from the remote computer to the local host; then downloading those files to their personal computer using the procedures required by the local host. Newer software, like Fetch for the Macintosh, and Minuet for IBM PCs, can simplify both using ftp commands and the process of downloading the files to the user's own computer.

Files that are downloaded may be text, data, graphics, sound, animation. The files or programs may be compressed (to speed up the transfer process) or encrypted, and when this is the case, special software will be needed to read or use them. Usually, this software is also available on the Internet via ftp. Text files are normally loaded into the user's word processing program for use.

"Anonymous ftp" sites on the Internet allow anyone to login, even though they do not have an account on that computer, using the name "anonymous" (and sometimes with the user's email address as the password). Once on the computer, they can search directories in the public sections of the computer, use public services on the system, and transfer files and programs to their own computer. These anonymous ftp servers may have computer software, documents, files of pictures or other material, and files or programs for configuring networks or using Internet facilities. These services are provided by the people responsible for the computers, as a public service, and in the public interest. As with most other things on the Internet, this is subject to change.

Transferring or "downloading" files or programs requires a knowledge of ftp commands and procedures. Some ftp commands are the same on all computers, while others are different. Once logged on to a remote computer, typing `help` (or a question mark, `?`) will usually result in a list of the ftp commands that can be used on that computer. The commands for ftp must be used in a defined sequence, and in a precise format. In addition, users normally need to know the filename of the file they are looking for, and its location (or directory) on the computer. That is, unless they are just "poking around" in a remote computer's public directories to see what is there. However, even this is not easy, since filenames on UNIX computers (and many other computers) tend to be rather cryptic, and the files themselves may have to be checked.

Files can be transferred in different modes, and a file transferred in the wrong mode may be unreadable when it is opened, or it may be read only with difficulty. When a file is transferred in ASCII mode, certain characters are translated between systems, so that the file is more comprehensible when it arrives. However, when binary files are transferred, this translation is undesirable, since it can render the files useless. Binary files are those containing information other than simple text. There are also different modes for picture files, sound files, and animation files, and each must be transferred in the correct format, and/or the user needs to have the appropriate software to read the file once it arrives. Often, this software is available on the Internet via ftp. Files are often stored in compressed format in order to save space; in addition, compressed files will be transferred more quickly. If files have been compressed using a compress program like zip, then a .Z or .zip suffix on the end of the filename will indicate this (for example, `filename.txt.Z`), and the user will need unzip to read them. Unzip (and other programs like it, such as pkunzip) is available on the Internet for all main types of computers.

An Internet search tool called ARCHIE was developed at McGill University in Canada several years ago to help users locate files in the ftp sites of the Internet. ARCHIE can be accessed by using telnet to log on to a mainframe computer that provides ARCHIE services—there are several of them around the world. While there are other methods, they are becoming less common as the Internet develops. ARCHIE servers are located in New York, New Jersey, Nebraska, and Maryland in the United States; in Australia; in Canada; in the United Kingdom; in Finland; and in other places. There are ARCHIE "clients" available for microcomputers; these are programs that users can run on their own computers to search the ARCHIE databases.

Ftpmail provides a free service for people who have access to electronic mail but not to ftp facilities—or for people who don't want to have to learn how to use ftp, or for people who find ftp a frustrating process. An ftpmail user sends a message, in a prescribed format, to the computer on which the ftpmail service is based. That computer then logs on to the remote computer where the file that the user needs is stored, collects the file, and delivers it to the user's electronic mailbox. There are some disadvantages though. When ftp is used, the files are delivered almost immediately; when ftpmail is used, the service may take more than 24 hours to deliver the files, depending on the number of requests that have been sent to it that day. However, as soon as the ftpmail computer receives a request, it will send a confirmatory message, giving an indication of the number of jobs in the queue, and of approximately how long it will take to deliver the file. Unfortunately, not all types of files can be delivered via ftpmail, but many (and particularly text files) can be.

What is the use of ftp? There is a wide range of information, and many resources, documents, and programs, that are available free on the Internet. Many of these have potential applications in schools and school libraries. The most up-to-date versions of any Internet guides are usually available by ftp. Computer software for Internet applications, including software for use with ftp, gopher, and World Wide Web, is available through ftp sites. Educational resources available via ftp include policy documents, lesson plans, photographs (such as photographs taken by astronomers, or photographs of animals and plants), the full text of books (anything from *Alice in Wonderland* to the Greek classics), computer software from Apple and IBM, and government statistics from the United States and Canada.

USENET NEWSGROUPS

USENET has been likened to "an electronic Hyde Park", and described as "an anarchy that relies on sharing, motivated by intellectual rather than economic competitiveness ... from endless chatter and flame wars, it distils collective wisdom" (Caywood, 1993). USENET is a UNIX-based international network, linked to the Internet, though not strictly part of the Internet. It supports the distribution of messages and newsgroups worldwide; these can be read through client software on the user's own computer, or through the host computer to which the user is connected. USENET started in 1979, and by December 1993 there were more than two million users worldwide, posting approximately twenty thousand articles a day in the various newsgroups. Not all Internet users have access to USENET. When they do have access, they may not have access to all groups. Some system administrators of host computers post only those categories of newsgroups that they feel will be of use to people who use their systems, while others don't post the alt (alternative) or rec (recreational) newsgroups.

Where people do have access to USENET, the commands that they use are different from the usual Internet commands. However, even this is an oversimplification, because different news reading software will be provided on different hosts, and sometimes this software will be command-driven, while on other hosts the software will be menu-driven. Users of the Netscape World Wide Web browser are able to use it to read newsgroups.

There are thousands of USENET newsgroups, each dealing with a particular topic, or a particular aspect of a topic, or discussing a topic from a particular point of view. There are newsgroups in the field of library and information science, covering particular types of libraries (public libraries, school libraries, music libraries, and so on); or covering particular issues like library management, or library automation, or censorship of library materials; or covering library resources such as CD-ROM, or science fiction, or local history materials. In addition, there are newsgroups that are related to the professional, vocational, informational or recreational of library users, in a wide range of fields, from game-playing to heart surgery. Like listservs, USENET newsgroups provide access to current information, discussion, and opinion. The messages contributed to USENET newsgroups are provided voluntarily by people all around the world who are interested in the particular topic covered by the newsgroup. Sometimes the newsgroups are used as a means of testing ideas or getting feedback on documents that will appear later in a more traditional format—as part of a book, or as an article in a print or electronic journal.

Information from selected USENET newsgroups is carried on some gophers and electronic bulletin boards where it is considered that that information will be of use to users of the gopher or the bulletin board. So the messages from some of the USENET newsgroups related to education or school libraries are carried on the CICNet K-12 gopher in Michigan and on the Canada SchoolNet gopher, for instance, and users of the gopher don't have to learn to use USENET commands in order to read the messages.

It can be very difficult for people who have never used USENET to comprehend what it is, and this difficulty tends to be compounded by the fact that USENET is often discussed in terms of what it is not, rather than what it is. For example, it is not an organization, but rather a network of linked computer systems, owned and managed separately, that pass on newsgroup messages from one to the other and make them available to users. Yet these things need to be said, because people who are expecting a structured organization will have difficulty in coming to terms with USENET (and with many other Internet resources and services). The transmission of news and messages is entirely co-operative and relies on the goodwill of systems managers throughout the world. Users can read messages posted to the newsgroups that are received by their system, and respond, or post their own messages. The procedures for doing these things vary from computer system to computer system, and most Internet users will need to consult the system manager of their own host computer for advice and information.

Many USENET newsgroups create a set of instructions for posting to the group, instructions which are posted at regular intervals so that users are reminded of them. Many groups also have a Frequently Asked Questions (FAQ) file, which is also posted regularly. This helps to avoid annoyance to regular readers who find new users asking the same basic questions over and over again. The FAQ files are an important information resource on the Internet, and, when they are compiled with care (some are even indexed), they can represent the "collective wisdom" of a worldwide group of enthusiasts or experts. Many of these FAQ documents are archived on ftp sites and gophers, as well as being posted to the newsgroup.

The usual question is, "How does a USENET newsgroup differ from a listserv?" Both are based on electronic mail, and both provide access to current information and discussion. However, USENET newsgroup messages can be read by all interested people who have access to appropriate software, whereas a listserv requires that the person join (or "subscribe"). Members of a listserv receive all messages sent to the listserv computer by other subscribers, in the form of electronic mail messages, usually within a few hours of their being sent, but people interested in the communications of a USENET newsgroup have to make the effort to log on to the USENET system and select the appropriate messages for reading. On the other hand, once logged on, the USENET user can read the communications of any USENET newsgroups, whereas that user cannot browse the messages of a listserv to which he or she does not subscribe (though they may be able to browse the archives of the listserv if those archives are on a public gopher). The electronic mail from a listserv will remain in the subscriber's electronic mailbox until it is read; the messages posted to a newsgroup will usually be deleted after a month or so, whether or not they are read, and so they don't clutter up an electronic mailbox. Both have their advantages and disadvantages. In some cases, both a newsgroup and a listserv are established as parallel groups, and the messages posted to one are also posted automatically, via a "gateway", to the other; when this happens, people can use whichever of the two is the more convenient.

There are several different categories of USENET newsgroups. Each has its own characteristics, and each is distinguished through the first few letters of the name of the newsgroups. The basic categories are as follows:

- **comp**—groups for discussion of computer hardware and software, and for discussion of communications protocols;
- **misc**—for discussion of topics that do not fit comfortably elsewhere, such as commercial use, fitness, job hunting;
- **news**—covering groups that provide announcements of new developments in networking or online services, newsgoups that make available documents related to USENET or networking, and network administration;
- **rec**—for discussion of recreational topics and hobbies, for example, interactive role-playing games, music, reading science fiction, stamp collecting;
- **sci**—for discussion of scientific subjects, including space research, physics, medicine, mathematics, and biology;
- **soc**—groups created primarily for social interaction, or for discussion of social or cultural issues;
- **talk**—groups concerned with long-term debates on such topics as politics, religion, the environment;
- **alt**—alternative groups of discussions, not carried by all USENET sites, including groups discussing topics that have be considered controversial by some commentators (these discussions are not always thought of as a regular part of the USENET categories).

Other categories of groups include **biz** (business), **k12** (related to elementary and secondary schools), or geographically based categories such as **aus** (Australia), **can** (Canada), and **is** (Iceland).

USENET newsgroups of interest to people in the field of school librarianship include `alt.censorship` (a discussion group covering all aspects of censorship and censorship attempts), and `K12.library`. In addition, there are many newsgroups that carry current information and discussion that will be of interest to the school library's users—for example, there are curriculum discussion groups that may well be of interest to teachers in schools.

LIBRARY CATALOGS

There are more that four thousand library catalogs available on the Internet, ranging from the LOCIS catalog of the Library of Congress to the catalogs of school libraries. Many of these public access catalogs contain not only bibliographic records for items in the collection, but also other useful information, such as periodical indexes, local history files, community information files, full-text reference works, bibliographies, and "ready reference" files. Sometimes access to the additional files is restricted to registered library users.

The online public access catalog of the Seattle Public Library in Washington State, for instance, has a community information file, a file of community events, and a "quick facts" file of answers to frequently asked reference questions. Information provided online by the Greater Victoria Public Library in Vancouver, Canada, includes a range of bibliographies (among them bibliographies of local material and a bibliography of murder mysteries set in libraries, called "Library Macabre"). This library also has an online reference service through which reference questions can be sent in; these questions are then posted on the library's electronic bulletin board along with answers provided by the librarians. The Library of the University of Saskatchewan in Canada provides access to the ERIC educational database through its DOBIS/LIBIS library system, in addition to the catalog of its own collection of books and other materials.

Probably the most comprehensive guide to library catalogs on the Internet is the book *OPAC Directory 1994, An Annual Guide to Online Public Access Catalogs and Databases,* published internationally by Meckler Corporation.

COMMERCIAL SERVICES

The number of commercial services on the Internet is increasing, and many services that were available previously only by direct-dial access with a modem through the telephone lines are now also available on the Internet. This can substantially reduce the costs associated with long-distance searching of online information services such as DIALOG or OCLC.

Not all the commercial services on the Internet are information services; users can go shopping with their credit cards for a wide range of goods and services. However, some of the commercial services such as bookshops, document delivery services, and software suppliers, are of particular interest to libraries, including school libraries. A major bookstore on the Internet, BOOKS.COM, has large stocks of books in the fields of computer studies, technology, and social sciences, of potential interest to schools. CARL's UnCover document delivery service provides free access to magazine indexes, but charges for copies of articles delivered by mail or fax. The Electronic Newsstand gopher allows users to read the contents pages of current journals free, and even to read an article from each issue for free, but promotes subscriptions to those journals and enables interested people to subscribe online.

Some commercial services carry special services that are aimed at schools or school libraries; America Online, for instance, a commercial service based in the United States, has the Scholastic Network online as part of its services. Scholastic provides resources for teachers (including resources for classroom activities), offers information services related to education, and has authors and other guests online from time to time.

DIALOG's Classroom Instruction Program, which provides schools with low-cost access to many DIALOG databases, is more appealing to many schools now that DIALOG is available through the Internet and communications costs are lower. Schools taking part in the Classroom Instruction Program also have access to instructional materials and manuals that are designed to help teachers and school library staff who are teaching children the basics of online searching. In early 1994, OCLC announced a special pilot program that gives schools cheaper access to the FirstSearch information databases, as a means of encouraging the use of online services in education; as with DIALOG's Classroom Instruction Program, OCLC's FirstSearch is accessible via the Internet.

Some of the commercial services allow users to browse catalogs free, but charge them for documents and special services; others, including online information services like DIALOG, require passwords for all services.

A monthly list of commercial services available via the Internet, called "The Internet Mall: Shopping on the Internet Highway", is maintained by Dave Taylor in the United States. It is available from different locations on the Internet itself, via ftp, gopher, and other means.

GAMES AND RECREATIONAL SOURCES

Everyone needs a break some time! When this time comes, there are many recreational resources available on the Internet that would be of interest to school librarians, teachers, and young people. For some people, including many young people, exploring (or "surfing") the Internet, and "chatting" via the keyboard with other explorers, is a time-consuming hobby in itself, and keyboard friendships may be formed in this way. Resources for young people on the Internet include games, listservs and discussion forums, bulletin boards, databases of information, and even specialized gophers that point them to resources that might meet their needs. While some of these resources are based on standard software or tools like listservs, there are other resources that are based on software that is definitely nonstandard.

There are many listservs and discussion groups that focus on hobbies and leisure activities such as coin collecting, listening to jazz, long-distance running, reading murder mysteries, travel, breeding dogs, collecting baseball cards, and growing rare plants. Examples include STARGAME (the STARTREK role-playing game listserv), STREK-L (the Star Trek Fan Club listserv), TOLKIEN (for readers of J.R.R. Tolkien's books), STAMPS (for postage stamp collectors), KIDCAFE (which aims to facilitate "youth dialogue"), and ROCK (the rock and roll music discussion list). USENET newsgroups also provide a forum for discussion of leisure interests and hobbies, including rock music, fantasy role-playing games, creative writing, test cricket, writing computer programs, and collecting postcards. However, the existence (and easy accessibility) or newsgroups such as `alt.sex` has made teachers and school administrators very wary of providing unsupervised access to USENET resources (and sometimes Internet resources in general) in schools.

The popularity of fantasy role-playing games such as "Dungeons and Dragons" led, in the early days of network computing, to the development of multiuser environments on mainframe computers or large minicomputers on the Internet, where ongoing role-playing fantasy games could be developed, with the games sometimes going on over several years. Today, MUDs (Multi-User Dungeons) are still popular, though not restricted to fantasy and gaming. Generally, MUDs allow many users to be logged on at one time, playing one game, with each user assuming an identity and character. Players can walk around, explore, chat with other characters, solve puzzles, outwit monsters, and even create their own rooms and tools. Some MUDs are simply devoted to online conversation on a theme. There are many variations on the MUD idea, including MUSH, MOO, MUCK, DUM, MUSE, and others. In addition, these interactive games have spawned a whole group of bulletin boards, listservs, and USENET newsgroups where players can discuss the games and develop strategies. There are online discussion groups, for instance, for users of LPMUD (for German-speaking MUD-ers), and for the people (some of them teenagers) who set up and administer the MUDs.

There are many other types of interactive games on the Internet, including chess, Scrabble, Go!, backgammon, and Diplomacy. On some chess and backgammon servers, users play against the computer; on others, they play in "real time" against human opponents. In addition, games of correspondence chess, via email, have been played by school students in many different countries; for example, elementary school children in the south of Iceland have played chess matches via electronic mail and Internet Relay Chat (see below) against children in schools in South Australia.

OTHER RESOURCES

While the discussion in this chapter has covered the major Internet tools, resources, and services that are likely to be of use to school librarians and others involved in the provision of library and information services in schools, there are a number of other Internet tools and services that meet particular needs. Some of these are described briefly below.

whois

The whois command enables Internet users to search a database of registered "domains" (for example, `ubc.ca`) and registered users. Run by the Network Information Center, the whois database is primarily for system managers (or their electronic mail postmasters) and listserv owners or moderators, so that they can find contact people at a computer site on the Internet. However, many educational sites, such as universities and research centers, run whois servers of their own, offering information about people who are on the staff of the institution, or attending the institution. In addition, there are directory information services based on whois, and whois services may be made available through an institution's gopher.

Finger

Finger is a very simple Internet tool that has several uses. The finger command, typed by itself, will return a list of people who are currently logged on to the computer that is being used. The finger command, when followed by the name and Internet address of another computer (for example, `finger @rhi.hi.is`), may return information about the users who are currently logged on to that computer. Some computers have the finger command implemented in such a way that it will provide information about a user who has an account on the computer, whether or not that user is currently logged in—sometimes by typing finger and a name (first name or last name), but sometimes only by typing the full user ID of the person. However, with an increasing emphasis on system security, many sites are blocking the finger command to outside access, and so a "Connection refused" message might be received in response to a finger command to a remote site.

The finger command has also been used as the basis of specific information services. For example, typing finger followed by the electronic mail address of a journal may get the table of contents of the current issue, plus subscription information. Typing `finger taylor@netcom.com` will get current information about how to locate a copy of the current version of the document "The Internet Mall: Shopping on the Information Highway". Typing `finger copi@oddjob.uchicago.edu` will get a list of events in history and birthdays of famous people that have occurred on that particular day. Typing `finger nasanews@space.mit.edu` will get the daily press release from NASA (particularly interesting during a space mission). And, in a much more light-hearted application, typing `finger xmastree@cygnus.com` just before Christmas 1993 from anywhere on the Internet returned information about the Christmas tree that was set up in the foyer of the offices of Cygnus Support in Mountain View, California: Internet users could see if the bubble lights, musical bells, and other decorations were switched on, though users of Cygnus's own network could also use commands to control the decorations, lights, and bells. This effort was repeated in 1994. While this seems trivial, it does give an indication of the ways in which the finger command could be used to provide information about the current status of a machine or experiment or service.

```
[51] % finger xmastree@cygnus.com
[cygnus.com]
                                                                    /\
The Cygnus Support Christmas Tree!                                 /\*\
                                                                  /\o\*\
Current state of the Christmas Tree is:                          /*/\/\/\
                                                                /\o\/\*\/\
Boring Blinking White Lights:    on                            /\*\/\*\/\/\
Less Boring Color Lights:        on                           /\o\/\/*/\/o/\
Tacky Bubble Lights              off                                 !!
                                                                     !!
Have a very wired Christmas!                                         !!
See the tree on the World Wide Web: http://www.cygnus.com/xmastree
Cygnus Support, "We Make Free Software Affordable."
```

Figure 2.7: Information Returned Through a Finger Command

For those accessing the Internet through a host computer that does not have finger, it is possible to install a version of finger on the microcomputer. There are several versions that are freely available via ftp, including GNU finger and BSD finger.

Internet Relay Chat (IRC)

Internet Relay Chat, or IRC, allows users to "talk" via the keyboard with other Internet users around the world, in "real time", that is, with messages being typed backwards and forwards when both users are logged on at one time. This is sometimes called "talk". Not all host computers that provide access to the Internet have facilities for IRC. In addition, when it is implemented, this can be done in different ways, so that the commands may vary from site to site.

When IRC is used in schools, it is usually as part of communications projects or projects involving students who are learning a foreign language. It is also the basis of some interactive Internet games.

CONCLUSION

Any list of Internet tools, resources, and services, is bound to be, on the one hand, confusing or intimidating for the novice, and, on the other hand, superficial for the experienced Internet user. The intention has been to provide an overview, with an indication of possible school library applications, as a basis for further discussion in later chapters of this book. Readers who wish to make use of the tools, resources, and services described will almost certainly find it necessary to consult one of the published guides to the Internet. The Bibliography at the end of this book lists several.

REFERENCES

NOTE: Quotations not followed by a reference are quotations from the information screens of the gophers, the headers of electronic journals, or the information messages supplied to new members of listservs.

Abrahamson, Andy and Tkachuck, Richard (1993), "AskERIC news", *TIE (Telecommunications in Education) News* 4, no. 3–4, p.23.

Bailey, Charles W. jnr (1994), Library-Oriented Lists and Electronic Serials, Document downloaded from the Library of Congress gopher LC MARVEL, 2 February.

Berry, John (1993), "K. Wayne's World: OCLC confronts the future", *Library Journal,* 118, 9, 15 May (conference reprint).

Birmingham, Judy (1993), Announcing the StarkNet Gopher from the Stark County School District, Canton, Ohio, USA, Message posted to the LM_NET listserv on the Internet, 15 November.

Broadhead, Rick (1993), Toronto Free-Net FAQ, Message posted to the EDTECH listserv on the Internet, 5 August 1993.

Bruce, Thomas R. (1994), Cello v1 Released, Message posted to the Net-Happenings listserv on the Internet, 17 February.

Caywood, Carolyn (1993), USENET, Message posted to the PUBLIB listserv on the Internet, 19 August.

Cisler, Steve (1993), Community Computer Networks: Building Electronic Greenbelts, File available from ftp.apple.com in the /ftp/alug/communet directory in Word (Macintosh), ASCII, and PostScript formats.

Clyde, Laurel A. (1993a), "Happy anniversary, Computer Pals", *Emergency Librarian* 21, no. 1, September-October, pp.57–58.

Clyde, Laurel A. (1993b), "The Internet", *Access* 7, no. 2, May, pp.26–29.

Clyde, Laurel A. (1994), *The Internet: An Introduction for Librarians,* Lindin, Reykjavík.

December, John (1994), Hypertext Index to Internet Resources, Document downloaded from World Wide Web, 27 February.

Eberlee, John (1993), "Backers of freenet hope to promote IS literacy", *Computing Canada,* 18 January, p.38.

FAQ—International E-mail Accessibility (1994), Document posted to the Net-Happenings listserv on the Internet, 24 June.

"FirstSearch discounted for school libraries" (1994), *OCLC Newsletter,* 207, January/February, p.27.

Geffert, Bryn (1993), "Community networks in libraries: a case study of the Freenet P.A.T.H.", *Public Libraries,* March/April, pp.91-–99.

Godin, Seth (1993), *The Smiley Dictionary,* Peachpit Press, Berkeley, California.

Harder, Ray (1994), Mosaic for Beginners, Draft document posted to the LM_NET listserv on the Internet, 20 March.

Harris, Judi (1992), "Mining the Internet: files for free! FTP file transfers on the Internet", *The Computing Teacher,* 20, 4, December/January, pp.50-52.

Harris, Judi (1993), "Mining the Internet: information by (electronic) mail order—FTP gateways and gophers", *The Computing Teacher* 20, no. 7, April, pp.29–32.

Hughes, Kevin (1994), Entering the World Wide Web: A Guide to

Cyberspace, Available on the World Wide Web at the URL http://www.eit.com/web/www.guide/

"Internet grabs big share of global market" (1994), *The Internet Letter* 1, no, 5, 1 February, pp.1, 3–8.

Kawasaki, Guy (1993), The Unofficial Smilie Dictionary. Document downloaded from the LM_NET listserv on the Internet, 23 August.

Korpinen, Heikki J. (1993), WYN—News Agency for Youth, Message posted to the LM_NET listserv on the Internet, 13 November.

Labovitz, John (1994a), What is an "E-Zine"?, Document available on the World Wide Web at http://www.ora.com:8080/johnl/e-zine-list/zine.html

Labovitz, John (1994b), Where You Can Find the E-Zine List, Document available on World Wide Web at http://www.ora.com:8080/johnl/e-zine-list/where.html

Mattison, David (1993), "The Victoria Free-Net: a report from Canada's first free-net", *The Reporter* (British Columbia Library Association) 36, no. 3, pp.37–38.

Morgan, David (1994), Free-Net List, Message posted to the USENET Newsgroup alt.internet.services, 10 June.

Nickerson, Gord (1992), "World Wide Web: hypertext from CERN", *Computers in Libraries* 12, no. 11, December, pp.75–76.

On Internet: An International Title and Subject Guide to Electronic Journals, Newsletters, Books, and Discussion Lists on the Internet 1993, Meckler, Westport, Connecticut.

Online Computer Library Center (1993?), *OCLC at a Glance*, OCLC, Dublin, Ohio (leaflet).

Polly, Jean Armour (1993), "ALUG online", *Apple Library Users Group Newsletter*, Spring, pp.33–35.

Rovers, Perry (1994), Anonymous FTP—Frequently Asked Questions (FAQ) List, Document posted to the Net-Happenings listserv on the Internet, 23 March.

Sanderson, David W. and Dougherty, Dale (1993), *Smileys*, O'Reilly and Associates, Sebastopol, California.

Scott, Peter (1994), The Free-Nets Home Page, Message posted to the Net-Happenings listserv on the Internet, 20 April.

Singh, Jagtar and Meadows, Jack (1993), "Electronic serials for library and information specialists on Internet", *ASLIB Proceedings* 45, no. 9, September, pp.234–241.

Strangelove, Michael (1993), "Free-Nets: community computing and the rise of the electronic citizen", *Online Access*, Spring, pp.46–47.

The Unofficial Smilie Dictionary (1994), Message posted to the LM_NET listserv on the Internet by Peter Milbury (author unknown), 14 February.

Valauskas, Edward J. (1993), "TurboGopher: Internet access with ease on the Macintosh", *Online* 17, no. 2, March, pp.87–89.

Ward, Lynn (1993), "Exploring the power of the Internet gopher", *Library Technology News*, 8, June/July, pp.1–3.

Whitman, Mark (1993), LinkWay and SI Images, Message posted to the EDTECH listserv on the Internet, 20 November.

World Wide Web Frequently Asked Questions (1994), Message posted to the Net-Happenings listserv on the Internet, 15 February; Document available on World Wide Web as `http://siva.cshl.org/~boutell/www_faq.html`

"Youth librarians go electronic" (1993), *yaacing (The Newsletter of the Young Adult and Children's Services Division of BCLA)*, Fall, p.18.

CHAPTER THREE

LM_NET ON THE INTERNET

WHAT IS LM_NET?

LM_NET is "a world-wide discussion group for school library media people" on the Internet. In Internet terms, it is a "listserv", one of many thousands of listservs that brings together people who are interested in particular subjects, or people who belong to particular professional or trade groups. Listservs enable their members, or "subscribers", to communicate with each other, and with all members of the listserv, via electronic mail. Messages sent to the listserv by any subscriber will be posted to all subscribers, and any subscriber can read the messages that others send to the listserv.

Started in June 1992, LM_NET had almost one thousand members in several countries just a year later. It is based on a computer at Syracuse University, New York, and operated, or "owned", by Michael Eisenberg, an Associate Professor in the School of Information Studies at Syracuse University, New York, and Peter Milbury, library media specialist and master teacher at Pleasant Valley High School in Chico, California. In advertising the listserv, the founders have commented that it is "open to all school library media specialists—worldwide—and people involved with the school library media field ... we want to keep the activity and discussion focussed on school library media" (Milbury, 1993f). Many of the members are people responsible for library/media services in schools, whether they call themselves, or are called, school librarians, teacher librarians, librarians, library media specialists, library media teachers, or any one of a number of other titles. Other members include people responsible for school library/media services at the district, state, or national level; school teachers; university and college faculty who are responsible for courses in school librarianship; students enrolled in formal university or college courses for school librarians; office-bearers in professional associations in the field of school librarianship; and people who provide commercial services for school libraries.

Early in 1994, approximately 25 to 40 messages were being posted to the listserv every day, and these were on a variety of topics related to school librarianship. As the founders noted in December 1993, LM_NET is "a list for practitioners helping practitioners, sharing ideas, solving problems, telling each other about new publications and upcoming conferences, asking for assistance or information, and linking schools through their library media centers" (Eisenberg and Milbury, 1993a). Through LM_NET, school librarians, who often work in isolation from other school librarians, have formed professional friendships and found support. The list has been used as a tool for lobbying: members alert each other to the need to take action on particular issues, such as funding cutbacks, new legislation, or censorship attempts.

In some cases, acquaintances or alliances formed through LM_NET have been consolidated through face-to-face meetings at conferences and other functions, organized beforehand through the net. For example, in a posting to LM_NET on 8 November 1993, Milbury announced the "First Annual LM_NET/CALIBK12 Meeting", a breakfast meeting of LM_NET members and members of CALIBK12, the California library media teachers' network, at the California Media and Library Educators Association State Conference, held that week in Pasadena, and later reported on that successful meeting in a posting on 16

November. An LM_NET breakfast meeting was held during the American Library Association (ALA) Midwinter Meeting in Los Angeles in February 1994, and reports were posted to LM_NET within 24 hours. Eisenberg commented, in a message to LM_NET on 6 February, that "the best part ... was meeting so many new people and putting faces with userids", while Carol Simpson, in a message on the same day, noted that "the wonderful thing about these meetings is that we all have an instant camaraderie" based on shared experiences on the net. Already, people who were at this meeting were planning for larger meetings as part of the ALA conference in Miami Beach later in 1994, and the American Association of School Librarians (AASL) conference in Indianapolis in mid-1994.

Eisenberg and Milbury have noted („LM_NET", 1993, p.1) that though LM_NET did start out as just "one more" electronic forum, "it quickly evolved into something much more that just a means for communicating information and ideas. Maybe it's due, in part, to breaking the isolation of school library media specialists (often only one to a school) or because library media types are quick to embrace and effectively use new technologies. Whatever the reason, LM_NET can truly be described as a community: a group of people who hold common interests, help each other, share problems and solutions and work together to fulfil individual and group goals". Shelley Lochhead, Librarian at Hopkinton High School, Contoocook, New Hampshire, USA, summed up her view of the features that make LM_NET more than just another listserv, in a message to all LM_NET subscribers in September 1993: she mentioned "the high level of conversation", "the sense of community", and the many special features of this listserv, including the face-to-face meetings of listserv members when this is possible.

Members of LM_NET who met together at the American Library Association Midwinter Meeting in Denver in 1993 discussed the ways in which LM_NET was already having an influence on the professional lives of practicing school librarians and on library educators and students in university and college programs for school librarians/ media specialists. The points of discussion were summed up by Eisenberg and Milbury („LM_NET", 1993, p.8):

* LM_NET overcomes isolation, by linking even the most remote library media specialist to colleagues throughout the world. Building-level practitioners are able to raise questions and discuss concerns with peers on a regular basis, as if they were in the same setting.
* LM_NET brings practice into the classroom of library media training programs. Already, library educators use the interactions on LM_NET as case studies of real events in real library media settings.
* LM_NET provides easy and open interaction between library media educators and researchers, those in professional leadership positions and those on the "front lines". This helps bridge the often-expressed gap between theory and practice.
* LM_NET helps develop technology skills among library media specialists. The listserv allows people to raise technology-related questions and provides information and assistance in using the Internet as well as other technologies.
* LM_NET creates a sense of belonging. Library media professionals and others involved in the field have a "home on the Internet" that is targeted specifically at their interests.
* LM_NET puts the library media profession into the center of the national networking movement. In many ways, the interactions and special efforts associated with LM_NET represent cutting-edge applications of listserv and Internet capabilities to professional practice.

It is important to note that participation in LM_NET is not restricted just to formal subscribers. LM_NET discussions are also carried on a number of educational bulletin boards and gophers, where school librarians and others who use the board or gopher can read messages, and in some cases participate in the discussion. For example, LM_NET discussions are posted to NEXUS, the national electronic information service for Australian schools. Australian teacher librarians can read the messages on a bulletin board on NEXUS, and then, if they wish, respond through the NEXUS electronic mail system to LM_NET itself. LM_NET messages are also posted to the Empire Schoolhouse (a NYSERNet bulletin board in New York), and to the Canada SchoolNet gopher (where messages can be read by school library personnel in Canadian schools that are linked to the Internet). LM_NET has been put onto the news and conference area of TENET, the Texas Education Network, and other school networking organizations have also been posting LM_NET traffic to conference areas so that their members who are working in the school library field can follow discussions. In addition, the LM_NET Archives (the archived messages posted to the LM_NET listserv) are available for public browsing on the AskERIC gopher in New York State. Thus the sphere of influence of LM_NET is wider than just its own registered subscribers.

ESTABLISHMENT OF LM_NET

Eisenberg and Milbury have given a very brief summary of the establishment of LM_NET in an article in *Information Searcher* (1993, pp.1, 6–9, 26). The idea for a listserv for people interested in school libraries was first raised by Eisenberg with Ann Weeks, executive director of the American Association of School Librarians (AASL) early in 1992. They agreed that the idea should be tried, and arrangements were made with Academic Computing Services at Syracuse University to set up the listserv on the University computers. LM_NET officially opened on Friday 5 June 1992, with 42 members, including local library media specialists from the Central New York area, colleagues of Eisenberg's at North American universities, and some "library media people" from New England who were recruited by a supporter, Carolyn Markuson.

Meanwhile, on the west coast of the United States, Milbury had established a "Leading Edge Librarian" Internet group, mostly people from California. At the suggestion of Markuson, Milbury and Eisenberg began to communicate on 8 June, and on 15 June, Milbury came on board as "co-owner" of the LM_NET listserv. The next day, the "Leading Edge Librarians" were officially merged with the existing LM_NET list, bringing the membership to around one hundred.

Over the northern summer of 1992, LM_NET membership grew, as a result of information spread through workshops, postings to other library-oriented listservs, brief articles in professional journals and newsletters, and personal contacts. By the start of the new school year in September, there were 250 members on LM_NET, and this had increased to around 400 by the end of 1992. In January 1993, LM_NET was mentioned in articles published in two professional journals, and more than one hundred new members were added that month.

GROWTH OF LM_NET

The growth of LM_NET through 1993 and into 1994 has been rapid; the total membership was close to one thousand by the time of the first anniversary of the listserv in June 1993, and it has continued to grow. The growth has not been quite as spectacular as that of the PUBLIB listserv, established on 2 December 1992 as a forum for people working in, or interested in public libraries. PUBLIB membership grew to 200 by the end of the first month, and after one year, the membership stood at approximately 1,400, with representation from every continent except Antarctica (Polly, 1993). However, professional librarians in public libraries are a large group, and in many states and countries they have more professional education in librarianship and more expertise in information retrieval, so that they are often in a better position to appreciate the benefits that listserv membership might bring. The comparative professional isolation of school librarians, who seldom work with others who have similar qualifications and interests, can be a barrier to finding out about Internet discussion groups, even though these are the people who may need them most.

While we know that the growth of LM_NET in its first year was rapid, it is difficult to trace accurately the growth in membership for that first year, because many of the quoted figures vary and may reflect the wide publication of membership numbers that were outdated even before they were published.

Any LM_NET subscriber can use the REVIEW LM_NET command to get a list of subscribers, and thus count the total membership on a particular date. However, while these lists are accurate, they do not include members who have temporarily stopped their subscription, and they provide only the email address and names of subscribers. Nevertheless, they have been used for some formal analyses of membership. Milbury undertook a "brief analysis" of LM_NET membership in late May 1993, for instance, at which time there were 963 subscribers. The author carried out two later analyses of the membership, on 1 October 1993 (1,137 subscribers) and on 7 February 1994 (1,411 subscribers). Table 3.1 shows the increase in LM_NET membership, based on these analyses. By late 1994, membership of LM_NET had reached 3,000, with the rate of increase being particularly impressive in the second half of the year.

While total membership is easy to see from the membership list, some subscribers elect to "conceal" their membership—that is, their name and email address do not show on any list of members, or any search for members, though they are included in the count of total membership. Thus, more detailed analyses of membership must be based only on "non-concealed" members. In fact, there were only two "concealed" subscribers to LM_NET in October 1993, and five in February 1994, so the effect on the analyses was not very noticeable, given the total number of subscribers.

However, even with the basic membership lists available in response to the REVIEW LM_NET command, it is

Table 3.1
Membership of LM_NET

DATE	TOTAL MEMBERS
Late May 1993	963
1 October 1993	1137
7 February 1994	1411

still difficult to answer questions like what is the geographical spread of LM_NET members, and from where do they enter the Internet? The electronic mail addresses might appear to answer these questions, yet they also present difficulties. Most electronic mail addresses are expressed in a coded format, using abbreviations and sometimes aliases. It is possible to verify the actual geographic locations (including site of the host computer, system, and/or network of origin) for electronic mail addresses, using Internet analysis tools such as Netfind or Network Information Center Gopher, but addresses must be verified one at a time, a daunting task even for a small list. But further, even when a geographic location is identified for the host computer or network through which the member enters the Internet, the essential nature of Wide Area Networks (WANs) defeats the notion of geographic location, since the users of a WAN are likely to be geographically dispersed. There are some extreme cases that illustrate this: for example, members of the United States armed forces serving abroad, and schools for the children of armed forces members abroad, usually have an email address on a United States host computer, at least indirectly, so that a subscriber with a United States armed forces electronic mail connection may be in Egypt or some other foreign location.

Nevertheless, as long as all this is borne in mind, it is possible to use the list of electronic mail addresses to extract some basic information about the membership of LM_NET and the growth of that membership over time.

Table 3.2 shows the geographic location of LM_NET subscribers by country (that is, the country in which their host computer or network is located) over the period May 1993 to February 1994. This information was extracted from the list of electronic mail addresses by counts based on the highest level (country) domain abbreviation for countries outside the United States, that is, the two-letter country code with which electronic mail addresses in most countries end. Thus, Canadian subscribers will have electronic mail addresses ending in ca, while subscribers in Iceland will have electronic mail addresses ending in is. Electronic mail addresses in the United States have tradi-

Table 3.2
LM_NET Membership by Country

	Late May 1993	1 October 1993	7 February 1994
Australia	5	10	13
Belgium	1	1	1
Brazil	1	0	0
Canada	31	39	75
Czech Republic	0	2	2
Denmark	1	0	0
Finland	2	2	1
Iceland	1	1	2
Italy	0	2	1
Japan	0	2	2
Malaysia	0	1	1
New Zealand	1	1	1
Singapore	0	1	1
United Kingdom	1	1	1
Netherlands	0	0	1
United States	919	1072	1304
Total "unconcealed"	963	1135	1406

tionally ended with a three-letter abbreviation for their general Internet classification, such as edu (for educational institutions), com (for commercial services), or org (for nonprofit organizations). Those people in the United States with access to the Internet via BITNET (the United States academic network) have electronic mail addresses in a slightly different format, usually with only one set of letters to the right of the @ sign in the address, or with the address ending with BITNET. However, it is now becoming more common for United States addresses to follow the international pattern, and newer United States electronic mail addresses often end in us.

It is clear from this that subscribers in the United States dominate LM_NET membership, just as United States users have dominated the Internet itself (though evidence quoted earlier indicates that this situation is now changing gradually, with non-United States Internet access increasing at a greater rate than in the United States). The other major (and growing) groups of subscribers are in Canada and Australia. In addition, Canada and Australia are the countries outside the United States where LM_NET traffic is carried on local networks, and so there are more people who read LM_NET messages in those two countries than the membership lists would indicate—just as there are in the United States. For each of the other countries, the membership is limited to one or two subscribers.

Table 3.3 shows that the total number LM_NET subscribers from outside the United States is growing, just as the number in the United States is growing. However, the number of foreign subscribers is increasing at a greater rate than the membership in general, and so where foreign subscribers accounted for 4.57 percent of the total membership in late May 1993, by 7 February 1994, they accounted for 7.25 percent of the total membership. The most spectacular growth was in Canada, where subscribers almost doubled between October 1993 and 7 February 1994. The 75 Canadian subscribers accessed

Table 3.3
Non-US Members of LM_NET

DATE	NUMBER	% OF TOTAL
Late May 1993	44	4.57
1 October 1993	63	5.55
7 February 1994	102	7.25

LM_NET from 26 different hosts across Canada, from Newfoundland, Nova Scotia, and Prince Edward Island in the east to British Columbia in the west, with the largest group from any one province coming from British Columbia.

MEMBERSHIP BASIS OF LM–NET

Further analyses of membership were carried out, based on the list of LM_NET members downloaded on 1 October 1993. As has been indicated, the total membership at that date was 1,137, though two of these subscribers were "concealed". Thus, information about them is not included in the Tables below.

Members of LM_NET access the Internet from a wide range of host computers, as indicated by the host abbreviation in their electronic mail address. A list of hosts with five or more LM_NET users as of 1 October 1993 is provided in Table 3.4. The information in the Table consists of that part of the electronic mail address that is to the right of the @ symbol (as in the example, `anne@rhi.hi.is`, where the host computer is located at RHI, the Icelandic abbreviation for the Computer Centre at the University of Iceland, at hi, the Icelandic abbreviation for the University of Iceland, at is, the Internet country code for Iceland). Thus this information indicates the address of the site or computer where the person has their Internet account, the institution, the network or section of a network, sometimes the type of organization or network, and, outside the

Table 3.4
Hosts With Five or More Members of LM_NET
1 October 1993

HOST	NUMBER OF MEMBERS
ALBNYVMS	5
CLASS.ORG	5
DUVM	5
ERIE	5
ISCSVAX.UNI.EDU	5
NORTHWEST.MISSOURI.EDU	5
NOVA.GMI.EDU	5
UAFSYSB.UARK.EDU	5
UAIVM.UA.EDU	5
UMAIL.UMD.EDU	5
UMAXC.WEEG.UIOWA.EDU	5
ALASKA	6
CBE.AB.CA	6
GUEST.NWNET.NET	6
MAIL.FIRN.EDU	6
NHGS.VAK12ED.EDU	6
SED	6
TJHSST.VAK12ED.EDU	6
UWWVAX.UWW.EDU	6
BIGCAT.MISSOURI.EDU	7
NHNET.UNH.EDU	7
ZODIAC.RUTGERS.EDU	7
CLEVELAND.FREENET.EDU	8
DESIRE.WRIGHT.EDU	8
RITVAX.ISC.RIT.EDU	8
BRAHMS.UDEL.EDU	9
CSN.ORG	9
NDE.UNL.EDU	9
MSUSI.MSUS.EDU	10
UTKVX	12
VDOE386.VAK12ED.EDU	12
AI.MEC.MASS.EDU	13
CLN.ETC.BC.CA	13
MACC.WISC.EDU	13
LIS.PITT.EDU	16
MAILBOX.SYR.EDU	17
CWIS.UNOMAHA.EDU	21
DELPHI.COM	23
CSD4.CSD.UWM.EDU	27
UNIVSCVM	29
SUVM	32
ONONDAGA	36
VAXI.MANKATO.MSUS.EDU	37
EIS.CALSTATE.EDU	71
TENET.EDU	119

United States (and sometimes in the States as well), the country code. Where only one set of letters is given (for example, SUVM), this usually indicates a BITNET address. However, as noted previously, it is not necessarily a simple matter to decode the information in an electronic mail address, though addresses on major hosts tend to be easily recognized.

Altogether, there were 45 hosts with five or more LM_NET users; these 45 hosts together accounted for 676 LM_NET users, or 59.56 percent of the 1,135 "nonconcealed" LM_NET users.

However, the total number of hosts on which LM_NET members were based was 363; of these, 45 had five or more users, and 318 had fewer than five users on LM_NET. Only nine hosts had 20 or more LM_NET members. Of these, TENET (the Texas Education Network) alone accounted for 119 members, or 10.48 percent of the membership. However, this was the exception; the next largest membership on any one host was 71 (or 6.25 percent) at `CALSTATE` (California State University), and after that, 37 (or 3.26 percent) at `MANKATO.MSUS`, and 36 (or 3.17 percent) at `ONONDAGA`. This illustrates the diversity of affiliations of LM_NET members, and gives an indication of their countrywide geographical location in the United States.

Only two of the addresses in Table 3.4 were non-United States addresses, `CLN.ETC.BC.CA` with 13 members, and `CBE.AB.CA` with six members. Both of these sites are in Canada, one in British Columbia and one in Alberta. Given that the Canadian membership of LM_NET almost doubled between 1 October 1993 and 7 February 1994, it seemed to be worthwhile to look at the Canadian members in the February listing to see if the Canadian membership patterns reflected those in the United States. Table 3.5 shows the Canadian hosts with the number of LM_NET members accessing the Internet through each.

Table 3.5
Canadian Hosts With Members of LM_NET
7 February 1994

HOST	NUMBER OF MEMBERS
ACS.UCALGARY.CA	1
CARLETONBE.OTTAWA.ON.CA	1
CRC.SD68.NANAIMO.BC.CA	1
EDNET.BC.CA	1
FREENET.VICTORIA.BC.CA	1
GATE2-WHISTLER.SFU.CA	1
JUPITER.SUN.CSD.UNB.CA	1
MALA.BC.CA	1
MORGAN.UCS.MUN.CA	1
NVANCVR.SCHDIST44.BC.CA	1
QUCDN.QUEENSU.CA	1
SASK.USASK.CA	1
SFU.CA	1
SHERIDANC.ON.CA	1
SOL.UVIC.CA	1
UNIXG.UBC.CA	1
UVVM.UVIC.CA	1
VENUS.CC.HOLLANDC.PE.CA	1
LIS.UTORONTO.CA	2
JESTER.USASK.CA	2
FIRST.ETC.BC.CA	3
MINET.GOV.MB.CA	4
CALVIN.STEMNET.NF.CA	6
FOX.NSTN.NS.CA	6
CBE.AB.CA	8
CLN.ETC.BC.CA	26

Table 3.5 shows that the 75 Canadian members accessed the Internet through 26 different hosts, and average of 2.88 members per host. Some 18 of those hosts had only one LM_NET member. The only host with a large number of LM_NET members was `CLN.ETC.BC.CA` with

26 members; the next largest group was eight members on CBE.AB.CA, followed by six members each on FOX.NSTN.NS.CA and CALVIN.STEMNET.NF.CA. As was the case for the United States, these figures indicate a dispersed membership, both in terms of host computers used and geographically. The Canadian host computers were located in nine different provinces, with British Columbia and Ontario being the only provinces to have LM_NET members on more than two host computers.

Apart from the United States and Canada, Australia was the only country to have more than one or two LM_NET members. However, the total Australian membership on 7 February 1994 was only 13, and so tabulation of the membership did not seem warranted. Nevertheless, small though they are, the Australian membership statistics do reflect those in the United States and Canada. The 13 Australian members were accessing the Internet through nine different hosts in five different Australian states and territories, with the largest group of LM_NET users on any one host being three.

Turning again to the United States subscribers on LM_NET, it is possible to deduce some further information from the list of electronic mail addresses returned by the REVIEW LM_NET command. Those United States addresses that do not end in .US end with an abbreviation that indicates the type of organization through which the person has access to the Internet. Table 3.6 shows the United States membership of LM_NET by type of organization through which they gain access.

Of the 46 LM_NET subscribers who had access to the Internet through a commercial service, 23, or 50 percent, used Delphi. Other commercial organizations had fewer LM_NET members using them for access; the next largest group was the group of four using America Online, while 11 commercial providers had between one and three people gaining access to LM_NET through their services. Among them were CompuServe, The World, and GEnie.

Table 3.6
United States Members: Access to the Internet

CODE	NUMBER OF MEMBERS	NOTES
BITNET	208	(An academic network linking universities and colleges in the United States)
COM	46	(Commercial organizations, including organisations that provide Internet access for a fee)
EDU	730	(Educational, including university and college, research organizations, schools, education authorities)
GOV	9	(Government agencies of all kinds)
MIL	1	(US Military)
NET	22	(Network, including statewide networks)
ORG	37	(Nonprofit Organization)
US	19	(The country code abbreviation for the United States, giving no reliable indication of affiliation)

Some LM_NET members in the United States (and some outside the states) were accessing the Internet through community freenets, including the Cleveland Freenet in Ohio, the Buffalo Free-Net in New York State, the Tallahassee Freenet in Florida, and the National Capital Freenet in Ottawa, Canada. Other organizations or services used to access the Internet included FrEdMail (Global SchoolNet Foundation) and other international electronic mail project connections.

All of this indicates diverse groups indeed! And while it would not be appropriate to draw conclusions about school users of the Internet in general on the basis of this analysis of LM_NET membership, nevertheless it is probable that school use does reflect this wide diversity of access patterns. Clearly, people involved in school librarianship find access in whatever way they can, in situations where they do not have institutional access through an educational network or a state network. The variety of access points and systems used make it difficult to provide firm guidelines or instructions, or even basic information, that will apply to all school users of the Internet.

FEATURES OF LM_NET

Many listservs offer a range of options and features for their subscribers. Some of these are created through the listserv software itself; others are created and maintained through the work of the listserv "owners" or the subscribers. LM_NET has a number of special features that have helped to make it the focus of an online community. These range from the Skills Index maintained by one of the listserv subscribers to the LM_NET Archives maintained on the AskERIC gopher for the benefit of the educational community as a whole.

LM_NET Digest

Many LM_NET subscribers find that receiving up to 25 messages a day is somewhat daunting, even though the discussions are useful. For these people, the "digest" option is often appropriate. They receive the same messages, but in batches of five or six (depending on the length of the individual messages). Thus, instead of 25 to 40 messages a day, they receive perhaps four or five. They can still respond to messages, either direct to the sender, or to the whole list of subscribers.

Targets/Hits

A large and active listserv can become chaotic without some means of focusing discussions. On LM_NET, one of the discussion tools adopted is called "TARGET->". While this is "a bit more formal than is common on most lists", it was felt by the list owners that such a tool would serve members well as the listserv grew. Initially, reactions were mixed, but the rapid growth in listserv membership and increasing traffic on the listserv, among other factors, have helped to convince the membership that some kind of mechanism for moderating discussion is needed.

The LM_NET owners have recommended that subscribers with queries related to a particular topic specifically TARGET-> their queries and request responses directed to their own personal email address. Then, after a few days, they should use a HIT-> summary to share the responses they had received with all LM_NET subscribers. So, when a subscriber needs information about a particular topic (such as writing a school library collection development policy, or selecting CD-ROM encyclopedias, or resources for deaf students, or public access catalogs designed for use by elementary school children), the subscriber posts a TARGET-> message, outlining the problem, and asking people to respond directly to the posting subscriber at their own email address. Once the subscriber has collected the responses, he or she summarizes them and posts the summary to the listserv as a HIT-> message, with the same subject heading as the original TARGET-> message. In this way, all subscribers to the listserv are informed about the topic, without being required to read through a number of messages that may be repetitive or confusing. It reduces the amount of electronic mail traffic on the list, while stimulating discussion about current issues and facilitating sharing of information.

Mentoring

For a large number of LM_NET subscribers, LM_NET is their first listserv, and their introduction to the Internet. One of the LM_NET members, Shelley Lochhead, has organized a mentor program to assist new subscribers. Mentors are simply "people willing to help out with new users or those needing a special hand", people who are not necessarily whiz-kids, but who "know a little" and are "willing to share". The program, which commenced in

October 1992, uses general postings to the listserv to recruit volunteer mentors and to identify the people who need help from mentors. Matches are made on the basis of applications used, operating system environments, and communications software. Most of the mentoring is done through the electronic mail system or by telephone. While much of the assistance given relates to technical problems and the skills required to use Internet tools, mentors also help in the process of finding resources. "Most of the mentoring is reactive, but mentors may also nudge mentees if there has been a hiatus of activity" (Wighton, 1993, p.14).

The LM_NET Skills Index (later the Telecommunications Skills Index or Internet Assistance for LM_NET Members Index) is created by Lochhead to help members to "become brave and independent surfers on the Internet". This list gives the names and electronic mail addresses of LM_NET members who have volunteered to answer questions in their areas of computer communications expertise. "These experienced network users are available to members who need assistance in getting acquainted with network resources" (Lochhead, 1994). The Telecommunications Skills Index file is stored in the LM_NET file list with the name "Skills Index". LM_NET subscribers can request a copy by sending an electronic mail message to the listserv computer.

Monitoring of Other Listservs

Many LM_NET subscribers also subscribe to other listservs on the Internet. However, few people can cope with the volume of electronic mail generated through more than a couple of active listservs. Yet important information, of interest to school librarians, is often posted to other listservs for people whose interests are related to those of school librarians, for instance, listservs in the fields of school administration, children's literature, curriculum development, educational technology, librarianship, information policy, and educational research. To overcome this problem, and to assist LM_NET subscribers to keep abreast of current developments, several LM_NET members monitor other listservs and information sources, and post useful messages and information back to LM_NET.

The listservs and other information services monitored include PUBLIB (for librarians in public libraries and joint-use libraries), PACS-L (for librarians interested in public access to computer-based services), EDTECH (for teachers and others interested in the use of information technology in educational settings), CoSN (for educators and others interested in computer networking in education), KIDS-NET (which provide opportunities for school students to use international computer communications), CDROM-LAN (for educators, librarians, and others interested in the networking of CD-ROM resources), HYPERCRD (for people interested in hypermedia and the use of HyperCard software), and the White House information postings (from the Office of the President of the United States).

LM_NET Archives

While many of the messages exchanged on LM_NET are purely ephemeral, others are of more lasting value, and the information provided by subscribers can be a wonderful resource. Some messages provide assistance at the point of need. However, other people, not part of the original discussion, may be able to use the earlier information when a problem arises in their own local setting. In addition, the discussions can provide a record of the range of viewpoints, or changing viewpoints, on important professional issues or concerns, like censorship, access to information, school/community libraries, volunteers in school libraries, school-based decision-making, and so on. However, for this to be effective, subscribers need access to earlier discussions and messages. This access is provided through the LM_NET Archives.

The LM_NET Archives are available to anyone who has

access to gopher, at the AskERIC gopher site in New York State. Most gophers have an option called "Other Information Services" or "Other Gophers" or "Gopher Servers all Around the World". From this, users can follow a path North America/ USA/ New York/ Syracuse University/. Another option is to use telnet to go to a public gopher server anywhere on the Internet, and then the series of gopher menus will lead to AskERIC and the LM_NET Archives. LM_NET can be found by taking the following gopher path:

```
- Access to the AskERIC Virtual Library via GOPHER/
 - AskERIC (Educational Resources Information Center)/
  - Education Listservs Archives/
   - LM_NET/
```

Here, the archives can be read, month by month. In addition, the directory of LM_NET members is available, along with a range of other documents, including information about LM_NET, and the "Checklist of Microcomputer Based Library Software".

LM_NET Directory

A directory of LM_NET members is maintained by Betty Dawn Hamilton and updated regularly. This list provides members with information about each other, to augment the very sparse information that is provided when the REVIEW command is used to get a list of members. Listing in the directory is voluntary, and members provide details of full name, the position they hold and the institution for which they work, their full postal address, telephone and fax numbers, professional memberships, and information about special interests. The directory is available online through the AskERIC gopher (from the same menu as the LM_NET archives).

NOTES: JOINING LM_NET

Subscriptions to LM_NET (requests to join) are handled automatically by the listserv computer at Syracuse University in New York State. Note that, although one "subscribes" to a listserv, the subscription is usually free. This is the case with LM_NET. To subscribe, send an email message to the listserv computer. For Internet users, the address of the computer is

`listserv@listserv.syr.edu`

Leave the subject line of the message blank. In the first line of the body of the message, type

`SUBSCRIBE LM_NET Firstname Lastname`

Substitute your own first name and last name for the words "Firstname" and "Lastname". Thus, the author's subscription message to the LM_NET listserv would read

`SUBSCRIBE LM_NET Anne Clyde`

The LM_NET listserv computer will respond to this within a day or so with a message that asks for confirmation of your subscription, and provides information about LM_NET. If the procedures are followed, you will be added to the list of subscribers, and you will begin to receive mail from the listserv.

At this point, you can also begin to send messages to the listserv for posting to all subscribers. To do this, you send your message to an address that is different from the administrative address of the listserv; for LM_NET, this address is

`LM_NET@listserv.syr.edu` (for Internet users)

Your message should be sent in the format in which you want it to appear on the listserv. In fact, to quote from the LM_NET "Welcome" message to new subscribers, "just send an email message as you would to anyone else with an electronic mail address". The difference is that this message will go out to thousands of subscribers. Because you are a subscriber to the listserv, you will also receive a copy of your message so you do not need to save a copy when you send the message.

To change to the digest format for receiving LM_NET messages, subscribers send a message to the administrative address of the listserv at `listserv@listserv.syr.edu` (not to the listserv itself) with the subject line blank and one line in the body of the message:

```
set lm_net digest
```

To cancel the digest format and return to the normal setting, the following message is sent to the administrative address of the listserv computer (the same address as above):

```
set lm_net mail
```

Other listserv commands enable subscribers to find out the email address of another subscriber, to get a list of subscribers (with their email addresses), to conceal their own name and email address (if they do not want other subscribers to be able to read their name and email address on a list), to temporarily cancel mail (for instance, when they are going to be away on vacation and unable to read their electronic mail), and to sign off from LM_NET. Information about these, and other commands, is provided in the "Welcome" message sent by the listserv computer to all new subscribers. Subscribers are advised to save this message for later reference.

REFERENCES

Biagini, Mary K. (1993a), "LM_NET, a lifeline", *School Library Media Quarterly* 21, no. 2, Winter, p.91.

Biagini, Mary K. (1993b), "A Midwinter Meeting", *School Library Media Quarterly* 21, no. 3, Spring, p.153.

DeCandido, GraceAnne (1993), "School librarians on the Internet", *School Library Journal*, January, p.10.

Eisenberg, Michael (1994), Midwinter Meeting, Message posted to the LM_NET listserv on the Internet, 6 February.

Eisenberg, Michael and Milbury, Peter (1993a), LM_NET: A World-Wide Discussion Group for School Library Media People, Message posted to net-happenings@is.internic.net, 23 December.

Eisenberg, Michael B. and Milbury, Peter (1993b), LM_NET: Bringing

Together the School Library Media Community Electronically, Draft document, Electronic mail communication, 29 July.

Eisenberg, Michael B. and Milbury, Peter (1994), "The Internet and library media programs: the technology is now!", in McClure, Charles R., Moen, William E., and Ryan, Joe (eds), *Libraries and the Internet/NREN: Perspectives, Issues, and Challenges*, Mecklermedia, Westport, pp.199–220.

Eisenberg, Michael B. and Milbury, Peter (1993), "LM_NET: the school library media electronic community", *Information Searcher* 5, no. 2, pp.1, 6-9, 28.

"Internet grabs big share of global market" (1994), *The Internet Letter* 1, no. 5, 1 February, pp.1, 3.

"LM_NET, a lifeline" (1993), *School Library Media Quarterly*, Winter, p.91.

LM_NET List: School Library Media and Network Communications 1993, List downloaded from the LM_NET listserv listserv@suvm.syr.edu on the Internet, 1 October.

Lochhead, Shelley (1993), Help, Message posted to the LM_NET listserv on the Internet, 28 September.

Lochhead, Shelley (1994), Internet Assistance for LM_NET Members Index, Document posted to the LM_NET listserv on the Internet, 1 June, and available in the LM_NET Archives on the AskERIC gopher.

Milbury, Peter (1993a), "LM_NET: a librarian's dream", *CMLEA Newsletter* 16, no. 8, April, p.7.

Milbury, Peter (1993b), LM_NET Membership Directory Now Available on Gopher, Message posted to the LM_NET listserv on the Internet, 16 May.

Milbury, Peter (1993c), LM_NET Statistics Regarding Message Postings and Membership, Message posted to the LM_NET listserv on the Internet, 24 May.

Milbury, Peter (1993d), A Brief Analysis of LM_NET Members E-Mail Addresses, Electronic mail communication, 28 July.

Milbury, Peter (1993e), CMLEA, Message posted to the LM_NET listserv on the Internet, 16 November.

Milbury, Peter (1993f), LM_NET: A Worldwide Discussion Group for School Library Media People, Message posted to the net-happenings listserv on the Internet, 23 December.

Milbury, Peter (1994a), LM_NET Archives Location, Message posted to the LM_NET listserv on the Internet, 23 January.

Milbury, Peter (1994b), Finding the LM_NET Archives and Related Information, Message posted to the LM_NET listserv on the Internet, 22 March.

NEXUS: A World of Learning, Telecom NEXUS, A National Electronic Information Service for Australian Schools (1993), Education Department of South Australia, Adelaide.

Polly, Jean Armour (1993), PUBLIB and PUBLIB-NET Are Now One Year Old, Message posted to the PUBLIB listserv on the Internet, 5 December.

Simpson, Carol (1993), Resolution Honoring LM_NET, Message posted to the LM_NET listserv on the Internet, 15 March.

"TENET: Texas Education Network" (1993), *School Library Media Quarterly*, Summer, pp.255–256.

Wighton, David J. (1993), "Telementoring: examining the potential for an educational network", *TIE (Telecommunications in Education)* 4, no. 3-4, pp.13–16.

CHAPTER FOUR

THE RESEARCH PROJECT

In 1993, discussions on Internet listservs such as LM_NET and EDTECH often referred to a perceived lack of information about how school libraries were making use of the Internet, and the frequent requests for such information that were appearing on these listservs supported this perception, as did a preliminary search of online databases such as ERIC (Educational Resources Information Center), British Education Index, and LISA (Library and Information Science Abstracts). It therefore seemed appropriate to undertake a research project to look at school library use of the Internet at present, to identify barriers to the use of the Internet in schools and opportunities provided by use of the Internet, and to identify trends and developments. Funding and facilities were available through the University of Iceland for such a project, and work commenced in August 1993.

Specifically, the aims of the research project, based on perceived needs for information and on an analysis of related research studies, were to:

- identify research that had already been completed in this area or was under way;
- identify policy documents related to school and library use of online services, from education authorities, library authorities, government agencies, and other organizations;
- identify and describe Internet resources that have

applications in school libraries, or that could be used within the context of the school library program or the provision of information services in schools;

- collect information about the users of an Internet listserv for "school library media people" and analyze it to determine the characteristics of these pioneer users, how they heard about the Internet, how they learned to use it, how they use it at present, and the purposes for which they use it;
- describe and discuss current projects based on the use of the Internet by school libraries;
- collect baseline information about the extent of teachers' and students' access to the Internet in schools and school libraries (as distinct from access for the school librarian);
- identify the barriers to the use of the Internet by school libraries, and provide suggestions (from the literature and from discussions on the listservs) for overcoming these barriers;
- identify issues associated with the use of the Internet by school libraries, and discuss those issues from different points of view.

It appeared that this information would be of use to school librarians (who were looking for ideas for using the Internet in a school library environment and for examples of successful use by school libraries), and to teachers, school administrators, educational administrators at the district and state levels, and others involved in policy decisions related to school libraries and information networks.

The research project was international in scope. However, since the main discussion groups on the Internet with school library membership operate wholly or partly in English, the scope is, in effect, almost totally English-language international, though some resources and services in other languages (including French, Spanish, Norwegian, and Icelandic) were explored, and documents were translated for the project from Russian, Japanese,

German, Icelandic, Finnish, and Hebrew. Because of the North American dominance of the Internet, despite its international character, material is more abundant from the United States (and to a lesser extent, Canada).

To achieve the aims of the project, several different research strategies and methods were used.

- A review and analysis of published and unpublished material related to the topic, including the research reports, government documents and legislation, reports and policy statements from school authorities and professional associations, reports describing individual school and school library use of Internet resources, and documents and information made available on the Internet. In addition, some quantitative analyses of citations were carried out to determine trends in the literature.
- A questionnaire survey of users of the LM_NET electronic discussion group for teacher librarians on the Internet. LM_NET had been operational for more than a year at the time of the survey and had more than one thousand members in several countries. The questionnaire was distributed through a posting on LM_NET itself, and people could respond by electronic mail (from LM_NET), or print out the questionnaire and respond by mail or fax.
- An analysis of LM_NET traffic for one month, with all LM_NET communications during that month being downloaded for analysis. The material collected in this way was to be used to place the questionnaire responses in perspective, and to provide additional information related to usage, the nature of the messages posted, the topics discussed, and the users as a group.
- A series of interview-based mini-case studies of users of LM_NET, selected as a result of an analysis of the questionnaire responses, an analysis of the postings to LM_NET, and the review of the literature. Interviews were carried out by telephone, email, and having the

subjects record their answers to some focus questions on audiocassette.

- Online exploration of Internet resources and services, using Internet search tools such as WAIS, Hytelnet, gopher, and Mosaic, and continued monitoring of the sources and services identified as being appropriate for school library applications or as having something to offer in terms of meeting the information needs of the various members of the school community.

THE LITERATURE REVIEW

A comprehensive literature review was carried out as a basis for the project. Sources used included online bibliographic databases (such as ERIC, British Education Index, Australian Education Index, LISA, Microcomputer Index, SCIS—Schools Curriculum Information Service), and bibliographies and documents available on the Internet itself (through such sources as the AskERIC gopher, the NYSERNet gopher, the Ontario Institute for Studies in Education gopher, and the FedWorld government bulletin board service). Other sources included White House and other United States government press releases and information services online, American Library Association and other professional association information services and press releases online, newspaper databases, and CARL's UnCover search and document delivery service.

The literature review had several purposes. The main aim was to identify relevant government reports and legislation and policy documents from governments, education authorities, and/or library authorities. In the United States, recent discussion has focused on the National Information Infrastructure (NII) and the provision that is to be made for schools and other educational institutions within any legislation. Vice President Al Gore has made several public statements on the NII. The "Administration White Paper on Communications Act Reforms" states that "it is a goal of this Administration that by the year 2000 all of the classrooms, libraries, hospitals, and clinics in the United States will be connected to the NII" (United States of America, 1994). Documents, policy statements, and discussion papers related to NII have been issued by the National Coordinating Committee on Technology in Education and Training (1994), the American Library Association (1994), the Committee on Applications and Technology Information Infrastructure Task Force (1994), Bell Atlantic (Cullen, 1994), the Electronic Frontier Foundation (1993), and others. Connie Stout provided an analysis of "NII and Education" for the EdPOL-D (Education Policy Digest) electronic journal (Stout, 1994), while the electronic newsletter Networks and Communities devoted the whole of its 26 December 1993 issue to a discussion of the White House legislative goals in relation to NII. There have been many others. Discussion is also ongoing in Australia in relation to the development of the AARNet national research and education network, and in Canada in relation to CA*NET and CANARIE. In the Canadian province of New Brunswick, a task force of the Electronic Information Highway produced a report in 1994 with the title *Driving the Information Highway,* in which opportunities for the province are highlighted. In Europe, a conference on the Use of Databases and Telecommunications in Education, held in Denmark in June 1993, incorporated official reports from 12 European countries on their policies and practices in relation to telecommunications in schools (Collis, 1993; Smedegaard, 1993). It emerged that "most of the countries in Europe have some kind of national plan and service to support telecommunications in education" (Collis, 1993).

Documents from education and library authorities shed some light on attitudes to the use of online or other computer-based information services in schools and school libraries, though the Internet is seldom discussed specifically. These documents and policy statements will be discussed further in the chapters dealing with Internet applications in school libraries and issues associated with access to the Internet in schools and school libraries. However, despite some notable exceptions like the TENET state telecommunications project in Texas, and VA PEN in Pennsylvania, a 1992 research study reported by Margaret Honey noted that "there is not widespread administrative support for telecommunications activities on either the district or the school level" (Honey, 1993), and this is supported by the small number of official documents available from this level in the United States.

A second purpose of the literature review was to identify research that had been completed or was under way in the area of school or school library use of the Internet, and in related areas, such as the use of online information services and CD-ROM in schools and school libraries, and the use of the Internet in public, academic, and special libraries. The literature review confirmed the lack of studies that specifically dealt with the use of the Internet in school libraries and indicated a possible reason for this: "the Internet is relatively new. Consequently information related to Internet lags behind the technology" (Benavides and Benavides, 1993). However, the review did reveal studies that shed some light on some aspects of this project. These included the Benavides's Louisiana study quoted above of staff development and its contribution to the success of educational projects on the Internet, Michael Anthony Gallo's doctoral dissertation for the Florida Institute of Technology on the effects on high school teachers of direct and unrestricted access to the Internet (Gallo, 1993), and a descriptive case study of the implementation of a technology education initiative in six Western Australian secondary schools, which identified factors that contributed to successful outcomes (Treagust and Rennie, 1993).

Nevertheless, we do know, from research in the more general field of computer mediated communication and the use of telecommunications in education that computer networking, including use of the Internet, offers significant benefits for schools and educators, in terms of resource sharing, resource management, faster access to information, access to more up-to-date information, and less paperwork at the local level (Bishop, 1990; Kinnaman, 1990). One of the most important benefits is the opportunity it provides for collaborative projects and the exchange of information and files, even across the world (Kinnaman, 1990). Internet access allows both teachers and students to reach outside the traditional classroom to share information and concerns, to seek advice, and to explore a range of information sources and services (Schuckel, 1990; Lehman, Campbell, Halla, and Lehman, 1992; Halla, Perceival, and Snyder, 1989), and it promotes new forms of social interaction that break down the isolation of teachers and open up the classroom (Halla, Perceival, and Snyder, 1989; Halla, 1990; Kurshan, 1991). Another major benefit is the access to information almost anywhere in the world (Kinnaman, 1990).

An international overview of the research related to telecommunications and student learning has been provided by Betty Collis and Jim Levin (1993). They cite other analyses of the literature (Collis and De Vries, 1991; Collis, 1992; Wellburn, 1992) to support their contention that most of the research studies are descriptive case studies, and the researcher is often someone who is involved in the project; analysis and discussion tend to focus on organizational challenges, barriers to effective use, and qualitative evidence of benefits in terms of student learning. This is probably due to the fact that the topic is a very new one, but, nevertheless, quantitative and predictive research, using more sophisticated methodologies, is needed as a basis for further development.

A third purpose of the literature review was to identify reports of surveys in related fields, such as the use of online information services or CD-ROMs in schools and school libraries, with the idea that these might provide a framework or basis for the proposed survey of the members of LM_NET about their use of the Internet. Charles McClure has carried out research projects related to the use of the Internet by public libraries, including a 1991/92 study (with others) that used a survey, focus groups, and site visits to collect data. In 1990, Roxanne Baxter Mendrinos surveyed 379 school library media specialists in Maine and Pennsylvania about their use of CD-ROM (Mendrinos, 1992). Among the results of this study were the identification of some barriers to the adoption of CD-ROM technology and issues associated with the use of the new technology, and these seemed to have some relevance in the context of Internet use as well. In 1993, Margaret Honey and Andrés Henríquez published a report of their United States study of 550 school teachers who were active telecommunications users. Because the proposed study was also to be a study of known users of the technology, both the methodology used by Honey and Henríquez and the findings were of some relevance. The findings of this survey will be discussed further in Chapter Five and Chapter Eight, in relation to school and school library use of the Internet, and barriers to the effective use of the Internet in schools. Another study that provided a partial foundation for the proposed project was a study carried out by the author in 1987 with Joyce Kirk, a survey of school users of electronic information systems in Australia (Clyde and Kirk, 1989). This involved a questionnaire survey of school librarians whose schools were known to be using online information services, to identify the services being used by those schools, and to collect information on the nature of that use. All of these, and particularly the latter, influenced the development of the questionnaire survey that formed part of the research project described in this chapter, though none could, by itself, be used as a model for the survey.

In addition to the literature review, some quantitative analyses of references (using online services, including

ERIC and Library and Information Science Abstracts) were carried out to determine trends in the literature over a period of time. This work is referred to in the Introduction to this book.

THE ONLINE QUESTIONNAIRE

A questionnaire survey was undertaken to collect information from the school librarians and others associated with school libraries who were using the Internet. The questionnaire was posted to the LM_NET listserv on the Internet, since it was the most significant discussion group or forum for "school library media people" on the net, and one that had been well publizised. LM_NET had been operational for more than a year at the time of the survey, and had more than one thousand members in several countries. The members included school librarians, teachers, school system administrators, library advisers, library school faculty and graduate students, and others who were associated in some way with school library services. Six months' monitoring of the listserv had shown that the membership was relatively stable and growing, and that the quality of the professional discussion was high.

The questionnaire was selected as the most efficient means of collecting basic information about the users of LM_NET, how they found out about LM_NET and the Internet, how they learned how to use them, the purposes for which they were using LM_NET and the Internet, the Internet sources and services they were using, any things that they would like to be doing or services they would like to be using, their perceptions of any barriers to the use of the Internet in school libraries, and their ideas for the future.

Distribution of the Questionnaire

The questionnaire was distributed to all members of LM_NET, through a posting on LM_NET itself, in October

1993. This month was selected because it is the first month of the new northern academic year that could be called a "normal" month, a time when it could be expected that schools would have settled down after the activities associated with the beginning of a new year. In Australia and other countries that follow the southern academic year, October is a month relatively free of holidays and examinations and other activities that might cause school librarians to miss their electronic mail reading. The day before the questionnaire was posted, a message was posted to LM_NET alerting members to the fact that the questionnaire would be coming and asking them to take the time to read it and respond. In keeping with the tradition of sharing that is so much a part of LM_NET and the Internet, the researcher indicated that summaries of the responses would be posted to LM_NET. A follow-up posting to LM_NET in late November summarized responses to date and invited any members who had not yet completed the questionnaire to do so. This not only resulted in further responses, but also in electronic mail messages from five people who had missed the questionnaire posting and who asked for a copy to complete. The explanations provided by those who missed the questionnaire reflect life on the Internet: two had their accounts set to "nomail" at that time for different reasons; two had recently joined the listserv and had not noticed the original message; and one was not receiving mail at that time because of technical problems with the local server that provided Internet access.

In all, 105 people responded to the questionnaire survey, representing 9.24 percent of the total LM_NET subscribers in October 1993. The response rate is approximately what was expected, based on the response rates achieved in other surveys of listserv members (for example, Sudamalis, 1992) and the comments of other researchers who have used this method (for example, Mitchell, Paprzycki and Duckett, 1993b).

Scott Heath (1993) discusses the issue of survey population and response in relation to questionnaires administered via electronic mail. He notes that the sample population would clearly be more likely to be random if a complete list of users of a service were obtained and individual users were randomly selected from that group. This would increase the validity of the results, but would make it more difficult to deliver the questionnaires, each of which would have to be addressed individually to the electronic mail address of the selected recipients. Creating a long mailing list and sending the questionnaire to all the addresses on the list can result in an unacceptably long mail header if a bulk mailing is used, and this may cause recipients to stop reading (Mitchell, Paprzycki and Duckett, 1993b), although there are software solutions to this problem. When a questionnaire is sent to all members of a listserv, it has to be understood that the respondents will be a self-selected sample that may not be representative of the listserv members as a group, let alone the wider professional groups represented by listserv members. This is true for the present study; nevertheless, as the analysis in Chapter Five shows, the survey respondents do generally reflect the different groups of people who are LM_NET members.

Unfortunately it is difficult to draw any conclusions about the extent to which the survey respondents represent the total membership of LM_NET since the information available about members through the listserv REVIEW command is limited to email address and name. However, the focus of the study was the collection of information about LM_NET users and their use of the Internet, rather than carrying out analyses and drawing conclusions about either LM_NET members or school librarians in general on the basis of survey responses. Nevertheless, when looked at in conjunction with the analysis of LM_NET traffic (described below), it is possible to draw some wider conclusions about LM_NET members and their use of LM_NET and the Internet.

In addition to these considerations, there were technical issues related to the administration of questionnaires via electronic mail that needed to be addressed if the survey were to produce results. Three different ways of handling an online questionnaire are discussed by Alejandra Rojo (1993). One is by having respondents download the questionnaire to disc, complete it on the computer, and then upload it to the electronic mail system again. Alternatively, the survey might be carried out interactively via telnet (those who were selected as part of the study would receive email asking them to telnet to the host computer and respond to the questionnaire online). Or the emailed questionnaire might be printed by the respondent (using the PRINT or PRINT SCREEN commands), completed on paper, and mailed. The option or options chosen would affect the design of the questionnaire, and would have implications for the instructions provided to the recipient as well.

The options suggested by Rojo, and others, were reviewed for this project. The telnet option was rejected, for two reasons: it was clear from their postings to the listserv and their requests for information that many LM_NET users had limited (though developing) Internet skills; it was also clear from comments in some postings that some members had Internet accounts with very limited capabilities. The aim was therefore to keep the response options simple and related to the electronic mail capabilities and skills that LM_NET members would have to possess in order to use LM_NET itself. Thus the introduction to the questionnaire explained how people could respond. "The first [option] is to complete the questionnaire on the screen, and then to FORWARD it to me.... The second is to download the questionnaire to your hard disc, complete it later, and then upload it and send it to my email address. The third is to print out the questionnaire, fill it in on paper, and then send it to me by mail." Offering the last option carried a disadvantage for the researcher, in that not all the survey data was returned in machine-readable format, and so some keyboarding and coding of the data was required. However, the fact that some 20 percent of the responses were returned by mail in this format suggests that, for this group at least, the response rate would have been much lower if the option had not been offered. This is supported by comments from some respondents who indicated that they did not have the skills to respond via computer, thus confirming the impression gained earlier that some new members, particularly, may have only limited skills; for instance, one respondent noted that "I don't know how to download, print, or mark the survey on the screen. I wrote down the answers and then put them on w/ the keyboard. I am a novice to say the least."

All three methods were used by different respondents, but while the printed and mailed responses were easy to distinguish, it was not always possible to tell if a respondent had completed the questionnaire on the screen, or had downloaded it to disc and completed it offline before uploading it again. Figure 4.1 indicates the numbers using the two basic response modes (response via electronic mail and response via air mail).

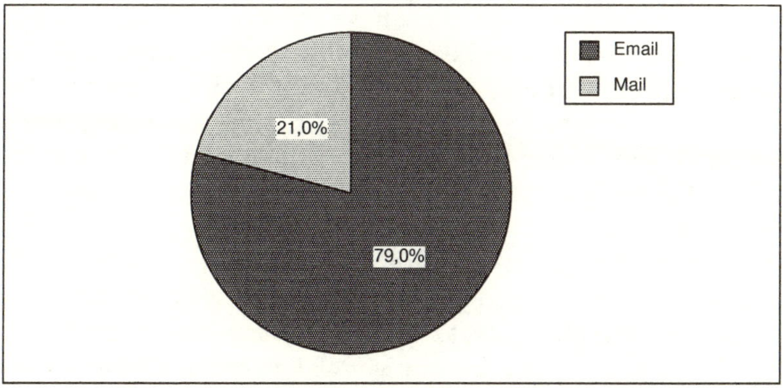

Figure 4.1: Methods of Response to the Online Questionnaire

In a 1993 research report, Heath raised the issue of anonymity in relation to online questionnaires, an important consideration in many studies. In fact, anonymity can be guaranteed only by the person who distributes the questionnaire and collects the responses, since most electronic mail message headers will include at least the electronic mail address of the sender. It is possible that a custom reader could be designed and written to replace the identifying code, and this method would provide anonymity; however, even this is not guaranteed, since many questionnaire respondents forget that an electronic mail "signature" that they have created for themselves is automatically attached to the bottom of every message that they send. For the present study, it was decided to admit that anonymity might be compromised and to ask the respondents to check a box to indicate if they could be quoted by name or otherwise in the publication that resulted from the project. This admission had a further advantage in that it allowed the researcher to identify, at least by electronic mail address, people who would be suitable subjects for a mini-case study and to contact them. It was noted, during the course of the project, that those respondents who wished to remain completely anonymous had printed out the questionnaire, written in their responses, cut off the header and any other material that might identify them, and returned the questionnaire by mail in an envelope that had on it only the researcher's address and a stamp. This seemed a reasonable solution, given the nature of the project.

Design of the Questionnaire

One of the challenges of the project was designing a questionnaire that would be attractive when it appeared on the computer screens of LM_NET members, that would be easy to read online (regardless of the electronic mail software being used by the member), that would have no formatting characters (which would be interpreted differently by different receiving software), that would result in the collection of useful information but would not require the respondents to leave their computers to find the information (in which case they would just hit the <DELETE> key), that would not occupy unnecessary space in the electronic mailboxes of those LM_NET members whose accounts have space limits, and that would still be reasonably easy to analyze.

Research indicates that "the appearance and arrangement of the survey form itself is vital to a successful study". A carefully constructed questionnaire that is "appealing to the eye" will increase the response rate and result in data that is easier to manage and code (Berdie and Anderson, 1974, p.31). Further, the form must be sufficiently interesting and have enough face-appeal so that the respondent will be inclined to respond to it and to complete it. However, to a large extent, the way in which an electronic mail questionnaire will appear on the screen of the reader is beyond the control of the researcher—at best, the researcher can take steps to ensure that the limitations of electronic mail reading software will not cause too much damage. Many LM_NET users in schools were known to have electronic mail software that was extremely limited in its visual presentation capabilities. In any case, display typefaces, and even such display features as bold or italic lettering, cannot be used in the electronic mail system. An additional factor was that "white space" could not be used for emphasis or to highlight sections of a questionnaire, since this space would occupy scarce space in some users' electronic mail accounts. Thus, while recommendations related to the design of printed questionnaires were taken into account in constructing the questionnaire for this project, those recommendations were also adapted where necessary to meet the requirements of the delivery medium.

Comparatively little material is available on the design of questionnaires intended for electronic delivery, as distinct from printed questionnaires, though studies have been done of questionnaire responses in mail and telephone surveys and "disk by mail" (or DBM) surveys (Saltzman, 1992; Zandan and Frost, 1989). In November 1992, Linda Sudamalis submitted a research paper for a masters degree at Kent State University with the title "The Electronic Survey as a Research Tool: A Case Study of BALT-L". The aim of this paper was to "create a user profile of one specific electronic conference/electronic mail discussion group using a survey administered, collected, and tabulated electronically"; the focus was on using the Internet to study an aspect of the Internet. While Sudamalis does not provide detailed discussion of the challenges of using the Internet for research, her work does provide an example of a successful study of a listserv. In July 1993, Alejandra Rojo posted a message to the METHODS listserv on the Internet requesting suggestions and information about questionnaires delivered via electronic mail, in order to maximize the rate of response. In August of the same year, she posted a summary of the responses she had received to METHODS; the following points made by her respondents were relevant to this project:

- Sending a separate introductory or explanatory message before the questionnaire is considered desirable, unless the questionnaire is very short.
- There is a need to offer information and explanations for respondents on how to go about downloading/uploading the questionnaire, or printing the questionnaire, or using telnet to respond to the questionnaire on the host computer.
- The use of email to do a survey is more appropriate if the topic under consideration is related to computer technology. If not, there could be a serious nonresponse bias.

With the aim of learning from the work of others, online questionnaires used by other researchers in the fields of librarianship, school librarianship, education, and information science were collected, through listservs,

USENET newsgroups, and research reports. These were examined, either online or in printout form or both, and their characteristics (particularly their on-screen characteristics) noted. Some were designed for simple opinion surveys for the purpose of supporting a submission or a project or a seminar presentation; others were large-scale surveys for books or postgraduate theses. While none could be used as a model for this project, the experience of completing the questionnaires and reviewing them on screen and in print form provided some insights into the requirements of the electronic mail distribution medium.

To test the ideas and suggestions about online questionnaire construction that were gleaned from many different sources, a draft questionnaire was developed, based on the aims of the research project. This was loaded into the EUDORA electronic mail software and then sent to computers at the University of Iceland and elsewhere that were running other electronic mail software, in order to check basic formatting requirements. The second version of the questionnaire was then sent by electronic mail to students undertaking a postgraduate course at the University of Iceland, a course called "Research in Library and Information Science". They were asked to complete the questionnaire and return it via electronic mail, and to make notes on the process. Then, in a group discussion session, they provided feedback about the layout of the questionnaire, the format of the questions, and other aspects of the questionnaire. The points that emerged from this discussion provide useful information for people designing questionnaires for online delivery:

- Questions must be kept simple and short, and where people are asked to check items in a list, the list should be kept short, so that all items fit on the screen at the same time.
- Layout and instructions must be clear, despite the fact that the limitations of the electronic mail system make this difficult. Some electronic mail software "wrapped

around" the text, so that the beginning of one question merged into the end of another, unless an extra space was used; some software truncated lines of text; and there were other problems. Lines of text need to be kept short, to accommodate the limitations of some of the software packages.

- Response boxes should be in a line on the left hand side of the screen, so that it is easy to move the cursor down from one to the next.
- The instructions for answering a question should appear on the same screen display as the question—the question should not be so long that the instructions disappear at the top of the screen by the time the reader reaches the end of the question.
- No questions should require the respondent to leave the computer to collect information (such as statistics) from somewhere else. Some people pay for their online time by the minute; some may be using a computer a long way away from their normal desk to read their electronic mail. In any case, there is a strong temptation for the respondent to hit the <DELETE> key if responding to the questionnaire proves too difficult. Thus the group suggested that questionnaires delivered by electronic mail were not an appropriate medium for collecting detailed factual material, statistics, or other material that required reference to other sources. However, it could be a good way to collect opinion, comment, and the kind of information that a respondent could be expected to have stored in (human) memory.
- In developing a questionnaire for delivery via electronic mail, the researcher should not assume more than basic electronic mail skills. In their everyday work, few people use more than a small proportion of the features of their electronic mail package—they tend to learn the functions that they need to do their daily work.
- Because electronic mail provides respondents with a virtually unlimited space in which to answer open-ended

questions, these questions can become dangerous; if the question is not carefully worded, responses may be longer than can be dealt with. Print questionnaires usually give an indication of the expected response by providing a certain amount of space for an answer; this is not possible with electronic mail, where the space will accommodate a message of almost any length. It is therefore suggested that the instructions for each open-ended question might provide an indication of the expected length of the answer, unless the researcher is prepared to deal with any and all information provided.

All of these considerations were taken into account in developing the final version of the questionnaire for this project. The result was a questionnaire form that was designed for presentation on the screen, rather than on paper. For those respondents who printed out the questionnaire before completing it and returned it by mail, the paper copy may have been less attractive than the usual questionnaire format; however, it could be argued that, had the questionnaire not looked easy on the screen, it would never have been printed out in the first place.

Nevertheless, despite all this, there is clearly a great deal of research work to be done on the design and development of questionnaires for online distribution and on the identification and further development of strategies that might result in increased response rates and the collection of more useful information.

ANALYSIS OF LM_NET TRAFFIC

All LM_NET traffic for one month was downloaded for analysis. The month selected was October 1993, for the same reasons that that month was selected as the time for the questionnaire survey of LM_NET members. Conducting both the questionnaire survey and the analysis of traffic in the same month meant that approximately the same population was the basis for both studies.

Members of a listserv (or "subscribers") receive all messages that are posted to the listserv by other members and by the listserv "owners" or moderators. These messages are delivered to the members' electronic mail accounts. In October 1993, members of LM_NET could set their membership parameters to receive copies of their own messages to the listserv as well (this is now automatic), and this feature was used to ensure that copies of the researcher's own messages were also sent to her electronic mail account. Thus the LM_NET messages received in the researcher's own electronic mail account were a complete record of the traffic on the listserv. This was confirmed by scanning the LM_NET archives for the month of October; as indicated in Chapter Three, these archives are publicly available on the AskERIC gopher. In all, 606 messages were posted to the LM_NET listserv in October 1993.

The messages posted to the listserv were captured in two ways: each message was printed out from the print function of the electronic mail package (EUDORA), and the print copies filed in the sequence in which they were transmitted; and machine-readable copies of all messages were saved as a series of text files on the computer. Because of the different ways in which the messages were captured, the analyses also had to be carried out in two ways. The printed copies were scanned visually by the researcher to identify particular features of the messages or characteristics of the senders, with the information being used as the basis of qualitative analyses and coded for use as the basis of quantitative analyses. Keyword analyses were carried out on the machine-readable versions of the messages, using the spellchecker function of the word processing package (WordPerfect Mac) on the computer, to identify issues and concerns, whether or not they were the stated subject of the message.

It had originally been intended that content analysis software would be used to augment the simple keyword search analyses of the machine-readable version of the messages that were carried out through the spellchecker. Various packages for this purpose were investigated, and information was sought through the METHODS listserv on the Internet (METHODS is a listserv for the discussion of research methodology). However, the content analysis packages identified appeared to be more suitable for the content analysis of literary works, or for producing conceptual maps or social schemata as a result of analyses of the writings of particular groups of people, or for analyzing communications in creative environments such as MUDs (the multi-user role-playing games on the Internet). Ultimately, it appeared that either a word processor with good keyword search facilities, or a full-text database package with good keyword search facilities, would be better for the fairly simple tasks of identifying the subjects or topics discussed on the listserv, identifying the people who were sending the messages (through their electronic mail addresses), and, when used in conjunction with a statistical package, for analyzing the patterns of communication.

The information obtained through these analyses of LM_NET communications was used to place the questionnaire responses in perspective, and to provide additional information related to usage, the nature of the messages posted, the topics discussed, and the users as a group.

MINI-CASE STUDIES OF INTERNET USERS

In order to collect more detailed information about particular school-based projects, or about the use of the Internet in particular school libraries, a mini-case study approach based on "interviews" was used. The particular cases were selected for more detailed study on the basis of responses to the survey questionnaire (responses returned by electronic mail almost always included an electronic mail address in the header of the message, even where there was no name given); messages posted to LM_NET that indicated some use of the Internet in the school library; and references in published articles or unpublished documents available on the net. In all, eleven small case studies were undertaken, each focusing on some particular aspect of the application of Internet sources and services in the school library setting. The results of these case studies are incorporated into the discussion in the four chapters that follow.

The subjects were located in the United States, Canada, Australia, the United Kingdom, Singapore, and Iceland. The "interviews" were carried out by telephone, by electronic mail, by mail, and by having the person record his or her answers to some focus questions on audiocassette. In six cases, more than one interview method was used.

ONLINE STUDY OF INTERNET RESOURCES

A preliminary search using various Internet tools (including VERONICA, Jughead, WAIS, Hytelnet, and Mosaic) located many guides to the Internet and its resources; some were available as conventional printed publications, others were available only on the Internet itself (via gopher, World Wide Web, ftp, or electronic mail), and some were available in both formats. Some of these guides were general, all-purpose guides to resources and services, often designed to help the "network neophyte". Some covered resources dealing with a particular subject or topic (for instance, there were guides to environmental information on the Internet, and to information in the field of mathematics); some were developed for the use of particular groups of people (such as teachers, or business people); and some were based on a type of Internet resource or service (such as resources available by ftp, or gophers).

This preliminary search revealed that there was then apparently no comprehensive listing of Internet resources to meet the needs of school librarians and people responsible for library and information services in schools. Further, messages posted to LM_NET and EDTECH provided an indicator of the frustration that school librarians felt at not being able to locate appropriate resources, or not being able to find them easily. The responses to the online questionnaire provided some information about resources that respondents were using; however, the number of resources identified in this way was relatively small in comparison with the number that were later identified by other means.

To guide the search for resources or services that would be appropriate for school library applications or that would have something to offer in terms of meeting the information needs of the school community, the members of the school community were identified as students, teachers, the school librarian, the school principal (and deputy principal), other professionals and support staff working in the school, volunteers, and sometimes parents. The information needs of the various members of the school community (Clyde and Kirk, 1989) are discussed at the beginning of Chapter Two. The school librarian has a role in meeting these information needs, and in providing a wide range of information and resource services in the school, though this by no means describes the totality of the role of the school librarian.

The following strategies were used to identify appropriate Internet resources and services.

- Existing Internet guides (printed and online) were examined for listings that might be appropriate for meeting some of the needs of school library users.
- All sources and services mentioned by respondents to the questionnaire survey (or, at least, those that could be identified from the information provided by respondents) were checked online.
- Some twenty listservs in the fields of education, librarianship, school librarianship, and Internet news, were monitored for one week, and on the basis of this, four (those that provided the most leads to appropriate

resources and services) were selected for ongoing monitoring. The four were LM_NET, EDTECH (a listserv for people interested in the use of information technology in education at all levels), PUBLIB (a listserv for people interested in public libraries, but one which nevertheless often has information or discussions related to resources for young people and for teachers), and Net-Happenings (a listserv that carries announcements of new Internet resources and services). Sources identified through these listservs were checked online.
- USENET newsgroups available on the network news server at the University of Iceland were reviewed once in total, and those that carried material of interest to school libraries were noted. On the basis of this, six newsgroups were checked on a monthly basis for new postings.
- Gophers and World Wide Web services in the field of education, such as the AskERIC gopher, the CICNet gopher, the Ontario Institute for Studies in Education (OISE) gopher, and Canada SchoolNet, were checked on a regular basis.
- Online exploration of Internet resources and services, using Internet search tools such as WAIS, Hytelnet, gopher, and Mosaic, was ongoing throughout the life of the project, as was continued monitoring of the sources and services identified as being appropriate for school library applications or as having a place in meeting the information needs of members of the school community.

The result of this is a comprehensive, but not complete, listing, or directory, of Internet resources that could be of interest to school libraries or that might be appropriate for meeting many of the information needs of members of the school community. This directory is seen as an important outcome of the project, and it will be maintained and developed further in the future.

CONCLUSION

The literature review, the questionnaire survey, the analysis of listserv traffic, the mini-case studies, and the online study of Internet resources all provided information about present and potential applications of the Internet in school library services. In the chapters that follow, the information collected through these strategies is used to discuss the use of the Internet by school librarians, applications of the Internet in school libraries, barriers that prevent the effective use of the Internet in schools, and issues and concerns related to the use of the Internet in education.

REFERENCES

Alfano, Vicki (1993), Internet User Survey, Message posted to the NETTRAIN listserv on the Internet, and cross-posted to the LM_NET listserv, 12 April.

American Libraries Internet Survey (1993), Message posted to the PUBLIB listserv on the Internet, 5 October.

American Library Association, Washington Office (1994), "National Information Infrastructure—Gore's January 11 speech", ALAWON: American Library Association Washington Office Newsletter (published online on the Internet) 3, no. 3, 22 January.

Bane, Adele F. and Milheim, William D. (1993), Internet Survey, Message posted to the CBEHIGH listserv on the Internet, 25 August.

Benavides, Otto E. and Benavides, Alba E. (1993), Internet and Curriculum Delivery: Training of Teachers and Administrators, Paper presented at the Tel*Ed 93 Global Connections International Conference, November. Proceedings available through the CoSN gopher on the Internet.

Berdie, Douglas R. and Anderson, John F. (1974), *Questionnaires: Design and Use*, Scarecrow, Metuchen, New Jersey.

Bishop, A.D. (1990), "The National Research and Education Network (NREN): promise of a new information environment", *ERIC Digest*, November, pp.3–4.

Clyde, Laurel A., Hannesdóttir, Sigrún Klara, and Klobas, Jane (1993), *Guidelines for Carrying Out National Surveys of School Libraries and their Needs*, UNESCO, (in draft form).

Clyde, Laurel A. and Kirk, Joyce (1989), "The use of electronic information systems in Australian schools: a preliminary survey", *School*

Library Media Quarterly 17, no. 4, Summer, pp.193–199.Collis, Betty (1992), "Supporting educational uses of telecommunications in the secondary school", *International Journal of Distance Education* 19, no. 1, pp.23–44.

Collis, Betty (1993), European Activity and Trends with Telecommunications in Education, Paper presented at the Tel*Ed 93 Global Connections International Conference, November. Proceedings available through the CoSN gopher on the Internet.

Collis, Betty and De Vries, P. (1991), *Exploratory Research on Telecommunications in Secondary Education*, (PRINT—Project for the Implementation of New Technologies), Ministry of Education and Science, The Netherlands, Hoevelaken.

Collis, Betty and Levin, Jim (1993), Research on Telecommunications and Learning: An International Perspective, Paper presented at the Tel*Ed 93 Global Connections International Conference, November. Proceedings available through the CoSN gopher on the Internet.

Committee on Applications and Technology, Information Infrastructure Task Force (1994), What it Takes to Make it Happen: Key Issues for Applications of the National Information Infrastructure, Document posted to the Net-Happenings listserv on the Internet, 25 January.

Cullen, James G. (Bell Atlantic)(1994), Response Statement to Vice President Gore's Speech on the Administration's Telecommunications Initiatives, Document posted to the PUBLIB listserv on the Internet, 12 January.

Dupuy, Luc (1993), Programmes for Content Analysis, Message posted to the METHODS (Research Methodology) listserv on the Internet, 29 October.

Electronic Frontier Foundation (1993), Gore Endorses EFF's Open Platform Approach, Press release issued by the Electronic Frontier Foundation and posted to the Net-Happenings listserv on the Internet, 21 December.

Gallo, Michael Anthony (1993), Assessing the Effect on High School Teachers of Direct and Unrestricted Access to the Internet: A Case Study of an East Central Florida High School, PhD dissertation, Florida Institute of Technology.

Gore, Al, *Vice President* (1993), Remarks by Vice President Al Gore at the National Press Club, 21 December, Message posted to the Internet by the White House, 21 December.

Halla, M. (1990), The Electronic School District Project: Wide Area Network for Primary and Secondary Education, Indiana University Computing Services, n.p.

Halla, M., Perceival, B., and Snyder, M. (1989), The Electronic School

District: A Statewide Computer Network for Public Schools, Indiana University Computing Services, n.p.

Heath, Scott (1993), Research Project Report—Schools and Change, Document (dated 6 December 1993) posted to the EDTECH listserv on the Internet, 9 January 1994.

Honey, Margaret (1993), American Teachers' Use of Telecommunications: Findings of a National Survey, Paper presented at the Tel*Ed 93 Global Connections International Conference, November. Proceedings available through the CoSN gopher on the Internet.

Honey, Margaret and Henríquez, Andrés (1993a), "Initial findings from a national survey on K-12 educators' use of telecommunications", *Information Searcher*, 5, 3, pp.9–12.

Honey, Margaret and Henríquez, Andrés (1993b), *Telecommunications and K-12 Educators: Findings From a National Survey*, Center for Technology in Education, Bank Street College of Education, New York.

Kahler, June (1993), Site Based Decision Making Survey, Message posted to TENET and LM_NET on the Internet, 13 July.

Kinnaman, D. E. (1990), "What is the research telling us?", *Classroom Computer Learning* 10, no. 6, pp.31–39.

Kurshan, B. (1991), Statewide Education Networks: Survey Results, Unpublished report.

Laughon, Sally (1993), "I am interested in the role of the moderator of online projects or of a network...", Untitled message re-posted to the LM_NET listserv on the Internet, 26 April.

Lehman, J. D., Campbell, J. P., Halla, M., and Lehman, C. B. (1992), "Doing science in the electronic school district", *Journal of Mathematics and Science Teaching* 11, no. 2, pp.193-198.

Levine, Sol and Gordon, Gerald (1958–59), "Maximizing returns on mail questionnaires", *Public Opinion Quarterly* 22, no. 4, Winter, pp.568–575.

Lucero, Kitty (1993), Internet Resources for HS Librarians, Message posted to the LM_NET listserv on the Internet, 26 July.

McClure, Charles R., Ryan, Joe, Lauterbach, Diana, and Moen, William E. (1992), *Public Libraries and the Internet/NREN: New Challenges, New Opportunities*, School of Information Studies, Syracuse University, Syracuse, New York.

Mendrinos, Roxanne Baxter (1992), "Applications and use of CD-ROM technology in secondary school library media centers", *Information Searcher* 4, no. 3, pp.17–19, 22–23.

Mitchell, Tony, Paprzycki, Marcin, and Duckett, George (1993a), An International Survey of Pre-Service Teacher Education: Computer Literacy Requirements for Certification, Message posted to the EDTECH listserv on the Internet, 13 September.

Mitchell, Tony, Paprzycki, Marcin, and Duckett, George (1993b), Research Methods Using Computer Networks: About the Computer Literacy Survey Document, Available for reading on the Internet gopher of the University of Tasmania, Hobart.

National Coordinating Committee on Technology in Education and Training (1994), The National Information Infrastructure: Requirements for Education and Training, Executive Summary, Document posted to the Net-Happenings listserv on the Internet, 25 March.

New Brunswick Task Force on the Electronic Information Highway (1994), Driving the Information Highway: The Report of the New Brunswick Task Force on the Electronic Information Highway, Department of Economic Development and Tourism, Fredericton, New Brunswick.

Powell, Ronald R. (1985), *Basic Research Methods for Librarians,* Ablex, Norwood, New Jersey.

Robinson, R. A. (1952), "How to boost returns from mail surveys", *Printer's Ink* 239, no. 10, 6 June, pp.35–37.

Rojo, Alejandra (1993), Summary on Online Questionnaires, Communication posted to the METHODS (Research Methodology) listserv on the Internet, 26 August.

Saltzman, A. (1992), "Improving response rates in DBM (disk by mail)", *Proceedings of the Sawtooth Conference,* n.p.

Schuckel, K. (1990), "Classroom computers in touch with the world", *Lafayette Journal and Courier,* 10 May, pp.B1–B2.

Smedegaard, R. (ed.)(1993), *Conference on the Use of Databases and Telecommunications in Education, Final Report,* Ministry of Education, Copenhagen.

Sproull, Lee and Kiesler, Sara (1991), *Connections: New Ways of Working in the Networked World,* MIT Press, Cambridge, Massachusetts.

Stout, Connie (1994), "NII and education: an analysis", EdPOL-D Education Policy Digest (an electronic journal sponsored by the Scholastic Network) 1, no. 2, February.

Sudamalis, Linda (1992), The Electronic Survey as a Research Tool: A Case Study of BALT-L, Masters Research Paper, Kent State University, Ohio, November.

Treagust, David F. and Rennie, Leonie J. (1993), "Implementing technology in the school curriculum: a case study involving six secondary schools", *Journal of Technology Education* 5, no. 1, Fall (no pagination). Downloaded from `listserv@VTVM1.cc.vt.edu` on the Internet.

United States of America (1994), Administration White Paper on Communications Act Reforms, Document posted by the White House to the Internet, 27 January.

Wellburn, E. (1992), *Information, Telecommunications, and Learning: A Review of the Research Literature,* Educational Technology Centre, Victoria, British Columbia.

Wignell, Dennis (1993), MUDs: Content Analysis, Message posted to the CMC (Computer Mediated Communication) listserv on the Internet, 14 November.

Wyatt, Bob (1993), Programmes for Content Analysis, Message posted to the METHODS (Research Methodology) listserv on the Internet, 29 October.

Zandan, Peter and Frost, Lucy (1989), "Customer satisfaction research using DBM (disk by mail)", *Proceedings of the Sawtooth Conference,* n.p.

CHAPTER FIVE

THE USERS OF LM_NET

INTRODUCTION

The LM_NET listserv for "school library media people" on the Internet was described in Chapter Three. Established in mid-1992, it had 1,137 members in 12 countries by 1 October 1993, and in excess of 1,400 members in 14 countries by February 1994. In addition, communications to the listserv were read by many hundreds, perhaps thousands, more people on educational bulletin boards and gophers in the United States, Canada, Australia, and other countries. While school librarians do belong to other Internet listservs, and/or read messages on the `K12.library` USENET newsgroup, LM_NET is the most significant Internet "meeting place" for school librarians and others interested in school libraries.

The questionnaire survey of LM_NET members was undertaken in October 1993 to collect information about the members of this listserv (over and above the information that could be gleaned from the online membership list), to find out how they had learned about LM_NET and the Internet, how they had learned their Internet skills, how they were using both LM_NET and the Internet, the purposes for which they were using it, and their perceptions of the barriers to Internet use in schools and the possibilities for the future. Information from the survey responses was augmented by information obtained through an analysis of messages posted to LM_NET during the month of October.

The school librarians on LM_NET are truly pioneers, and some of the survey responses and, on occasions, the messages on the listserv, demonstrate that they are often conscious of this. Two recent studies show that even among technology-using teachers and school librarians, users of the Internet are a minority. In 1993, Margaret Honey and Andrés Henríquez published the results of a United States national survey of 550 educators in elementary, middle, and high schools who were users of telecommunications technologies; only 48 percent of this group of generally experienced technology users had access to the Internet (Honey and Henríquez, 1993, p.30). In a 1994 survey of readers of the regular "Computers in School Libraries" column of the Australian school library journal *Access*, only 25, or 7.49 percent, of the 334 respondents who were working in school libraries where computers were being used said they had access to the Internet (Clyde, 1994). When the proportion of Internet users is so low among groups of educators who are using information technology, then it is certain to be a great deal smaller among the total population of educators or school librarians. However, there is evidence that interest in the Internet within schools is growing, and the growth in LM_NET membership is in itself an indication of this.

THE SURVEY RESPONDENTS

A total of 105 people responded to the questionnaire survey of LM_NET members, as indicated in Table 5.1. United States respondents comprised 95.23 percent of the total, a proportion that was very similar to the United States membership of LM_NET (94.45 percent on 1 October 1993). The five non-United States respondents came from Canada and Australia, the countries with the second and third largest groups of members respectively.

Table 5.1
Survey Respondents by Country

COUNTRY	NUMBER
United States	100
Australia	3
Canada	2
TOTAL	105

It has already been noted (see Chapter Three) that LM_NET members, even within the United States, are geographically dispersed, when looked at in terms of the host computers through which they access the Internet; the total number of hosts was 363, of which 318 had fewer than five LM_NET members. The questionnaire responses reinforce this impression of geographic diversity. The United States respondents came from 30 different states and the District of Columbia, with the mean number from each being 3.2; there were ten states (and the District of Columbia) with only one respondent.

The large number of respondents from Texas (15.24 percent of the total respondents) is a result of the work of TENET (the Texas Education Network) and the number of people in Texas who have joined LM_NET through their membership of TENET—in October 1993, subscribers through TENET represented 10.48 percent of the total LM_NET membership. TENET provides educators in Texas with access to worldwide electronic mail, news and electronic conferences, Internet resources in the field of education and in curriculum-related fields, freenets, online library catalogs, gophers, ftp, the Library of Congress, United States government information, Texas legislative information, weather services, and a range of other services. It also provides access to LM_NET and similar listservs in virtually all school curriculum areas (Webb, 1994).

The majority of the survey respondents (63.8 percent) were working in elementary, middle, or secondary

Table 5.2

United States Respondents by State

STATE	NUMBER
Texas	16
New York	11
California	8
Iowa	5
Missouri	4
New Hampshire	4
North Carolina	4
Wisconsin	4
Florida	3
Indiana	3
Maryland	3
Michigan	3
Minnesota	3
Pennsylvania	3
Virginia	3
Georgia	2
Illinois	2
Massachusetts	2
Nebraska	2
New Jersey	2
Oregon	2
Alaska	1
Arkansas	1
Colorado	1
Delaware	1
District of Columbia	1
Ohio	1
Rhode Island	1
South Dakota	1
Tennessee	1
Utah	1
(No State Given)	1
TOTAL	100

schools. It should be noted, though, that some of the people whose primary employment was in a school also held another position which involved wider responsibilities (for instance in a district office or as a regional adviser). The other respondents came from a wide range of work environments. They included university or college professors or instructors responsible for school librarianship or librarianship courses, graduate students, people working in university or college instructional media services or computing services, personnel from school district offices, personnel from library authorities or library systems, personnel from state or national education authorities, a paraprofessional working in a public library and studying library science, and the owner of a software company. All appeared to have some reasonable connection with school libraries or school librarianship.

The 67 people who were working in schools held a wide range of positions. They included people who held positions in more than one school, or in both a school and a school district office or other authority. However, most held a position that could be at least roughly equated with that of "school librarian", though many different titles were used, as indicated in Table 5.4. The most frequently used title, at all school levels, was "school library media specialist", with the next most frequently used being "librarian". Many people provided additional comments about their title, indicating that this is perhaps a sensitive issue. Certainly the matter of titles, or "what we are called", has been discussed several times and at length on LM_NET. Sometimes different titles reflect essentially different jobs or roles; sometimes they hide roles that are basically similar. Sometimes, however, the title is a matter of certification: in one state, "school library media generalist" was the name for a school librarian who did not have an MLS. Sometimes the title was related to an industrial award. It was noted by two respondents that, in Texas, the official name for a school librarian is "learning resources

Table 5.3
Work Fields/Environments of Respondents

WORK FIELD/ENVIRONMENT	NUMBER	TOTALS
SCHOOL LEVEL:		67
Secondary School	40	
Elementary School	17	
Middle School	7	
Other (volunteer, substitute)	3	
UNIVERSITY/COLLEGE LEVEL		21
Professor/Instructor/Lecturer	12	
Graduate Student	4	
Instructional Media Services	1	
Learning Resources Center/Educational Resources /Curriculum Lab	3	
Computing Center	1	
CENTRAL SERVICES/AUTHORITIES		15
School District Office (Including District Media Center)	6	
BOCES Library System	1	
Regional School Library System	2	
State or National Education Authority	3	
Library Authority	2	
Regional Library System	1	
OTHER		2
Public Library—Paraprofessional	1	
Software Company	1	
TOTALS	105	105

specialist", but not all respondents from Texas used this title. The same is true of California: it was noted that "school library/media teacher" is the official designation, but respondents also used other titles.

However, the school level respondents were, with only a few exceptions, people who were working in school libraries or in charge of school libraries, though some also taught in the classroom or had other duties in the school or in a school district office.

Table 5.4
Positions Held by Respondents Who Work in Schools

POSITION	NUMBER	TOTALS
SECONDARY SCHOOL		40
School Library Media Specialist	15	
Librarian	7	
School Library Media Specialist and Teacher	2	
School Library/Media Teacher	2	
Media Director	2	
Cataloger	1	
Media Technologist/Specialist	1	
Learning Resources Specialist	1	
School Media Specialist	1	
School Librarian	1	
Teacher Librarian	1	
Chief Media Specialist	1	
Director of Libraries	1	
Teacher	1	
Librarian/Coordinator of Library Services (Secondary School and District Office)	1	
Unspecified	2	
ELEMENTARY SCHOOL		17
School Library Media Specialist	7	
Librarian	3	
Teacher Librarian	2	
School Library Media Generalist	1	
Media Specialist	1	
Librarian/Information Specialist	1	
Art Teacher/Technology Coordinator	1	
Unspecified	1	
MIDDLE SCHOOL		7
School Library Media Specialist	3	
Librarian	3	
School Media Director	1	
OTHER	3	
Volunteer	1	
Substitute	1	
Unspecified	1	
TOTALS	67	67

Many people have noted that the Internet, "cyberspace", has been essentially a masculine environment. In mid-1994, it was observed that "despite hundreds of thousands of new users in the last year, men still dominate the Internet and commercial services such as Prodigy and CompuServe" (Kantrowitz, 1994, p.42). In fact, it has been estimated that, overall, only around 10 percent of Internet users are women, though some research suggests that the proportion of women may be even less: a survey of World Wide Web users, carried out in January 1994 by James Pitkow and Mimi Recker, found that only 6 percent were female. Even in the field of education, where only 29 percent of the teachers in the United States schools are male (NCES, 1992, p.36) men are more likely to be users of telecommunications technology than women. Honey and Henríquez (1993, p.7) found, for instance, that though women dominate the teaching profession, there were many more male teachers in their sample of active users of telecommunications technology in schools "than are represented in the national averages" (p.6); in fact, 43 percent of the teachers in their sample were male. However, contrary to this trend, LM_NET appears to be very much a female dominated domain, as Table 5.5 shows.

Table 5.5
Sex of the Respondents

WORK ENVIRONMENT	MALE	FEMALE	N/A	TOTAL
School Level	7	59	1	67
University/College Level	7	14		21
Central Services/Authorities	4	11		15
Other	1	1		2
TOTALS	19	85	1	105

Over all, nearly 81 percent of respondents were women. At the school level, the preponderance of women was even more apparent: 88 percent of respondents working in

Table 5.6
Women as a Percentage of Respondents

WORK ENVIRONMENT	PERCENTAGE
School Level	88.06
University/College Level	66.66
Central Services/Authorities	73.33
Other	50.00
TOTAL	80.95

schools were women. Does this reflect LM_NET membership? It is hard to tell from the membership data that is provided in response to the listserv REVIEW command, and the names appearing on messages cannot be taken as a reliable indication of the sex of the participant. However, the figure for school-level people does mirror the composition of the profession of school librarianship, where the great majority of the practitioners are women. For example, in Iceland, of the people who have completed courses for school librarians at the University of Iceland, faculty statistics show that 91.3 percent are women.

In March 1994, there was a discussion on LM_NET about women and computers in response to a posting that suggested that women were less likely to use computers than men. Not surprisingly, several women responded, indicating that they were not among those who fitt into the category of reluctant computer users, and some said that they were "truly hooked". However, the replies did illustrate a difference between male and female attitudes to computers that has been noted by researchers (Kantrowitz, 1994). Research has shown that, for men, the technology itself tends to matter most; they tend to be interested in the machine, the size of the processor, the speed, the exotic capabilities. For women, on the other hand, the computer is "meant to be *used,* like the microwave oven or the dishwasher" (p.38). These are, of course, general observations, and there are many exceptions, male and female. However, the women's responses to LM_NET in the March discussion indicated that, although they "love their computers", they love them for what they can use them for. For instance, one person commented that "I think I drive people crazy at school talking about what I'm doing on it, what has come over LM_NET, and on and on", while another said, "I think that anyone involved with the Internet knows its power; like so many others, I am hooked and can't find enough time in my daily routine to enjoy the pleasures of all that is available to us". In other words, they were hooked, not on the machine, but on what they could do with it, and above all on the fact that they could use it for communication and access to information.

What has been the effect on LM_NET of a largely female membership? The characteristics that distinguish women's groups generally from groups dominated by men include a spirit of cooperation and an emphasis on communication and group problem solving. Things that are striking about LM_NET are the almost total absence of "flaming", and the helpful lists, documents, and mentor program created by the members themselves to assist people new to the net. A "flame", according to the LM_NET netiquette document, is "an emotionally charged posting ... often directed at someone". Flames "come in many different flavours" (Roelands, 1994), and they may contain inflammatory, abusive, or obscene language. The intention is not to solve a problem but to humiliate. There were no messages that could be described as "flames" among the 606 messages posted to the LM_NET listserv in the month of October 1993; in fact, one of the list owners, Peter Milbury, noted in a posting on 24 July 1994 that "we have now had our very _first_ flame on LM_NET, after more than two years of existence", and he went on to outline procedures for dealing with flames on LM_NET. Yet on some other listservs and newsgroups, and in some discussion forums on online services, "flame wars" have made life "on the net" so unpleasant for the majority of participants that groups have disintegrated or been abandoned. Kantrowitz (1994, p.42) has noted that men on the net are not usually "out to win sensitivity contests", and she quotes André Barcard, a Californian technology writer, as saying that "In the computer world, it's 'Listen, baby, if you don't like it, drop dead'." While this may be the way many men talk to each other, it is not normally the way women operate, and it makes women uncomfortable. In addition, as Susan Herring (1992) has found, men are much more likely to get angry when newcomers to the net pose basic questions or otherwise show their ignorance than are women; women are generally more tolerant of people who don't know what they are doing and are more likely to create strategies or resources to help. This tolerant attitude, the spirit of cooperation, and the resources created by members are features of LM_NET that are remarked on frequently by participants and by people (men and women) who read the postings on bulletin boards and gophers.

In the national survey referred to earlier of United States teachers who use telecommunications technology (Honey and Henríquez, 1993, p.6), the people in the group were older, on average, than the nation's teachers as a whole; their average age was 44.9 years, as against 40.2 years for teachers generally. The members of LM_NET are by definition users of telecommunications technologies, since that is what is required to access LM_NET. They, too, as a group, appear to be older than the United States average. The majority of respondents who were working in schools (60 percent) were aged between 41 and 50 years, and a further 33.84 percent were older than 50. The one respondent who was under 26 years of age was a graduate student.

As a group, then, the survey respondents are predominantly school librarians or school library media specialists or people with similar positions in elementary, middle, or secondary schools, but with significant groups of professors, graduate students, and media or curriculum services

Table 5.7
Age of Respondents

AGE IN YEARS	School	University	Central Services	Other	Total
	WORK ENVIRONMENT				
Under 26		1			1
26-30	2	1	1		4
31-35	4	1		1	6
36-40	5	4		1	10
41-45	20	3	8		31
46-50	19	3	2		24
51-55	8	5	2		15
56-60	4	1	2		7
61-65	3	2			5
Over 65					
No Answer	2				2
TOTALS	67	21	15	2	105

supervisors from universities and colleges, and personnel from central (regional or district or state or national) school or library authorities. Most live in the United States, with a few from other countries, generally reflecting the widespread geographical distribution of LM_NET members, in so far as that can be determined from email addresses. They get their access to LM_NET through a wide range of services and host computers. They are mainly female, especially at the school level, and they are mostly over 40 years of age.

JOINING LM_NET

Established in mid-1992, LM_NET was promoted in the professional literature and at conferences and meetings, as well as on the Internet itself. There were short articles about LM_NET in school library journals like *Emergency Librarian,* and in educational computing journals like *The Computing Teacher.* However, only 19 of the survey respondents first learned about LM_NET through an article in a professional journal or newsletter, and only 15 through a conference or workshop. More people (36) learned about LM_NET through a colleague or friend than by any other means. Superiors in the school, school district, or other authority seem to have played a very minor role; people generally seem to have learned about LM_NET outside the formal continuing education or advisory structures—with the exception of some of the "others" who learned about LM_NET through their use of TENET.

Five people learned about LM_NET through a formal course of study, usually a postgraduate course at a university or college, where the use of LM_NET was part of the course requirement; two respondents mentioned that they had been enrolled in courses taught by one of the LM_NET founders, Michael Eisenberg, at Syracuse University. However, their attendance at these courses was in their own time, and on their own initiative—even when the information came formally, it came from outside the school system or established advisory systems.

Table 5.8
How People First Found Out About LM_NET

METHOD	RESPONDENTS IN		
	SCHOOLS	OTHER PLACES	TOTAL
An article in a professional journal or newsletter	9	10	19
A colleague or friend	17	19	36
A superior in my school	1	0	1
A superior in my school district or other authority	0	0	0
A workshop or conference	12	3	15
Information posted to another listserv or bulletin board on the Internet	17	4	21
A formal course of study	4	1	5
Other	7	1	8
TOTALS	67	38	105

Two people, already Internet users, more or less stumbled on LM_NET while experimenting with Internet tools. One "Went gophering one day and found a list of lists... and picked out a couple to see what happened". Another said, "I was trying out a VERONICA search and used the keyword library. I just stumbled across some listings!"

School librarians and others may hear about LM_NET, or read about it, but they still need some motivation for joining, some reason for subscribing and then taking part, even to the extent of just reading the electronic mail generated through the listserv. Table 5.9 summarizes the main reasons cited by survey respondents for joining LM_NET. It should be noted that many people gave more than one reason, and so the results have not been totaled. Only those reasons given by four or more people are included in the Table.

Table 5.9

Reasons for Joining LM_NET

REASON	NUMBER
Communication with colleagues, to reduce isolation	32
To keep up to date with developments in the field	23
To share information and ideas	11
Curiosity—to see what is was all about	6
To see what others are concerned about or doing	6
Because it seemed to be designed for school librarians	5
For library school faculty, as a way of finding out "what is going on out there"	5
As part of a graduate school course or assignment	4
Collecting information that is relevant to my position as a faculty member teaching school librarianship courses	4
To find information about library automation	4

"Communication with colleagues" emerges as the major reason for joining LM_NET. It is clear that school librarians feel a sense of isolation, even when they are working in comparatively large schools (500 to 700 students). One commented that "as the only librarian at our middle school, I get lonely. It's great to hear from the rest of the world!", while another said, "As the only librarian in my high school, I feel isolated. I wanted contact with colleagues who had similar concerns." Other comments echo these sentiments. "One of the reasons I attend my state library association conference is to meet other librarians and discuss solutions to various situations. LM_NET allows this year-round instead of just one week a year." People wanted "to network with other library media specialists throughout the world", and to gain a "sense of community". One respondent put it much more forcefully: she joined LM_NET "to put an end to 22 years of isolation!"

Another important reason for joining, and one cited by school librarians, university faculty and graduate students, people working in school district offices and education authorities, the owner of a software company, and a paraprofessional working in a public library, is "to keep up to date with current developments in the field". Related reasons given include a desire to "see what others are concerned about or doing", and "to learn from others and their experience".

For university faculty, the need to "know what's going on out there" was an important factor in joining; one commented that "as a professor of library science, I feel this listserv will keep me abreast of the concerns out there in the real world as opposed to what some may see as my Ivory Tower". Three graduate students saw it as a way of learning more about "the real world" and the profession they would be joining. The need to know what was happening in school libraries was also a factor for three people who were working in district offices or central school library services.

Some of the members had been drawn to LM_NET because they needed information about library automation. These people included school librarians, library advisers, library school faculty, and a graduate student. For one person, this provided an immediate incentive for joining: "I needed information quickly about a circulation system. It was during summer, when my professional contacts are hard to contact. I wanted a variety of opinions and experiences". Others hoped to get information about CD-ROMs and CD-ROM networking through LM_NET.

Several people (though a minority) were led into LM_NET through a desire to see how the Internet worked, or to use their newly acquired electronic mail accounts, or to find out more about listservs—in other words, they came to it through interest in the medium, rather than the content, at least initially. Three respondents saw it as an opportunity to practice using electronic mail; two saw it as a way of "participating more fully in the Internet"; one wanted to find out more about the Internet; one was looking for "a way the Internet could be specifically useful to me"; two were interested in computer communications; one wanted to gain experience with listservs; and one wanted "to find more ways to use the computer".

Some members joined LM_NET because they had to, or because they found that membership had been obtained for them or made available to them. Four people had joined as part of a course or assignment in graduate school; one said as a library media teacher in California, she "found herself subscribed" as part of a more general enrollment; another took part in LM_NET because it was provided as an interest board on the school district's local FrEdMail network; and another read LM_NET communications through the Australian NEXUS school service.

Other reasons given by one or two people for joining LM_NET included professional growth, having access to a listserv that dealt just with issues related to school librarianship, its apparent relevance to the job situation, its usefulness as a source of information to meet the needs of others in an organization (like the Department of Public

Instruction), the desire to "plan for the day when we have access from school and can get students and faculty on the net", assessing it as a possible teaching tool (within university courses in library science), and simple curiosity.

The emphasis that respondents placed on communication and professional contact as a reason for joining LM_NET and taking part in professional telecommunications activities are supported by the results of the study of technology-using educators reported by Honey and Henríquez. For them, the major "incentives for using telecommunications as a professional resource" included the "opportunity to communicate with other educators, share ideas, obtain information, and get feedback", "access to information", and access to "an effective tool for combating isolation that so many educators experience as part of their jobs" (Honey and Henríquez, 1993, p.18). Clearly, school librarians are not alone in their feelings of isolation and their need for professional contact, or in their desire to share information and ideas, though school librarians may be more conscious of their isolation, since they are more likely to be working alone in a school.

USING LM_NET

People may join a group for one reason, and then continue their membership for quite another reason. And so the questionnaire asked LM_NET members to indicate all the various reasons for their continued membership of and use of LM_NET. In this case, the initial purposes for which people joined, that is, professional contact and communication, the desire to keep up to date, and information sharing, continued to be important factors for LM_NET members. However, it is also clear that, as their experience of LM_NET increased, they became aware of its value as a means of locating information about resources, of finding solutions to library management problems, and of finding answers to thorny reference questions. Table 5.10 summarizes the responses.

Table 5.10
What People Are Using LM_NET For

USE OF LM_NET	RESPONDENTS IN SCHOOLS	RESPONDENTS OUTSIDE SCHOOLS	TOTALS
For contact with other professionals outside my school	65 (97.01%)	29 (76.32%)	94 (89.52%)
To discuss professional issues	53 (79.1%)	26 (68.42%)	79 (75.23%)
To get information about resources for the school library media center	56 (83.58%)	16 (42.11%)	72 (68.57%)
To find solutions to problems related to the running of a school library/media center	55 (82.09%)	14 (36.84%)	69 (65.71%)
To get information for other people	47 (70.15%)	16 (42.11%)	63 (38.09%)
To have fun	49 (73.13%)	12 (31.58%)	61 (58.1%)
To get information about library automation	35 (52.24%)	15 (39.47%)	50 (47.62%)
To find answers to reference questions	35 (52.24%)	5 (13.16%)	40 (38.09%)
Other	5 (7.46%)	7 (18.42%)	12 (11.43%)

It has already been noted that the respondents who were not working in schools formed a very diverse group. As might be expected, their reasons for using LM_NET were often different from those of the people who worked in schools and were certainly much more diverse. For both groups, contact with other professionals was important, as was the discussion of professional issues and ideas. However, more of the people who worked outside schools provided "other reasons" for using LM_NET, and for five of these people, this "other reason" was the most important reason for its use. These included assessing LM_NET to see if it could be a useful teaching tool in library school courses, finding out what others are discussing or doing and how they are solving their problems, keeping track of the issues that are of concern to practicing school librarians, making contact with other library educators involved in courses for school librarians, and collecting information to help other school librarians in the district or state to "learn the power of telecommunication".

The "other reasons" mentioned by people working in schools included the enjoyment of "associating with those who subscribe to LM_NET", learning about conferences, updates, and other events, brainstorming "with other thoughtful, creative people about problems and issues common to the profession", helping to "build a stronger local network", and so that information could be collected in order to "inform others of the value of LM_NET". One person had the specific aim of communicating with others who use the Mandarin library management software. These "other reasons" are mostly related to communication and networking, in various guises, and they reinforce the pattern of the other responses.

As well as asking LM_NET members to indicate all the purposes for which they used LM_NET, the questionnaire also asked them to indicate which of those purposes was the most important for them. Table 5.11 summarizes the responses. As might be expected, contact and communication were highlighted. For the school-based people, "contact with other professionals outside my school" was the most important reason for using LM_NET, and this is in line with the reasons that so many gave for joining LM_NET—the need for communication, for contact with people who shared their ideas and understood their goals, and to reduce their perceived isolation. For people outside schools, this was less important, though still a reason cited by some 42 percent as the most important. However, it is interesting to note that the reason considered most important by people outside schools was a related one, the desire to "discuss professional issues" (cited by 68.42 percent of this group as their most important reason for using LM_NET). Other important reasons for this group were directly related to their own work—for instance, library school professors using LM_NET as a teaching tool and as a way of making contact with other faculty who are teaching courses related to school librarianship, a graduate student monitoring it as part of a research job, and library advisers using it as a way of demonstrating the effective use of electronic mail and telecommunications in workshops for school librarians and others.

Table 5.11

Respondents' Most Important Reason for Using LM_NET

USE OF LM_NET	RESPONDENTS IN SCHOOLS	RESPONDENTS OUTSIDE SCHOOLS	TOTALS
For contact with other professionals outside my school	35(52.23%)	8(21.05%)	43
To find answers to reference questions	0	0	0
To get information for other people	3	3	6
To find solutions to problems related to the running of a school library/media center	8	2	10
To discuss professional issues	7	16(42.11%)	23
To get information about resources for the school library media center	4	1	5
To get information about library automation	1	2	3
To have fun	2	0	2
Other	0	5	5
No answer	5	1	6
"Couldn't pick the most important use"	2	0	2
TOTALS	67	38	105

The use being made of LM_NET by school librarians will be discussed further in Chapter Six, which deals with the use of the Internet in general in school libraries.

ACCESSING LM_NET AND THE INTERNET

Once subscribed, how often do the respondents use LM_NET and the Internet, how do they get access, where is the equipment through which they access the Internet, and what Internet tools do they use?

As Table 5.12 shows, many respondents had a relatively long experience of using LM_NET, with most respondents (63) having used it for more than six months, and 28 having used it for more than a year. The LM_NET membership is growing rapidly, and so at any point in time there will be large numbers of inexperienced users on the listserv. However, it is possible that the questionnaire was off-putting to the less experienced users, since it required some email skills or skills in printing from the email system. Nevertheless, it is clear from the responses that some people who have only basic skills did complete the survey questionnaire. It may be that some of the people who had been using LM_NET for many months still had limited skills, especially if their Internet connection was restricted or if they had had few opportunities to develop their skills further through formal courses.

Table 5.12
Length of Membership of LM_NET

LENGTH OF MEMBERSHIP	NUMBER
More than a year	28
10-12 months	20
7-9 months	15
4-6 months	16
1-3 months	16
Less than a month	9
Not applicable	1
TOTAL	105

While respondents tended to come from among the more established members of LM_NET, they also tended to be people who logged on to their email system relatively frequently. Table 5.13 shows the frequency of logging on; the largest groups are of those who log on once a day or more than once a day. Figure 5.1 shows the relationship between length of membership of LM_NET and frequency of logging on. Clearly, the respondents were generally active users of their email system.

Table 5.13
Frequency of Logging On to the Email System

TIME INTERVAL	RESPONDENTS IN SCHOOLS	RESPONDENTS OUTSIDE SCHOOLS	TOTALS
Less than once a month	0	0	0
About once a month	0	0	0
Between once a week and once a month	1	0	1
About once a week	2	1	3
More than once a week	13	1	14
Once a day	27	13	40
More than once a day	24	23	47
TOTALS	67	38	105

One person who logged on at least once a day, and also posted messages relatively frequently, said, "I go thru over 200 email messages a day ... am an Internet scout" (as part of a job with an education agency). Some of the other people who logged on daily or more often were people who monitor other listservs and newsgroups for postings related to school librarianship. This illustrates a previously mentioned feature of LM_NET: several members regularly scan other listservs for messages of interest to school librarians and post those messages back to LM_NET, thus making information from other lists available to LM_NET members.

The respondents were mainly people who post the occasional message to LM_NET—somewhere between once a week and once a month or even less frequently. "Lurkers" (people who read the messages sent to a listserv but do not themselves take part in the discussion) comprised 11.43 percent of respondents. Lurkers are often people new to the listserv or to the Internet in general, and so it is interesting that a questionnaire drew some of them out. However, patterns of participation do change as people gain more experience: as one respondent noted, "I lurked for the first six months and now I find I am beginning to respond more frequently". And then, things are not always what they

	More than once a day	Once a day	More than once a week	About once a week	Between once a week and once a month	About once a month
More than 1 year	17	9	2	0	0	
10-12 months	10	9	1	0	0	0
7-9 months	7	3	4	0	1	0
4-6 months	5	7	3	1	0	0
1-3 months	7	7	1	1	0	0
Less than 1 month	3	4	1	1	0	0

Figure 5.1 Relationship Between Length of Membership of LM_NET and frequency of Logging On

seem: another lurker had "sent answers to individuals" who had posed questions, but had not posted those answers to the whole list. At the other end of the scale, some of the people who contributed more often than once a week were people who monitored other listservs.

It has come to be an accepted notion that on any listserv or discussion forum, around 90 percent of postings will be made by around 10 percent of the members, and that the majority of members or subscribers will take little if any part in the discussions. However, it is possible that even this may be an optimistic estimate, and the case of PEN would support this. PEN, a community bulletin board in Santa Monica, California, was established in 1989 to provide local information and a forum for discussion of community issues. In 1991, when a formal evaluation was carried out, there were more than 3,000 subscribers, but only 500 to 600 logged on each month, most made no contributions to conference discussions online, and conferences had come to be dominated by around 50 "hard core" users (Rheingold, 1993, p.271).

Table 5.14
Frequency of Contributions to LM_NET

TIME INTERVAL	RESPONDENTS IN SCHOOLS	OUTSIDE SCHOOLS	TOTALS
I just "lurk"	7	5	12
I have only posted a message or or replied once or twice	11	12	23
I post a message or reply about once a month	15	9	24
Between once a week and once a month	14	8	22
About once a week	14	1	15
More than once a week	4	0	4
Once a day	1	1	2
More than once a day	1	1	2
No answer	0	1	1
TOTALS	67	38	105

An analysis of LM_NET traffic for the month of October 1993 showed that 606 messages were posted to the listserv during the month, an average of 19.55 messages per day. These messages were posted by 228 different people, representing 20.05 percent of the subscribers to the listserv as of 1 October. For the 228 people who posted messages, the average number posted by each person during the month was 2.66, though 123 people posted only one message and 38 people posted two. Almost two-thirds of the messages (370, or 61.06 percent) were posted by people who posted five messages or fewer during the month. This would seem to reflect the responses to the survey question that asked people how often they contributed to LM_NET discussions, if allowance is made for a slightly increased likelihood of response from people who were accustomed to responding to listserv messages.

However, just ten people contributed almost a quarter (22.93 percent) of the messages posted to LM_NET in October. One of the list owners contributed only four messages, while the other posted 12 (the majority of which were related to ongoing discussions on the list, rather than just to list management). The other large contributors (those who posted between nine and 25 messages) were people who are recognized on the listserv as making a positive contribution to the information sharing and to the professional tone of the list, and people who forward items of interest from other listservs, so that their dominance is not as marked as it might be. Nevertheless, while a few people make a relatively large contribution to the listserv discussions, they do not dominate the discussions, and a comparatively large proportion of the membership made at least one contribution during the month.

In addition, it became clear from references in "thank you" messages posted to the listserv, and in HIT->s (long messages that summarise all the responses received by a

Table 5.15
Number of Messages Posted by LM_NET Members
October 1993

NUMBER OF MESSAGES	NUMBER OF PEOPLE
1	123
2	38
3	26
4	12
5	9
6	4
7	5
8	1
9	3
10	0
11	0
12	2
13	0
14	0
15	2
16	1
17	1
—	
25	1
576	228

member who posts a TARGET-> question), that many other LM_NET members responded directly to the people who posted questions to the listserv rather than replying to the whole list. This indicates that the electronic mail traffic generated by the listserv discussions is certainly much greater than the traffic to the listserv itself would suggest. It may also involve more people; certainly, many apparent "lurkers" sometimes sent messages directly to people in response to questions posted to the listserv, as has already been noted.

This analysis is generally supported by the results of an analysis of LM_NET traffic carried out in May 1993 by Peter Milbury to see if LM_NET was "dominated by any individuals or groups of individuals" (Milbury, 1993). Between 5 May and 23 May, 119 people posted 281 messages, the average being 2.36 per person, and most of the messages were posted by people who sent five messages or fewer during the period. He commented that "among those who posted", this distribution appeared "to be pretty balanced". However, he also noted with concern that the 119 active people represented only 13 percent of the membership, a proportion that would seem to be good by the standards of many other services. This level of participation may be related to what is perceived to be the generally friendly atmosphere of the listserv, and the support given to new members who need it. It may also be that many members participate in LM_NET in their own time and at their own expense, and so they are determined to ensure that it works for them.

The majority of the people who worked in schools (73.13 percent) usually used a computer at home to access the Internet, and an additional 13 people working in schools often used a computer at home as well as a computer in the school or the school library for access. However, even when a computer could be used at school, access was sometimes a problem. One respondent who mainly used a computer at home to access LM_NET and the Internet commented that "I also have a modem in my office but

3.1 Professor Michael Eisenberg, Founder and Co-owner of the LM_NET listserv. (Photograph: Michael Eisenberg)

3.2 Peter Milbury, Co-owner of the LM_NET listserv. (Photograph: Peter Milbury)

3.3 Betty Hamilton, LM_NET Member and producer of the LM_NET Directory. (Photograph: Betty Hamilton)

3.4 Linda Joseph, LM_NET Member and editor/producer of the World Link Internet newsletter for schools. (Photograph: Linda Joseph)

5.1 Ken Schrieber's 7th Grade Class (1994), Bemidji Middle School, Bemidji, Minnesota, USA. This group took part in a Subject Matter E-Mail Project in 1994. (Photograph: Edee Miller)

5.2 Brandie and Joe, students at Bemidji Middle School, Bemidji, Minnesota, USA (1994). They took part in an electronic penpal project with Japanese school students. Brandie is pointing to Japan on the globe of the world, while Joe is holding up a printout of their work. (Photograph: Edee Miller)

5.3 Participants in the Computer Pals Across the World Environment Watch, being greeted by HRH the Duke of Edinburgh. (Photograph: Malcolm Beazley)

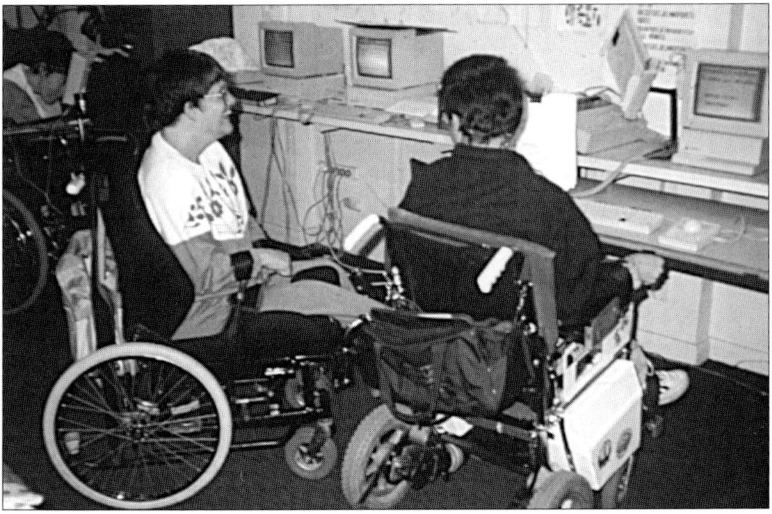

5.4 The Computer Pals Across the World electronic mail project has participants who are disabled, participants who are in hospitals, and participants who are isolated for various reasons. The photograph was taken in Australia. (Photograph: Malcolm Beazley)

5.5 Delegates to an international seminar on "Young People and Information", held at the University of Iceland in May 1993, are introduced to the KIDLINK Internet project. (Photograph: Sue Sherif)

5.6 The KIDLINK Project—young participants in Akureyri, northern Iceland, May 1993. (Photograph: Robyn Redman, DAGUR, Akureyri)

Table 5.16
Location of the Equipment Used to Access LM_NET and the Internet

LOCATION	RESPONDENTS IN SCHOOLS	OUTSIDE SCHOOLS	TOTAL
At home	49(73.13%)	11(28.95%)	60
In my school	5 (plus 2)	5	10
In my school library	10 (plus 11)	0	10
In a university or college	2	10	12
In a public library	0	0	0
Other:			
In office or on desk	1	13	14
Computer lab	0	0	0

I don't usually have the time during work hours. I do use it to answer quick questions (like accessing a university OPAC to see how they cataloged something)".

People working in universities or district or state authorities were much more likely to have access via a computer in their office or on their desk than people working in schools. Thus the people in schools, with less access to facilities, had to be more committed to the value of the Internet to take the additional trouble needed to use it at home—and in some cases to bear the expense of long-distance telecommunications and/or a personal subscription to a commercial access provider.

USING THE INTERNET

For some people, membership of LM_NET was their introduction to the Internet; others found out about LM_NET through exploring the Internet online. There was some confusion about the relationship between LM_NET and the Internet, suggesting limited experience. For instance, two people wondered if a question in the survey that asked "How did you first find out about LM_NET?" was the same as the question "How did you first find out about the Internet?", suggesting either that they thought that LM_NET and the Internet were one and the same thing, or that LM_NET was their introduction to the Internet, and so the introduction to the two was linked.

Table 5.17
How Respondents First Found Out About the Internet

METHOD	RESPONDENTS IN SCHOOLS	RESPONDENTS OUTSIDE SCHOOLS	TOTAL
An article in a newspaper	0	1	1
A book	1	1	2
An article in a professional journal or newsletter	10	5	15
An article in a popular or general magazine	1	0	1
A colleague or friend	21	19	40
A superior in my school	4	0	4
A superior in my school district or other authority	1	0	1
A workshop or conference	16	7	23
A formal course of study	6	3	9
Other	7	2	9
TOTALS	67	38	105

As had been the case with LM_NET, people frequently found out about the Internet through a colleague or friend, or through their reading of professional journals and newsletters. However, in the case of the Internet itself, workshops or conferences were frequently the source of the respondents' information, whereas this had not been so in relation to LM_NET. Some respondents first learned about the Internet, as they had learned about LM_NET, through formal courses of study.

Once again, as had been the case with LM_NET, the formal channels of the school, school district, or other authority were seldom the channels of the initial information about the Internet. Sometimes the channels were very informal indeed: one example of this is provided by the respondent who commented, "I found out about the Internet itself through a STUDENT at my school!" However, some respondents who were working in schools did comment about formal or semi-formal sources. One was "selected to participate as one of six librarians whose library was to gain access as a result of a NYSERNet grant". Two others found out through grant writing workshops or through the awarding of a grant. Another found out about the Internet through Massachusetts LearnNet/MCET (just as other respondents had found out about LM_NET through TENET).

Two people could not recall when they had first heard about the Internet: "the word was sort of floating in the ether". This is not surprising, given the growing number of articles about the Internet in popular magazines and newspapers and increasing public discussion of it, often in relation to government policy. It is clear, however, that some people began to use a particular Internet service (such as electronic mail or a listserv) before they realized that it was, in fact, part of a wider entity called the Internet. The comment of one respondent illustrates this: there was, she said, no one time when the Internet first impinged on the consciousness, but rather, "there was a ... gradual realization as I began to play around on LM_NET".

As had been the case with learning to use LM_NET, the majority of the respondents (72.38 percent overall) were partly or wholly self-taught, whether through unaided exploration of the Internet or through using books and other Internet guides. The second most important learning method was instruction from a colleague or friend (37.14 percent overall). Many people used both self-instruction and instruction from colleagues or friends (including sons, husbands, and a brother). And some people learned their

Internet skills through several methods, including, for instance, self-instruction, the help of a colleague, and an Internet workshop. Table 5.18 provides details of the methods by which people learned to use the Internet.

Table 5.18
How Respondents Learned to Use the Internet

METHOD	RESPONDENTS IN SCHOOLS	RESPONDENTS OUTSIDE SCHOOLS	TOTAL
Self taught	46 (68.66%)	30 (79.95%)	76
Taught by a colleague or friend	23 (34.33%)	16 (42.11%)	39
Attendance at conference/s and/or workshops in my own time	25 (37.31%)	4 (10.53%)	29
Attendance at workshop/s or other activities in the school	3 (4.47%)	6 (15.79%)	9
Attendance at workshop/s and/or other activities arranged by the school district or authority	18 (26.86%)	3 (7.89%)	21
Other	12 (17.91%)	3 (7.89%)	15

Again reflecting the situation in relation to LM_NET, the people in the universities and colleges and in the central services or authorities tended to have more opportunities to gain Internet skills in the course of their work than did the people working in schools. Some 37.31 percent of the respondents in schools, but only 10.53 percent of the other respondents, had attended conferences and/or workshops in their own time. On the other hand, while only three school-level respondents had been able to attend a workshop or other activity in their schools, six of the university-level faculty and staff had been able to attend such activities. More school-level people attended workshops and/or other activities in their own time than were able to attend workshops of activities run by the school district or authority. This presents a picture of school-level people reaching out to find help and information in various ways, mostly informally or in their own time.

The heading "Other" in Table 5.18 covers a range of activities or opportunities. Five people (all school-level people) had learned to use the Internet through a formal course at a university or college. Three people had taken a course in their own time that was provided via electronic mail or offered via the Internet itself, on "Navigating the Internet" or using the Internet. One had learned some skills through the online help of an LM_NET mentor; one had used online lists and guides; and three (again, all school-level people) had watched or had help from family members (son, cousin, brother).

Several respondents mentioned books that they had found helpful, and one noted that he had bought two books about the Internet and spent the whole summer reading them again and again. It seems that almost every week some new guide to the Internet appears, or a guide to a particular Internet tool or type of service, and there is also no doubt that they are well used by people who are new to the net. Although many of these publications duplicate information that is available free online, new users seldom have the skills needed to locate such information or to download the documents successfully.

These findings are supported by those of Honey and Henríquez (1993, p.12), who found that the majority of the "telecommunicating educators" in their national study were self-taught. They are also supported by the work of Vicki Alfano, who carried out a survey (by electronic mail) of members of several listservs (including LM_NET, EDTECH, NETTRAIN) in late 1993. She found that most of the 141 respondents in her survey used two or more methods to learn how to use the Internet, though self-instruction was the most common method. Some 121 respondents indicated that they had taught themselves, often with help from others, or with the assistance of books, documents, and handouts. Alfano notes that this "is consistent with other findings" (McClure, Bishop, Doty, and Rosenbaum, 1991) and is reflected in the number of "self-help" books and articles that have been written about the Internet.

Table 5.19
Internet Tools/Services Used by Respondents

TOOL/SERVICE	RESPONDENTS IN SCHOOLS	RESPONDENTS OUTSIDE SCHOOLS	TOTAL
Gopher	59 (88.06%)	34 (89.47%)	93 (88.57%)
Telnet	57 (85.07%)	32 (84.21%)	89 (84.76%)
ftp	29 (43.28%)	22 (57.89%)	51 (48.57%)
VERONICA	27 (40.29%)	18 (47.37%)	45 (42.85%)
ARCHIE	20 (29.85%)	13 (34.21%)	33 (31.42%)
World Wide Web	15 (22.38%)	8 (21.05%)	23 (21.9%)
ftpmail	9 (13.43%)	6 (15.78%)	15 (14.28%)
WAIS	3 (4.48%)	4 (10.53%)	7 (6.66%)
USENET	3 (4.48%)	1 (2.63%)	4 (3.81%)

The Internet tools and services that were most used by respondents were electronic mail and listservs (all respondents, by definition), gopher (88.57 percent), telnet (84.76 percent), and ftp (48.57 percent). Few people in schools had access to World Wide Web browsers such as Mosaic or even Lynx. Very few people were using USENET. Tools not listed in Table 5.19 but used by between one and three respondents were Hytelnet, whois, finger, and Jughead. Most respondents used only two or three Internet tools, and many commented at this point that their "Internet skills" were very basic. Some even indicated that they had not heard of some of the tools or services listed on the questionnaire form, and others asked questions about some of them. In fact, several respondents used the questionnaire to ask questions themselves about some of the Internet tools and services mentioned in it.

In her survey of listserv members, Alfano (1993) also found electronic mail and electronic mail-based services such as listservs, to be popular Internet applications. She comments that "the popularity of these applications is widely acknowledged", and cites Ed Krol in saying that "most users begin their network experience through email" (Krol, 1992). Other popular applications among her respondents were gopher, ARCHIE, WAIS, VERONICA, and Hytelnet, and Alfano notes, in explanation, that "the development of these client/servers has helped to make the searching and retrieval of information on the Internet more user friendly".

It would appear that, despite their occasionally limited skills, the members of LM_NET are often leaders in the use of telecommunications technology in their schools and sometimes in the school district as well. Although the survey questionnaire did not request information about the extent of the use of the Internet in the respondent's school, many of the respondents did in fact make a comment to the effect that they were either the first, or the only, staff member to use the Internet. Some also commented that with (at least at first) comparatively little knowledge to back up their position, they had become by default the school or district "Internet expert", and this provided an incentive for ongoing exploration and self-instruction. "As media specialist, I have led the way on use of the Internet and training for individual teachers and students; in fact, I have also led the way for other media specialists in Rhode Island. I am now writing a column called 'Caught in the Net' for our professional bulletin. Teachers are gatekeepers so I try hard to open their eyes up to the possibilities of the Internet. It takes time" (Carol Anderheggen as quoted in McClanahan, 1994). Many LM_NET members were introducing teachers and students to the resources and services available on the Internet; there is evidence of this in responses to a survey of members carried out by Eisenberg and Milbury in January 1993. Even when school librarians could only access the Internet at home in their own time, they were still attempting to provide printouts and other material "as a selling point". One commented that "I am using printouts for teachers and administrators to convince them of what we are missing by not having access at school", and another noted that "I have introduced the Internet by way of printouts. I have about convinced my administration that we really must have telecommunications at school or be left behind all of those schools who already have it" (Eisenberg and Milbury, 1993).

SUMMARY

The LM_NET survey respondents included people whose work involves providing library and information services in schools, and people whose work is outside schools (in such fields as education for school librarianship and the provision of central services for school libraries). School-level respondents dominated, though the other groups were significant. In keeping with the geographical distribution of members of LM_NET, most respondents were from the United States, though there were responses from other countries. Respondents were predominently female (mirroring the sex distribution of the profession), and mostly experienced professionals. The majority of respondents who work in schools described themselves as "self-taught" Internet users, and this may help to explain their dependence, as a group, on a small number of Internet tools and their possession of relatively limited skills. It appears that people had taught themselves to use basic tools in order to make contact, to communicate, and to get the information they needed. Some respondents had been helped or taught by a colleague or friend, and 37.31 percent had attended a demonstration or workshop in their own time. Only around a quarter of the people in schools had been able to attend an Internet workshop or other activity arranged by the school district or other authority. Overall, respondents in schools seem to have begun using the Internet on their own initiative. This observation is supported by the fact that three-quarters of the school-level respondents were accessing the Internet via equipment in their own homes, even though their use of it was related to their jobs. In the absence of any effective support at the school, district, or state/national levels, school librarians need a high degree of self-motivation to learn about the Internet and to use Internet resources and services in their schools.

In a presentation at the Tel*Ed 93 conference, Margaret Honey (1993, p.1) summarized the findings of the national study that she and Henríquez carried out of telecommunications-using educators, and her summary of the characteristics of the people in her study (14.4 percent of whom were library media specialists) reflects the characteristics of LM_NET users to a large degree. It is, she said, "the technologically knowledgeable computer and library media specialists who are taking the lead for telecommunications activities, serving as resource people and facilitators for colleagues in their schools". The data from their project also suggested that there was "not widespread administrative support for telecommunications activities on either the district or the school level", and that although the schools and districts represented in that national study had invested in training teachers in general computer-based applications, training in specific telecommunications techniques was extremely limited. The great majority of respondents in the study were self-taught, and they usually collected information about telecommunications activities by attending conferences or workshops in their own time. While personal motivation for using telecommunications in education was extremely high, the findings of the Honey and Henríquez study also suggest that these teachers were enouraged to continue their use of telecommunications by the enthusiasm that their activities generated in the classroom and the professional stimulation that they found through their contacts and projects.

The next chapter discusses the present applications of

the Internet in school libraries, and the potential for further use of the Internet in the school library setting.

REFERENCES

Alfano, Vicki (1993), Internet Survey Summary, Document received from the author via email, 30 December.

Benston, Margaret Lowe (1987), "Women's voices/men's voices: technology as language", in Kramarae, K. (ed.), *Technology and Women's Voices*, Routledge and Kegan Paul, London.

Clyde, Laurel A. (1994), "Computers in school libraries survey", *Access* 8, no. 3, August,pp.30–35, 29.

Eisenberg, Michael and Milbury, Peter (1994), "The Internet and library media programs: the technology is now!", in McClure, Charles R., Moen, William E., and Ryan, Joe (eds), *Libraries and the Internet/NREN: Perspectives, Issues, and Challenges*, Mecklermedia, Westport, pp.199–220.

Herring, Susan (1992), "Gender and participation in computer-mediated linguistic discourse", Paper presented at the Annual Meeting of the Linguistic Society of America, Held in Philadelphia, Pennsylvania, 9-12 January.

Honey, Margaret (1993), "American teachers' use of telecommunications: findings from a national survey", Paper presented at the Tel*Ed 93: Global Connections Conference (Proceedings available on the CoSN gopher).

Honey, Margaret and Henríquez, Andrés (1993), *Telecommunications and K-12 Educators: Findings From a National Survey*, Center for Technology in Education, Bank Street College of Education, New York.

Kantrowitz, Barbara (1994), "Men, women, and computers", *Newsweek*, 16 May, pp.36–43.

Kirkup, Gill and Keller, Laurie Smith (1992), *Inventing Women: Science, Technology and Gender*, Polity Press, Cambridge.

Krol, Ed (1992), *The Whole Internet: User's Guide and Catalog*, O'Reilly and Associates, Sebastopol, California.

McClanahan, Gloria (1994), Internet Use, Electronic mail message, 14 June.

McClure, Charles R., Bishop, A., Doty, P., and Rosenbaum, H. (1991), *The National Research and Education Network (NREN): Research and Policy Perspectives*, Ablex, Syracuse, New York.

Milbury, Peter (1993), LM_NET Statistics Regarding Message Postings and Membership, Message posted to the LM_NET listserv on the Internet, 24 May.

(National Center for Educational Statistics) (1992), *Schools and Staffing in the United States: A Statistical Profile, 1987–1988,* United States Department of Education, Office of Educational Research and Improvement, Washington, DC.

Pitkow, James and Recker, Mimi (1994), World Wide Web User Survey, Quoted in the document How Popular is the Web?, Available on the World Wide Web.

Rheingold, Howard (1993), *The Virtual Community: Homesteading on the Electronic Frontier,* Addison-Wesley, Menlo Park, California.

Roelands, Duane Willem (1994), The Grip—Social Dynamics of the New Frontier, Refractions (weekly electronic magazine) 1, no. 11, 20 July.

Turkle, Sherry and Papert, Seymour (1990), "Epistemological pluralism: styles and voices within the computer culture", *Signs: Journal of Women in Culture and Society* 16, no. 1, pp.128–157.

Webb, Lynn Judson (1994), "TENET—Texas connection to the world", *Information Searcher* 6,no. 3, pp.24–26.

CHAPTER SIX

THE INTERNET IN SCHOOL LIBRARIES

INTRODUCTION

"K-12 is one of the fastest growing communities connecting to the Internet. As a result, ... education is being revolutionized. Teachers have new tools and new ways to inspire students, and students are using the Internet to learn about the world" (NYSERNet, 1993). At the NYSERNet conference in Rochester, New York, in October 1993, Deborah Newkirk from the University of Alaska described "some of the major successful K-12 networking projects" that illustrated the "new tools" and "new ways to inspire students". At the SLOC (School Library Organisations Council) conference in Perth, Western Australia, in June 1994, Carol Tenopir of the University of Hawaii presented an opening scenario of the networked school librarian trawling the Internet for information for all the school library's client groups and taking a proactive role in identifying information needs, planning information services based on the Internet, and teaching the information skills required for "netsearching" and using online information.

The Internet has much to offer schools, in terms of currency and availability of information and the opportunities for networking and sharing information. As a management tool, the Internet offers considerable savings in time and often in costs, and it may also result in access to information that could have been located in no other way. Probably most importantly in the educational context, use of the Internet can help students to develop information skills (Clyde and Kirk, 1987). Current curriculum theory draws heavily on ideas about resource-based learning, individualization of instruction, and the need for all people to develop lifelong learning strategies to cope with a rapidly changing world. The application of the Internet to the school curriculum enhances students' physical and intellectual access to information.

The results of the research project on which this book is based suggest that, while most LM_NET members share this vision of the Internet in education and are enthusiastic advocates for educational and school library use of the Internet, the reality often falls far short of the vision, for a number of reasons. In this chapter, the use of the Internet in school libraries and by school librarians is discussed, based on information from the online survey of LM_NET members (specifically on information provided by the 67 respondents who were working in schools), and on evidence from downloaded LM_NET messages, documents posted to other Internet listservs, to gophers and USENET newsgroups, on reports of research projects or pilot projects, and the review of the literature. In addition, some of the information about Internet resources is based on online exploration of the Internet itself.

SCHOOL LIBRARIANS' USE OF THE INTERNET

How are school librarians actually using the Internet and for what applications? The questionnaire survey of LM_NET members asked respondents to indicate all the purposes for which they used the Internet (above and beyond their use of LM_NET). Table 6.1 summarizes the responses.

Once again, as it was with the use of LM_NET itself, it is notable that professional contact and communication are important factors, as is the use of the Internet for information searching to answer reference questions or to

Table 6.1
Respondents' Use of the Internet
(67 School Respondents)

USE OF THE INTERNET	NUMBER OF RESPONDENTS	PERCENTAGE
For email contact with people outside my school	65	97.01
Exchanging information on listservs and/or bulletin boards	57	85.07
To get information about resources	51	76.12
To get curriculum-related information for teachers	46	68.66
To get information about educational research or developments for teachers or school administrators	44	65.67
To discuss professional issues	43	64.12
To expand the range of resources available in the school	41	61.12
To have fun	40	59.70
To get information that it would be difficult to get otherwise	35	52.24
To get information for students	34	50.75
To find answers to reference questions	32	47.76
Student projects (group or individual) based on the Internet	29	43.28
To expand students' awareness of the world	23	34.33
Student research	22	32.84
To develop students' information and enquiry skills	15	22.39
To play Internet games	1	1.49
Other	3	4.48

provide other people with information. In addition, in some school libraries, the Internet is being used for student projects and student research. Information skills instruction was sometimes mentioned in this context, as was the need to expand students' awareness of the world, but in the overall context of the responses, these aspects remained secondary to professional contact and information services. This may be related to the fact that so many school librarians were accessing the Internet mainly through equipment located in their own homes, rather than in their school or school library: they were able to get information for library users, and provide printouts for them, but they did not always have the facilities within the library to allow users direct access to the Internet, or even to watch a search being carried out.

Which of these applications did the respondents in schools regard as the most important? See Table 6.2 for a summary of responses. Fourteen people found this ranking exercise too difficult: "Too many are important—impossible to rank" and "There is no single most important use—all are important to me". However, of those who did answer, 35.29 percent indicated that for them, the most important application of the Internet was for electronic mail contact with people outside the school. Other applications listed as most important by five or more respondents were exchanging information on listservs and/or bulletin boards, discussing professional issues, and use of the Internet to expand the range of resources available in the school. Only the last is not directly related to communication and professional discussion, though it is, of course, important in terms of school library service.

The "other" applications of the Internet that were mentioned by respondents fell into no recognizable pattern. Two people were using the Internet "to complete independent study coursework through Syracuse University"; one was using it to provide students in the school with access to the DIALOG service; one was using it "to see what issues are being discussed among media specialists"; and one had used it to organize "a sonnet contest using the Internet last spring". For two people, their "other" application was the most important for them.

Comments by respondents also make it clear that an application that is important at one stage may become less

Table 6.2
Most Important Application of the Internet
(67 School Respondents)

USE OF THE INTERNET	NUMBER OF RESPONDENTS
For email contact with people outside my school	18
Exchanging information on listservs and/or bulletin boards	9
To discuss professional issues	5
To expand the range of resources available in the school	5
To get information that it would be difficult to get otherwise	3
To get information about resources	2
To get information for students	2
To find answers to reference questions	2
Student projects (group or individual) based on the Internet	1
To expand students' awareness of the world	1
To develop students' information and enquiry skills	1
To get curriculum-related information for teachers	0
To get information about educational research or developments for teachers or school administrators	0
To have fun	0
Student research	0
To play Internet games	0
Other	2

important over time, as people become more familiar with the technology and with Internet resources, and try new Internet tools and services. In addition, the need that drew people into using the Internet may just be the beginning, and they may come to use it for a wider range of applications than would have seemed possible at first; for example, one person said, "I began using the Internet largely to expand the resources for students and teachers", but "I have since become very involved in co-ordinating student projects between our schools and schools in Russia."

Table 6.3
LM_NET Traffic
(October 1993)

TYPE OF MESSAGE	NUMBER OF MESSAGES	%
Professional contact and communication	55	9.08
Discussion of professional issues	151	24.92
Reference and information services	50	8.25
Locating information about resources	146	24.09
School library administration (including automation)	128	21.12
Curriculum applications and student projects based on the Internet	24	3.96
Miscellaneous	35	5.77
LM_NET administration	17	2.81
TOTAL	606	

The analysis of LM_NET traffic for the month of October 1993 supports the general picture given in Tables 6.1 and 6.2, particularly the emphasis on professional contact and discussion of professional issues, and the use of LM_NET to locate resources and to find information. Table 6.3 shows the messages for the month divided into major categories that generally reflect those in Tables 6.1 and 6.2, but which draw together several related categories. For instance, finding "answers to reference questions" and locating information for students, teachers, and school administration, have all been brought together under the broader heading "reference and information services", while "email contact with people outside my school" and "exchanging information on listservs and/or bulletin boards" have been brought together under the broader heading "professional contact and communication". The headings used in Table 6.3 will also be used as the basis for discussion later in the chapter. Some messages proved unclassifiable, and they have been included under the "miscellaneous" heading (which also includes messages clearly sent to the wrong place, incomplete messages, messages unrelated to the usual topics of the listserv).

The survey respondents were all reading messages posted to the LM_NET listserv for "school library media people"; this was how they came to be involved in the research project. However, apart from LM_NET, what Internet resources and services were being used?

Table 6.4
Number of Listservs to Which Respondents Belonged
(67 School Respondents)

NUMBER OF LISTSERVS	NUMBER OF RESPONDENTS
One (LM_NET)	36
Two	10
Three	6
Four	4
Five	5
Six	0
Seven	1
Eight	4
More than eight	1

Only 31 respondents (fewer than half) belonged to another listserv or listservs in addition to LM_NET. So while LM_NET members have clearly discovered listservs and know their value, they have not, on the whole, explored widely. This may be related to the type of Internet accounts that some LM_NET members have, with limited space in their electronic mailboxes. In addition, some members of LM_NET have expressed the fear that they might not be able to cope with a lot of electronic mail, and so they may, as a result, be selective about what they join.

In all, more than 50 different listservs were listed by the 31 people who belonged to more than one listserv. The most popular were:

- K12Net (8 people), an electronic bulletin board and conferencing system linked to the Internet, for discussion of curriculum, classroom-to-classroom projects, and language exchanges between children learning a language and native speakers of the language;
- EDTECH (6), a listserv for people interested in technology and its use in educational settings at all levels from preschool to university;
- KIDSPHERE (6), an international listserv for schoolchildren and their teachers;
- EDNET (4), a listserv or "forum" based at the University of Massachusetts, for "exploring the educational possibilities of electronic communication and the Internet";
- KIDLIT-L (4), for those interested in literature for children and young adults—members include university and college teachers of children's literature, publishers, school librarians, librarians, reviewers, and others;
- PACS-L (3), the Public-Access Computer Systems Forum, a listserv focusing on library automation and online services;
- PUBYAC (3), a listserv that deals with issues related to the provision of services for children and young adults in public libraries.

Other listservs that were mentioned were related to librarianship and to particular aspects of librarianship (such as cataloguing or technical services), to education and to particular aspects of education (such as vocational education or curriculum development), to books and reading, to computing and the use of microcomputers, and to hobbies and recreational interests. Listservs to which one or two people belonged included ifreedom (also known as "Snoopy", an intellectual freedom listserv based in Canada), Net-Happenings (a "read-only" listserv through which Gleason Sackman, the noted Internet scout, posts information about new Internet resources), Stumpers-L (the listserv where librarians post their truly difficult reference questions), K12ADMIN (for people interested in school administration and issues associated with school planning and development), MIDDLE-L (for people working in middle schools), PUBLIB (a listserv for people involved in public libraries, but which nevertheless discusses many issues that are also of interest to people in school libraries), DYNIX-L (for personnel in libraries where the Dynix automated library system is being used), CDROMLAN (where people who are mounting CD-ROM drives on networks meet up to discuss their problems and to exchange information), FEMINIST (a list for people interested in feminist issues), ROOTS-L (for people interested in genealogy), and HUMOR (probably self-explanatory).

Some people were able to read listserv postings through their local network (for example, NEXUS in Australia), and so though they did not subscribe to any listservs themselves, they still had access to the information that came through them. In relation to this, one person commented that "I used to subscribe to KIDSPHERE but requested that it be added to the newsgroups at our host university, and I then unsubscribed." Others had access through local FrEd-Mail services. However, some found their local Internet provider to be either unhelpful or negative about listservs and newsgroups; for instance, one respondent noted that "our FIRN network strongly discourages subscription to listservs". Looking at the issue from a system administrator's point of view, it is easy to see why this might be so: listservs can generate a lot of electronic mail, and if the subscribers do not read their mail regularly, or do not stop their listserv mail when they change address or go on vacation, then electronic mailboxes can fill up and the system administrator has to deal with the problem. However, given the value that survey respondents placed on communication and professional contact, it is easy to see why access to listservs and newsgroups is important for some of them.

Table 6.5
Subscriptions to Electronic Journals
(67 School Respondents)

SUBSCRIPTION?	NUMBER OF RESPONDENTS
Yes	25
No	41
No answer	1

Electronic journals and newsletters can be produced and distributed more quickly (and often more cheaply) than print journals. When an electronic journal or newsletter is an online version of a printed equivalent, it usually reaches its subscribers before the printed version is distributed. Many of these publications are free and give their readers quick access to valuable current information. While some provide only digests or compilations of information available elsewhere, they often do so in a way that makes it easier for the subscriber to keep abreast of particular issues. It has been said that "the greatest need on the nets is for filters", agents that sift information and organize what is relevant in a way that meets the needs of particular groups of users. Filtering "has been the traditional role of print journals"; it is already becoming clear that electronic journals could help to fill this same role on the Internet (Kessler, 1993). In a sense, these publications are a possible answer to the problem of information overload mentioned by so many members of LM_NET, rather than an addition to the problem. The very successful EDUPAGE electronic newsletter is an example of an Internet filter that highlights important information in its field of interest and provides summaries and pointers to articles, reports, and other print and electronic publications. Yet only a little more than one-third of the school-based respondents in the survey of LM_NET members subscribed to any of these electronic publications.

Although only 25 respondents (37.31 percent) subscribed to an electronic journal or newsletter, more than 30 titles were listed by those 25 people. While most people who subscribed, subscribed to only one or two, there were a few people who listed five or six titles and then indicated that there were others but they had forgotten the details. The largest number subscribing to any one title was six (for the award-winning EDUPAGE newsletter).

Electronic journals or newsletters that were mentioned by three or more people included:

- EDUPAGE, a free electronic newsletter produced three times a week by EDUCOM, a consortium of colleges and universities, which carries summaries of current news items related to information technology;
- ALAWON, a free electronic newsletter from the American Library Association's Washington office, produced once a week or more often, with a focus on United States government policy as it relates to libraries and information access;
- RPTCRD Daily Report Card News Service, an electronic publication distributed three days each week, that reports on developments in education around the United States, covering issues such as funding, curriculum change, political developments, school management, student achievement, social issues;
- ALCTS Newsletter, an irregular free electronic newsletter of the American Association for Library Collections and Technical Services, a division of the American Library Association;
- PACS Review, the Public-Access Computer Systems Review, a refereed electronic journal devoted to end-user computer systems in libraries, including public access catalogs, online searching, and CD-ROM access.

Other electronic journals or newsletters mentioned by respondents included Bits and Bytes (the "electronic newsletter for information hunter-gatherers" produced by Jay Machado, which has articles and news summaries), Infobits (an electronic newsletter that monitors a number of technology and educational technology information sources), CNN Classroom Guide, Somalia News Update (used for social studies classes), China News Digest, and NetTEACH News (a subscription newsletter for teachers in elementary and secondary schools who are interested in telecommunications in education).

Most of these electronic journals and newsletters mentioned are available free. However, despite this, it is clear that these Internet resources are not being used as much as they might be in schools—perhaps because school librarians seem to have little information about what is available.

Table 6.6

Use of a Community Freenet

(67 School Respondents)

USING A FREENET?	NUMBER OF RESPONDENTS
Yes	18
No	42
No answer	2

In places where they exist, community freenets provide local citizens and community organizations with free online access to local information, electronic mail services, and Internet access. Some schools are using a local community freenet at their Internet access provider. Because comunity freenets are linked to the Internet, people from outside the region can also log in (via telnet) and use the information services. There may, however, be a limit placed on the online time allowed to online visitors from outside the community; in addition, visitors may not have access to all databases and facilities provided through the freenet. Some school librarians were using remote freenets for particular information services that they provided, such as environmental information, or, in the case of the Victoria

Freenet, Canadian government information. However, there were also comments that the freenets were "always busy" or "often busy" and difficult to access via the Internet because of this. Nevertheless, 12 different freenets had been used by the 18 respondents who had used one, including the Cleveland Freenet (the oldest of the freenets, and the one most often mentioned by respondents), the Denver Free-Net in Colorado, Canada's Victoria Free-Net, the Tallahassee Freenet in Florida, and the Youngstown Freenet.

Table 6.7
Use of Commercial Information Services via the Internet
(67 School Respondents)

SERVICE	NUMBER OF RESPONDENTS
DIALOG	10
OCLC	1
Other (Unspecified)	2

Commercial online information services such as DIALOG have existed for more than 20 years, though in the last five years many new services have been established, and the older services like DIALOG have expanded their databases and services, while the provision of access via the Internet has made them more attractive for users who were previously disadvantaged by high telecommunications charges. When they were first introduced in the early 1970s, the online information services were mainly used by academic and research libraries and the larger public libraries, but by the late 1980s their use in small libraries like school libraries was increasing. Reflecting this pattern, some major publications on the use of online information services in schools emerged at the end of the decade. In the United States, these included Doris Epler's *Online Searching Goes to School* (1989), Beverley Hunter and Erica Lodish's *Online Searching in the Curriculum: A Teaching*

Guide for Library Media Specialists (1989), and Ann Lathrop's *Online and CD-ROM Databases in School Libraries* (1989). In Australia, the School Libraries Section of the Australian Library and Information Association had published *Online Information Services for Schools: Implications for School Libraries* as early as 1987, while in the United Kingdom, there were several publications on this topic, including Ann Irving's research-based book, *Wider Horizons: Online Information Services in Schools* (1990). In some schools, online information services have been introduced as part of "computer awareness" or "technology studies" courses. However, the use of online information services has a place and a value in the school curriculum and the school library, independently of technology studies or computer studies courses, both as a source of current information for teachers and students and as a means of teaching information skills that are relevant to today's world, and it is on this basis that many schools are using online services.

Among the online information services traditionally used by libraries, DIALOG, Data*Star, OCLC, and others can now be accessed via the Internet, and some, like DIALOG, offer delivery of search results by Internet email. Among the general online information services, the services, like America Online, Prodigy, CompuServe, and Mindlink, designed to appeal to the general public now offer Internet services as part of their "service package", along with their databases, conference systems, and other services.

In the last few years, several of the online information services have been marketing extensively to schools, and some have established special programs for schools. In some cases, these special deals extend well beyond special prices to include sophisticated teaching materials and support services. DIALOG's Classroom Instruction Program supports the use of online services within the educational program of the school, and OCLC established a special trial program in 1994. Meanwhile, among the newer general information services, both America Online (through its Scholastic Network) and Prodigy (through Classroom Prodigy) have special sections and services for schools.

DIALOG's Classroom Instruction Program is a well-established program that allows schools to search its databases cheaply for educational purposes. In all, DIALOG has more than 400 databases, most of which can be used through the Classroom Instruction Program. Databases of potential interest to schools include AP News, America: History and Life, Enviroline, Magazine Index, Time Publications, ERIC, British Education Index, A-V Online, Bowker Biographical Directory (formerly American Men and Women of Science), and the full-text newspaper databases such as the *Washington Post* and the *Times and Sunday Times* of London. The searching must be done in a supervised setting, it must be related to the curriculum, and it must be done as part of a formal course of study. The guidelines for the program specify that, apart from demonstrations by the teacher or school librarian, students either conduct their own planned searches or be active participants in the search process. To assist teachers and school librarians, DIALOG provides a range of material in support of the Classroom Instruction Program. This includes teaching material such as sample lesson plans, overhead projection transparency masters, and suggested demonstration searches. Newsletters provide additional information and ideas for the use of DIALOG databases in the school setting.

In August 1994, Evie Funk posted a HIT-> message to LM_NET which collated information provided by 16 LM_NET members who were users of DIALOG; the general consensus was that The Classroom Instruction Program was useful in the school setting and provided value for money. One middle school librarian had been using DIALOG "for a long time (10–15 years)", a high school librarian for ten years, another for seven years, so there was some depth of experience behind the responses. The Classroom Instruction Program was being used in these schools for teaching online search skills to students (for example, in the context of a special unit on controversial issues, in which students did their own searching, and in classes in critical thinking skills), to demonstrate online searching for senior students, to locate information for teachers and students doing research projects, for access to the Magazine Index and Books in Print databases, to locate the full text of newspaper articles. In one school, "the Official Airline Guide database is used a lot by a particular group of social studies teachers for a simulated travel program". In another school, it was found to be "a particularly good resource for topics which are current in nature—environmental concerns, political research, etc.". The advantages of DIALOG were listed by a high school librarian as "currency, retrospective searches, extremely specific searches due to the Boolean operators and other limiters ... ease and efficiency of retrieval", while others added speed of retrieval and "low cost" for "all the information you get". The disadvantages were seen to be the high investment of staff time required in learning and teaching the necessary skills, and the cost—though some schools, when they found that they were making frequent online use of a database like Books in Print had purchased that database on CD-ROM in an attempt to reduce costs.

The OCLC (Online Computer Library Center) program for schools is more recent than that of DIALOG. Announced in January/February 1994, it is a two-year pilot program which, in conjunction with the OCLC regional networks, gives school libraries (in all types of schools, K-12) access to the OCLC FirstSearch Catalog at a special rate. The program, called FirstSearch for School Libraries, is designed to enable teacher librarians to "evaluate the feasibility of providing FirstSearch to students". There are currently more than 40 databases available through FirstSearch, many of which would appear to have some value for school use; these include Reader's Guide to Periodical Literature, General Science Index, the Concise Columbia Electronic Encyclopedia, Library Literature, Book Review Digest, and PsycINFO.

However, despite the advantages of these and other special services for schools, the results of the survey of LM_NET members indicate that only 13 of the 67 school libraries represented were using services like DIALOG or OCLC via the Internet. There were indications that lack of knowledge of what is available may be a factor in this—several respondents wrote comments like "Is this really possible?" beside the question on the survey form. In addition, while the DIALOG Classroom Instruction Program has been operational for some years, the OCLC pilot program had not been officially announced at the time of the survey. Another factor may be the many school librarians who were using home equipment to access the Internet, and the consequent reluctance to incur too many charges, no matter how good the deal might be. Within schools, where people are not normally accustomed to paying for information, it often takes some online experience before they come to recognize that paying for well-organised, well-indexed, and carefully selected information can in fact save time and increase the range of quality resources available, out of proportion to the actual cost. Then, too, most schools are not accustomed to budgeting for the cost of online services, and administrators can become nervous about budget lines that represent access to resources (often hard to estimate) rather than the resources themselves. They are under pressure to show what they have done with the money allocated to them, and it is difficult to show anything concrete as a result of a budget line for an online service. Thus school librarians may have to work hard to "sell" the value of these services to administrators.

There is evidence that membership of the newer general commercial online services that provide Internet access as part of their service package is higher than the traditional services associated with libraries, such as DIALOG and OCLC. In July 1994, a discussion on LM_NET highlighted the school services offered by America Online, and several members indicated that they got their LM_NET access (and access to other listservs, gophers, and USENET newsgroups, though not to telnet and ftp) through America Online. The list of LM_NET members provided through the REVIEW LM_NET command on the listserv supports this (see Chapter Five). However, in these cases, people are buying their Internet access as well as their access to online information; to access DIALOG, OCLC, and other similar services via the Internet, they already need to have Internet access.

Table 6.8
Internet Access for Teachers in the School
(67 School Respondents)

PLACE OF ACCESS	NUMBER
In the school library	44
In a computer laboratory	8
In the classroom	6
In the staff room	1
Other	6
No access	13
Not applicable	1

Table 6.8 shows the extent of Internet access for teachers in the schools. In some schools, teachers had access to the Internet in more than one location, sometimes in several locations. In 44 schools, teachers had access of some kind in the school library. Of those 44 schools, one of the school's teachers also had access in a computer lab and a staff room, in two they also had access in a computer lab and the classroom, and in three they also had access in a computer lab. In the six schools in which teachers had

access in the classroom, they also had access in the school library.

However, the situation was not quite as attractive as these figures make it appear. In most of the schools, only a few teachers had access, not all teachers. Sometimes their access depended on their having money from grants or funded projects to pay for the computers and the telecommunications charges. In some schools, only the school library and one or two classrooms and/or the computer lab had telephone lines. In California, some teachers were paying the telephone company for a phone line to their classroom so that they could use the Internet. There were schools where teachers had access in theory, though in practice it was difficult: for example, one respondent reported that "the school has email access but it's difficult to get to a computer", while another said, "five teachers have accounts, [but] access is through one of two workstations at school or from home computers". Another respondent noted that, though "most classrooms have a phone jack, we have two travelling modems [and] only about half the teachers yet have a computer to call their own to use the modem with. We have a setup in the office too … with a dedicated modem. All that equals four systems, two phone lines." Even the access through the school library was sometimes difficult. One school librarian reported that access was possible "only after school" for teachers, another that "there is no access unless I log them onto my home account using the school's modem". In one school library that had Internet access, that access could be used only for library applications, and there was no access to services like electronic mail.

However, there were also some very bright spots. In one school, teachers had Internet access from 220 terminals located throughout the school, and via modem from their personal computers at home.

Table 6.9 shows the schools which provided some type of Internet access for students, and the location of the equipment used for that access. In all, 40 schools provided Internet access of some kind for students. In some of those schools, access was possible in two or three different places; in one school, students had access from 220 terminals throughout the school. In 24 schools, students had access just in the school library, though that access was sometimes very restricted. In one school library, the access was limited to library applications, and in another it was possible only with the school librarian doing the keyboarding. In 11 other schools, students had access in the school library as well as in the classroom and/or computer lab. As was the case for the teachers, though, not all students in the school necessarily had access even when access was possible in a computer lab or in some classrooms. Even in one school where the students had access through the computer lab, it was reported that "the teacher does the actual typing in of messages" for the students' electronic mail exchanges with another school, though "the kids compose" the messages. It is significant that whereas there were only 13 schools where teachers had "no access", there were 26 schools in which students had "no access".

Table 6.9

Internet Access for Students in the School

(67 School Respondents)

PLACE OF ACCESS	NUMBER
In the school library	35
In a computer laboratory	4
In the classroom	9
Other	1
No access	26
Not applicable	2
No answer	1

In the 40 schools where students had access to the Internet, access was generally supervised, though in three schools, students were allowed unsupervised access, as Table 6.10 shows, while in another three, access was both supervised and unsupervised.

Table 6.10
Student Access to the Internet in Schools
(40 Schools)

SUPERVISED OR UNSUPERVISED ACCESS	NUMBER OF SCHOOLS
Supervised	29
Unsupervised	3
Both Supervised and Unsupervised	3
No Answer	5

In early 1994, Gloria McClanahan posted a query to LM_NET about Internet use in schools. One of her four questions asked "Did you actually use the Internet with students in the past year?", while another asked "How does your school connect to the Internet for student use?" The responses generally support the picture that emerged from the survey, of supervised student access to the Internet through a computer in the school library and/or classroom and computer lab. "Most sites had only one modem set up...in the library. Some sites had additional modems in classrooms; most were working toward more modem stations set up in classrooms" (McClanahan, 1994b). In a Missouri high school, there were "connections in our library and also in our TV studio"; in a Texas middle school, "the only access" was from a workstation on the librarian's desk (operating as a standalone unit, not on the network); in a Texas high school, the telephone line used for Internet searching (via the University of Alabama at Birmingham) was in the library; in a Missouri high school, there was only one modem "right now", in the library media center office, and students used it through the school library media specialist. In a Kentucky middle school, the librarian said there was "one telephone line and modem in the media center, at my desk, I search while the student sits beside me, we confer on the search strategies, and I basically follow their desires in the direction of the search". Some of the school librarians were in districts where a WAN (wide area network) with Internet access was in the process of development, but meanwhile they were using a modem in the school library to get access to a local university system or a freenet.

While the responses to McClanahan's posting support the general picture of Internet use in schools that was presented by the survey results, they also support an earlier comment that much of the Internet activity in schools appears to take place at the middle school and high school levels; all but three of the respondents to McClanahan appeared to be working with students at middle school level and upwards.

Table 6.11
Internet Skills Instruction for Students
(67 Schools)

LOCATION OF INSTRUCTION	NUMBER OF SCHOOLS
In the classroom by the class teacher	1
In the computer lab as part of a computer class	2
In the computer lab as part of another class	0
In the school library	19
By the school librarian outside the school library	3
Through a computer club at school	0
More than one location including the school library	7
More than one location not including the school library	0
No specific instruction	1
Other	3
Not applicable/no answer	31

Although students had some kind of access to the Internet in 40 of the 67 schools represented in the LM_NET survey, not all of those schools provided them with instruction in Internet skills. In addition, in some schools where specific instruction was offered, this was described as "just beginning". In one school, "students who have use for Internet resources are taught on an ad hoc basis by teachers or librarian", while in another, Internet access was "brand new and we are only now developing mechanisms for instruction", though a range of instructional strategies was being planned. One Canadian junior high school librarian described a co-operative teaching plan involving the school computer consultant, the teacher librarian, and use of the school library's Internet connection (via modem). "She [the computer consultant] does the introduction, then gives them the assignment and sends them to me. I work with a small group at a time. ... we explore the Internet for about 40 minutes, then they send [a] message. I do the most on the Internet because I'm on it every day. She's only on at the most once a week" (McClanahan, 1994b). However, the information skills instruction and practice in this case was limited to the sending of a message. Nevertheless, there were also schools where cooperative, planned programs were well established, for example in the school where the librarian was teaching the skills "in co-operation with the Math Department Chairperson and classroom teachers who have participated in workshops". In other schools, such programs were being developed: in a posting to LM_NET in August 1994, Ronnie Pastecki indicated that "a curriculum and course outline for a half year telecommunications class at our high school" was being organized.

In summary, then, although LM_NET members were generally convinced of the value of the Internet in the school setting, it was often, of necessity, being used in limited ways. The most valued uses of the Internet were for professional contact and communication, for exchanging information with other professionals, for discussing professional issues, and, in terms of library services, to expand the range of resources available in the school, to get information about resources, and to find answers to reference questions. Although many school librarians were using the Internet with students, and were aware of the need to teach information skills through use of this medium, at this stage work with students generally ranked lower in the list of priorities. Sometimes this was simply because the facilities were not available in the school. The range of electronic resources used by LM_NET members was fairly limited, perhaps a result of lack of knowledge of what is available (many survey respondents indicated that they were "just beginners"), possibly reflecting the type of Internet accounts that some members have, and the fact that many pay for their own access. Fewer than half belonged to listservs (apart from LM_NET), only a little over one third subscribed to an electronic journal or newsletter, only a little over a quarter had used a community freenet, and only one fifth were using the Internet to access commercial online information services (including those offering special services for schools). In many schools, access to the Internet was restricted to a computer in the librarian's office or to the library and/cr a computer lab or one or two classrooms. Even in schools where teachers had Internet access, this was seldom easily available to all teachers. Generally, students were less likely to have access than teachers, and their access was normally supervised. Not all schools where students had Internet access provided Internet skills instruction, and where this instruction was provided, it was sometimes quite limited, largely, it seems, because of the restrictions on access to hardware. However, it appears that the need for students to be able to develop appropriate skills was more widely recognized, and it is clear that new programs are being developed in some schools for this purpose.

What is disturbing about all this is that there is evidence that LM_NET members are often leaders in the use of the Internet in their schools and sometimes their districts and states as well. If they are struggling to increase awareness of the possibilities and to make better facilities available for their schools, then what of the other schools? While much has been done by small groups of people, the vision is a long way from general realization.

In the rest of this chapter, the major applications of the Internet in school libraries will be discussed, under the broad headings used in Table 6.3, covering use of the Internet for professional contact and communication, for the discussion of professional issues, for finding answers to reference questions and providing information services for the various members of the school community, for locating information about resources, for help in school library management and administration, for curriculum applications across the different subject areas, and for student projects. An additional section discusses schools and school libraries as initiators in the information process, as suppliers of information on the Internet, rather than as just consumers of information that is provided by others. The information about applications of the Internet in school libraries comes from the responses to the questionnaire survey of LM_NET members, from the analysis of LM_NET traffic for October 1993, from other sources on the Internet (such as listservs and gophers in the fields of education and librarianship), and from the literature.

PROFESSIONAL CONTACT AND COMMUNICATION

The survey respondents, particularly those working in schools, placed a strong emphasis on professional contact and communication as a reason for using the Internet. This was also an important factor in their membership of LM_NET, and it is reflected in the number of messages posted to LM_NET that would appear to have their basis in just "keeping in touch". In fact, LM_NET in itself could be said to exist primarily because of this, and all messages to a certain extent illustrate this need.

However, there were some 55 messages posted to LM_NET in October 1993 (of a total of 606) the major purpose of which was obviously professional contact and communication (see Table 6.3). Some of these messages related to conferences: information about forthcoming conferences; summaries of conference highlights from those who attended a conference (including "news from the front" sent during the conference itself); messages related to plans for a group of LM_NETters to get together at a conference; and requests for information about possible speakers from people who were planning a local conference. Other messages in this category provided information about books and articles that members of LM_NET were recommending for professional reading; information about job vacancies and requests from people seeking employment; requests for LM_NET members to send greetings to workshops being run by a member; and information about activities that members of LM_NET had undertaken (research, workshop presentations, an experimental project). Another group of messages related to current political and educational developments, and these were usually posted with the intention of encouraging LM_NET members to lobby for a desirable outcome. An example is a message posted on 25 October 1993 to alert LM_NET members to elementary and secondary education legislation that was being discussed in the United States Senate and in committees, asking them to send letters to the decision-makers about particular aspects of the legislation.

In the context of professional contact and communication, it has been good to note the increasing presence on the Internet of the professional associations. During 1993/94, the International Federation of Library Associations and Institutions (IFLA) established a gopher at the Royal Library in the Netherlands; IFLA has a section for school libraries which is represented (though only in a small way) on the gopher. Later, a World Wide Web server was established for IFLA. The American Library Association and the Library Association (United Kingdom) were early supporters of electronic communication. The American Library Association now has a gopher and a Web server, and its Washington office publishes the well-known electronic newsletter ALAWON (which some LM_NET members indicated that they subscribed to); Library Association documents are made available electronically via the BUBL library science gopher at the University of Bath. The American Association of School Librarians (AASL) has Web pages. It also posts documents and other information to the AskERIC gopher server at Syracuse University in New York, where they can be read or downloaded; in addition, AASL announcements are sometimes posted to LM_NET, as are announcements from the Association for Teacher Librarianship in Canada (ATLC). A few American state associations have their own gopher server, for instance, the Minnesota Educational Media Organization (MEMO) (which also has a listserv) and the related Minnesota Society for Technology in Education (MSTE), while other state associations post announcements through their state electronic bulletin board or network (such as TENET in Texas) and/or Web servers.

DISCUSSION OF PROFESSIONAL ISSUES

Closely related to the use of LM_NET and the Internet for professional contact and communication is the use of these telecommunications resources for the discussion of professional issues. In all 151 of the 606 messages on LM_NET in October 1993 (or 24.92 percent) related to discussion of a variety of professional issues of concern to school librarians and others interested in the provision of school library services. Table 6.12 provides a summary of the issues discussed and the number of messages related to each. However, when the messages are looked at more closely, it becomes clear that this type of usage is even more important for participants than the raw numbers would suggest. Two of the messages that fell into the category of discussion of professional issues were HIT-> messages, messages that summarized a number of responses sent to the person who had raised an issue of concern by posting it as a TARGET-> message and asking people to respond direct rather than to the list. One of the HIT-> messages contained summaries of 17 responses, and the other, 13.

Table 6.12
Professional Issues Discussed on LM_NET
(October 1993)

ISSUE	NUMBER OF MESSAGES
Censorship and Challenged Books	24
Reading Incentives for Elementary Students	20
Revision of "Information Power"	17
School Libraries and Democracy	17
Management of School Networks	1 HIT> (17)
Popular Fiction in School Libraries	14
"Overworked School Librarians"	14
Technology Training for School Librarians	1 HIT-> (13)
Enquiry vs Research	10
Networks and Libraries	6
Vandalism in School Libraries	5
Teacher Training and Practicum in SLMC	5
Other	17
TOTAL	151 (179)

The topic that inspired most messages was the never-ending one of censorship and challenges to books and other material in school libraries. The "banned books" mentioned during the month included Judy Blume's *Forever*, Rosemary Guilley's *Encyclopedia of Witches and Witchcraft*, Christopher Pike's *Chain Letter*, and Zuckerman's *Tiger Kittens*. Messages in response to requests for assistance provided advice about district and school resource selection policies and policies for dealing with challenged material, suggested procedures that had worked in other places, and provided information about support material from the American Library Association's Office of Intellectual Freedom and other organizations. Discussion of a related topic, popular fiction in school libraries, dovetailed with the discussion of censorship attempts. Beginning as a discussion of whether or not horror stories and other books by authors like Christopher Pike, R. L. Stine, and Stephen King had a place in elementary school libraries, it broadened into a discussion of popular fiction in general in libraries. It connected with the censorship discussion in relation to school library selection policy statements (should students be given what they want to read or what is good for them?) and in relation to discussion of challenges to specific titles such as those of Pike.

Some of the discussions of professional issues originated in a reference question posted to the list, or in what appeared to be a simple request for information. For example, a request for information about reading incentive programs for elementary school children drew several responses that described programs that had been successful in particular schools, such as the Accelerated Reader Program, local programs such as a reading program in Oregon sponsored by the Portland Trailblazers, and the Book-it program sponsored by Pizza Hut (through which students received a coupon for a free monthly pizza if they reached their personal reading target for the month). However, the request also lead to a discussion about the value of reading incentive programs in general, with some participants quoting research evidence that showed that extrinsic rewards fail to encourage the long-term development of reading habits, and others citing some of the range of literature on this topic (either in support of incentive programs or against them).

Other discussions that originated in requests for information, or in reference questions, included the discussion about the nature of inquiry and research in school libraries, and the discussion about the place of a practicum in the school library in the training of teachers.

However, some of the issues were raised with the stated intention of sparking ongoing online conversation and debate. One of these was the discussion that focused on the American school library document, *Information Power: Guidelines for School Library Media Programs,* a discussion which began as the result of a message that solicited input for an American Association of School Librarians committee that was looking at the document. Messages on this topic were often longer than usual, and the writers went to some pains to make a case for their point of view, presenting clearly argued and documented discussion points related to *Information Power,* its contents, and/or the need for any amendments. In fact, a great deal of discussion centered around whether or not amendments were needed at all, when, as some people saw it, school libraries were "just starting to fulfil the promise" of a document that was still "dynamic, powerful, and right on target".

Other issues that were raised with the deliberate intention of stimulating discussion were the problems of vadalism in school libraries, the management of school networks (which usually include the school library), the related topic of technology training for school librarians, and the topic that came to be titled "overworked school librarians" (a discussion of the number of hours that school librarians work and the responsibilities that they have in the school).

Table 6.12 shows that 17 messages dealt with "other" issues. These were issues that were discussed on LM_NET during the month of October, but which generated fewer than five messages each in the month. They included outcomes-based education and school libraries, performance-based curriculum, student plagiarism in assignments and projects based on library resources, the role of district or regional school library coordinators, "underutilized school librarians" (the problem of school librarians being used as "babysitters" in the school, rather than being viewed as professionals who can "make a difference"), faculty reading groups, reading teachers and their relationship to the school library, and "gender" issues in information technology.

Given the United States dominance of LM_NET (despite the increasing membership from other countries), it is probably inevitable that discussion of professional issues on the listserv will largely reflect American concerns and viewpoints. The ongoing discussion of the issue of censorship, for instance, demonstrates this. Clearly, censorship is important to people in the United States, but in countries like Iceland, censorship of reading materials is generally not an issue ("Why would anyone want to interfere in someone else's reading?"), and professional librarians in Iceland who belong to international listservs for librarians often comment (in amazement) on the amount of bandwidth that is taken up with discussion of what to them is at best a peripheral topic. By the same token, while people in other countries recognize that discussion of a local document like *Information Power* is important for the American members of the listserv, they themselves would be more interested in discussing an international document or one of their own local documents.

It is not only on LM_NET that issues related to school libraries are discussed; there are several other Internet listservs, newsgroups, and newsletters where issues of concern to school librarians are raised, though Table 6.4 suggests that school librarians on LM_NET are not making as much use of them as they might. The USENET newsgroup `K12.library` carries discussions about topics of concern to school librarians, including library automation, selection of resources, and school library management. Within California, school library media teachers have a listserv called CALIB12 (on which discussion is focused on "issues and events which affect and interest those involved with California school libraries"), while in Minnesota, MEMO has a listserv called MEMO-net for its members, as well as a gopher. In Australia, there is a listserve called OZTL_NET (Australian Teacher Librarians Network) and a school library bulletin board on the NEXUS national online service for schools (which also carries LM_NET traffic). In Canada, both the Canadian School Library Association and the Association for Teacher Librarianship in Canada have listservs. Issues of interest to school librarians are also discussed on other librarianship listservs, including PUBLIB (where censorship, cooperation between school and public libraries, information skills, the promotion of reading, and other topics familiar to LM_NET members, have been addressed), LIBADMIN (for library administrators), and PUBYAC (which deals with topics related to children's and young adult services in public libraries), and on education listservs, including K12ADMIN (discussion of all aspects of school management and administration), EDTECH (for people interested in the use of technology in education at all levels), ELEMUG (for people in elementary schools), and INFED (for people interested in the use of computers in education, including topics such as artificial intelligence in education and the philosophical and sociological implications of the use of computers in schools). There are also forums for the discussion of particular issues that concern school librarians and other people. For example, the USENET newsgroup `alt.censorship` deals with reports of incidents of censorship, while listservs devoted to this topic include ALAOIF (the listserv of the American Library Association's Office of Intellectual Freedom) and Canada's ifreedom (also known as "Snoopy"). For school librarians who want to discuss children's literature in some depth, there is the KIDLIT-L listserv and Scholastic's BookBraG, and for fantasy fans, the USENET newsgroup `alt.fan.tolkien`, among others. And then, the work done, school librarians can relax with other like-minded people (maybe including some of their library clients) on the USENET newsgroups `rec.games.mud` or `rec.arts.books`.

REFERENCE AND INFORMATION SERVICES

More than half the school-level respondents to the questionnaire survey of LM_NET members indicated that they used LM_NET to find answers to reference questions, though noone listed this as the most important reason for using LM_NET. In addition, almost half the school-level respondents said that they used the Internet itself to find answers to reference questions, though only 2.99 percent of respondents listed this as their most important Internet application. The analysis of LM_NET traffic for the month of October 1993 shows that school librarians do indeed use LM_NET as a means for getting answers to their difficult reference questions, or to those questions that require the use of a reference work to which they do not have local access. In addition, there is evidence that school librarians who have access to the Internet use a range of sources and services to find answers to reference queries and to provide information services in their schools.

Table 6.13

LM_NET Messages About Reference Questions

(October 1993)

ORIGIN OF THE QUESTION	NUMBER OF MESSAGES
Teacher	16
Student	3
School Administrator	9
Parent	2
Other	13
Information Not Provided	7
TOTAL	50

Not all people who posted reference questions to LM_NET in October 1993 provided information about the person who had asked the question. However, those questions whose source was identified represented queries from all sectors of the school community—teachers, school administrators, the guidance counsellor, the janitor, students, parents. The "others" on behalf of whom questions were asked included unspecified colleagues at the school and district level, family members, and friends. It is interesting to note that relatively few messages relate to questions from students in the school (only three) in comparison with the number that relate to questions from teachers and school administration. This may mean that students were encouraged to find their own answers to questions, or that resources were more likely to be readily available to answer the type of questions that came from students. On the other hand, the emphasis on using LM_NET to get answers for teachers and school administrators could reflect the fact that many school librarians were actively seeking to convince their school decision-makers of the value of an Internet connection and were even using their own personal Internet connection from home in order to do this. Support for this conjecture can be found in one of the messages posted to LM_NET in October that began "I'm a high school librarian looking for ways to hook my faculty into using telecommunications available in the library", and then went on to pose a question on behalf of a special education teacher.

Many of the questions posted to LM_NET were factual questions: the bibliographic details for a research report written by a professor at the University of Southern California; the author and text of a poem called "Roots and Wings"; the words of the state song of Pennsylvania; information about a manufacturer of robotic arms. Others were more complex and required either lists of resources (the names and addresses of high schools with student-run courts) or some evaluation (a request on behalf of a language arts teacher who needed pointers to literary passages that provided good examples of character description, for reading to a class).

In Chapter One, the use of the Internet in reference services in libraries in general was discussed briefly, with examples drawn from a document created by Karen G. Schneider, "Twenty-two Internet Reference Success Stories", in which she collected and collated information from librarians about how they were using the Internet in reference work (Schneider, 1993). Early in 1994, Gail M. Szeliga attempted a similar project on LM_NET, targeting successful school library use of the Internet for reference. While there were fewer responses from LM_NET members, possibly indicating that reference use of the Internet in school libraries is not as well developed as in major public and academic libraries, nevertheless there were some interesting examples of reference use from school libraries. In a Missouri high school history teachers were provided with a list of Cabinet members "within seconds of their asking". The full text of Martin Luther King, Jr.'s "I Have a Dream" speech was downloaded for an American grade 7/8 class. A high school library in California uses the Economics Bulletin Board (via LC MARVEL) to get current economic data, particularly economic indicators over and above those that appear in the newspapers. A Syracuse, New York, school library used the *World Fact Book* via the University of Texas gopher to find information about Hong Kong. Senior English classes at a Texas high school used the *Oxford English Dictionary* online regularly; it is not available in print form in the school library or any local public library, and the school library could not afford to buy it. Other reference questions were answered through the full text of speeches (both current and historic) retrieved online, through the PDQ system (for information on alternative cancer treatments), and through online consultation with knowledgeable individuals (on USENET newsgroups and listservs). One school librarian commented, after describing her "reference success story", that "within five months of first using the 'net it became my lifeline", while another noted that, even in the reference work context, "the immediacy of communication with persons all over the globe is still a source of wonder", supporting the idea that communication is particularly important for this group of people.

LOCATING INFORMATION ABOUT RESOURCES

More than half of the questionnaire respondents who were working in schools indicated that they used LM_NET to "get information about resources ... for the school library", and 5.97 percent of these respondents indicated that this was their most important reason for using LM_NET. In addition, just over three-quarters of the school-level respondents indicated that they also used the wider Internet for this purpose. Their responses to the questionnaire are confirmed by evidence from the analysis of LM_NET messages: in October 1993, some 146 of the 606 messages, or 24.09 percent, were requests for information about resources, responses to such requests, general postings about resources that people had found helpful in their school library, and information about new resources (including informal advertisements).

As Table 6.14 indicates, the major resource formats that could be found in a school library were mirrored in the messages posted to LM_NET in October 1993. Since LM_NET members are users of information technology, it is not surprising to find information and requests for information about computer software (including educational games), CD-ROMs (full text databases, encyclopedias, periodical indexes, among others), and laser discs. However, there were also a considerable number of messages related to print resources, including professional periodicals, foreign language magazines for students, biographical reference sources, books for young people about

Table 6.14
LM_NET Messages About Resources
(October 1993)

TYPE OF RESOURCE	NUMBER OF MESSAGES
Books	25 HIT-> (9)
Reference Sources	6
Periodicals	10
Audiovisual Materials	1
Computer Software	15
CD-ROMs	24
Laser discs	4
Internet Resources	56
Other Resources	3
General Requests for Resources	2
TOTAL	146 (154)

the Holocaust, reading materials for fifth- and sixth-grade children who read at the first- to third-grade levels (the subject of a HIT-> message with nine responses), books for children about dwarfism, books in French or Spanish for young people, among others. In addition, there were requests for information about good resources (no specified format) about AIDS and about sexual harrassment awareness.

Since all the survey respondents were using the Internet, it is also not surprising that more than 50 of the messages related specifically to Internet resources. There were requests (and replies) for information about other listservs, including requests for information about listservs for middle school teachers (MIDDLE-L), for people involved in special education (one response listed more than 20 relevant listservs, including BEHAVIOR, BLIND-L, DEAF-L, and MOBILITY), for students of library and information science (LIS-L), and for people interested in the history of the American Civil War. One LM_NET member wanted a pointer to lists of listservs, while another commented that "since joining LM_NET I have become interested in (fascinated with) listservs—is there a listserv about listservs?" There were also requests for information about gophers and electronic bulletin boards on the Internet, including the Library of Congress gopher LC MARVEL, the BOOKS.COM electronic bookstore on the Internet, CARL's UnCover magazine index and document supply service, and Scholastic's online news service for schools. All these services have many potential applications in school libraries. LC MARVEL provides access to the Library of Congress catalogs, to United States and international government information, and to information about the Internet itself. BOOKS.COM provides a bibliographic verification service for current book details as well as an online ordering service. CARL's UnCover allows librarians to search an online index of more than 50,000 periodicals and to order copies of articles online for delivery by fax or air mail. The Scholastic Company began building its Internet presence in 1993/94, and now offers a range of electronic publications aimed at schools, online ordering services, and information services, via America Online and the Internet. The Scholastic-sponsored BooKBraG electronic newsletter about children's books, still in its first year as this book was being prepared, is impressively useful.

SCHOOL LIBRARY ADMINISTRATION

Some 82 percent of the 67 school-based survey respondents indicated that one of their reasons for using LM_NET was "to find solutions to problems related to the running of a school library/media center", and in the case of eight of those respondents, this was the reason cited as being the most important. In addition, for a small number of people, a reason for membership of LM_NET was "to find information about library automation"; for a few of those, an urgent need for information on this topic was a compelling reason for membership. It is therefore not surprising to find that 128 out of a total of 606 messages posted to LM_NET in October 1993 were related to school library administration and management (including the automation of school library functions). Again, though, given that all people who belong to LM_NET are computer and telecommunications users, it is not surprising to find that in the group of messages related to school library administration and management, the emphasis was on computers in library administration, or the management of computers and automation.

In the messages related to general library administration, major topics were scheduling of the school library (and the school), planning a new school library facility, budgeting, developing a policy and procedures manual, and evaluation of school library media programs. Eleven messages were related to the development of technology plans at the school and district level (how this should be done, what should be in them, who should be on the planning team, how should the team work). Other topics discussed included management of computer networks, software for networked CD-ROMs, printers, software for word processing and page-making, charge cards for laser printers connected to CD-ROM stations, and software copyright. The networking of CD-ROM stations was the subject of a TARGET-> during the month, and the corresponding HIT-> message incorporated input from 16 people.

Some 44 of the messages to LM_NET in October related to school library automation. There were discussions of the different types of library automation software available (and specifically of UNIX-based systems), and questions were asked about some of the different systems themselves. Kid's Catalog, a graphical user interface designed for children and young people in school and public libraries, available with the Dynix library automation system, attracted some favorable comment, not just for itself, but as a foretaste of future offerings. There were also questions (and answers) about computer catalog access for the visually handicapped (software that provides magnified images of the characters on the screen), printed user guides to help young people to search an online public access catalog (OPAC), a slow automated check-out problem in an elementary school, purchasing catalog records on CD-ROM, and the staffing implications of school library automation. Ongoing monitoring of LM_NET has shown that issues related to school library automation continue to be discussed in a significant number of messages each month, so that, after two years, the LM_NET archives are now a valuable source of information on this topic.

There are also many other sources of information about school library automation available on the Internet. The Library of Congress gopher LC MARVEL has a section containing documents that deal with aspects of library automation, including a substantial annotated list of library automated systems software. In the United Kingdom, the BUBL Bulletin Board for Libraries, based at the University of Bath but administered by Strathclyde and Glasgow University Libraries, has documents and information on this topic, with leads to relevant listservs, electronic journals, bibliographies, and software. For those who are automating their libraries, or have automated, there are listservs where users of particular automated system software can get together to discuss problems, ideas, plans for the future; these listservs include DYNIX-L, MANDARIN, LIBSPLUS, and MULTILIS. Other listservs where issues related to the use of computers in libraries are discussed include CDROM-L (use of CD-ROMs), CDROMLAN (using CD-ROMs on local area networks), and PRO-CITE (the Personal Bibliographic Software discussion list).

CURRICULUM APPLICATIONS

The responses to the questionnaire survey of LM_NET members give some idea of the use of the Internet for curriculum-related purposes in schools. Respondents working in schools where Internet resources and services were being used for curriculum applications were asked to indicate the school subject areas that were the main users. The responses are summarized in Table 6.15. Science was the subject area where most use was being made of Internet resources, with 17 respondents citing science as one of the main users. When biology and physics are combined with science, then science was one of the main areas of use in 20 schools, that is, in more than half of the schools where the Internet was being used for curriculum applications. The area of social studies and social science was another curriculum area where use was being made of the Internet, with 16 respondents indicating that social science or social studies was one of the main uses in their school. The third area in which the Internet was being used was the area of language arts/language education and English.

Many different projects and curriculum units were described by respondents. In science, the Internet was being used for access to SciNet and to science databases on DIALOG, to collect weather information from weather servers, and for current earthquake information. Economics students were using an economics bulletin board via the Library of Congress LC MARVEL gopher, and agriculture students used an electronic bulletin board for information about commodities futures for a contest. In language classes, students were using electronic mail to correspond with students in Estonia, in Germany, and with Spanish-speaking students. Two respondents mentioned the use of the Internet in interdisciplinary units that had a computer literacy component. In one school, integrated units on the 1940s (history, social studies, literature, science, mathematics) and the homeless (social science, research, social action, community service curriculum) had incorporated Internet resources. In the same school, classes had undertaken science fair projects in cooperation with other schools via the Internet.

Table 6.15
Curriculum Applications of the Internet
(34 Schools)

CURRICULUM AREA	NUMBER OF SCHOOLS
Science	17
Social Studies/Social Science	16
Foreign Languages	6
Language Arts	5
English	4
Economics	3
Business	2
Biology	2
History	2
Geography	2
Mathematics	2
Debate	2
Agriculture	1
Physics	1
Computer Literacy	1
Advanced Computer Applications	1

One of the survey respondents made a useful distinction between the direct use of the Internet by students in class and the use in class of Internet resources supplied in printout form by the school librarian who had downloaded them (usually on a computer at home) for the teacher. Some of the use recorded in Table 6.15 in fact represents the latter type. In these instances, the students get the benefit of access to a wider range of resources for their class work and research than would have been possible otherwise, but they do not themselves learn to locate and evaluate Internet resources, nor do they gain any real appreciation of the Internet itself (unless the two approaches are both used in the school for different classes and at different times).

The analysis of LM_NET traffic for the month of October 1993 showed only 24 messages that were directly related to curriculum applications or student projects – though one of these was a HIT-> message which collated responses from ten people about "K-12 access to the Internet". However, it could also be said that many of the messages related to reference questions or information provision also had direct curriculum applications in that they arose out of classroom work. Basically, the curriculum-related messages formed three groups: requests for penpals (or keypals), requests for participants in Internet projects, and discussion of the practicalities of such use of the Internet in the K-12 school environment, including project management, supervision of students, and potential problems.

The requests for penpals were mostly for exchanges between classes, either within the United States or international exchanges, though one of the requests was for a principal-to-principal exchange. For class groups, the exchanges were to be part of American history, English, or Spanish classes. There were two requests for schools to take part in collaborative projects. One request was for schools interested in doing a hawk migration census and sharing data. The other was for classes to collaborate on an international exchange of autobiographies as a basis for cultural exchange. Some of the people who posted these messages indicated that "there is probably a better list on which to post this request, however, I cannot find out which list", and "feel free to let me know … how to post to a more appropriate list". Most of these requests would probably be better posted on one of the lists created especially to facilitate email exchanges. And so, while school librarians might use LM_NET for this purpose when they don't know a better list, once they are more familiar with the range of Internet resources, and the finding tools, they may begin to use more appropriate lists for curriculum-related activities and student projects.

Among the listservs and groups that exist primarily for

the purpose of facilitating electronic mail contact is Intercultural E-Mail Classroom Connections (IECC), a listserv that functions as a "meeting place" for "teachers seeking partner classes for international and cross-cultural electronic mail exchanges". It does not duplicate the functions of listservs like PENPAL-L, which is for anyone interested in establishing one-to-one electronic links. Rather, it helps people who are looking for a partnership between entire classes, in different countries, usually for curriculum-related activities. A related listserv, IECC Project Announcements, is a forum for announcing, describing, or requesting help for, international or intercultural projects based in electronic mail. Another avenue for organizing school or class participation in electronic mail projects is provided by organizations that have been set up chiefly for that purpose, such as Computer Pals Across the World (CPAW), or KIDSPHERE, or KIDLINK. Information about Computer Pals is provided in the next section of this chapter, as is information about KIDLINK. In addition, from time to time, special cooperative projects that schools can join are announced on the Internet via appropriate USENET newsgroups and educational listservs. Such projects have included an electronic mail exchange associated with the 1994 Arctic Drift Stream Expedition, a project related to a multinational expedition to Antarctica, and several environmental monitoring projects.

In a wider context, there are now several gophers on the Internet that are designed partly or wholly to provide teachers with easy access to the educational resources on the Internet, including policy documents, lists and directories of resources, databases of educational information, collections of lesson plans, information about professional associations, the contents lists or full text of electronic journals and newsletters, and bibliographies. The NYSERNet gopher in New York has a substantial collection of K-12 education resources, as well as documents related to the Internet itself and its use in education. It provides an easy link to the AskERIC gopher at Syracuse University, New York, which carries an enormous amount of educational information, including the full text of ERIC digests, hundreds of lesson plans and curriculum guides, directories, information about K-12 networking, a list of listservs related to education, lists of books and journals, and the archives of professional listservs (including LM_NET). The CICNet K-12 gopher in Ann Arbor, Michigan, designed specifically for school teachers, has a large collection of resources for schools (including resources written by teachers), plus links to many Internet project files (including those of the Mount Vaughan Antarctic Expedition, the Bosnian/Croatian Exchange Project, the Wolf Study Project, and the Russian Far East Exchange). There is a substantial collection of lesson plans, including many that involve the use of Internet resources. Another gopher with collections of lesson plans, plus other curriculum documents and documents related to the educational use of the Internet, is the gopher of the Ontario Institute for Studies in Education (OISE) in Canada. One particularly useful document is "Reasons to Make Telecomputing Part of the Curriculum" (which incorporates leads to appropriate materials); another is "The World at Your Fingertips" by Yvonne Marie Andres, both from the FrEdMail Foundation. Other useful education gophers, or gophers with a large section of educational information include the Canada SchoolNet gopher, the TENET (Texas Education Network) gopher, the California Department of Education gopher, CoSN (the gopher of the Consortium for School Networking in Washington, DC), the Education Gopher at Florida Tech, Íslenska menntaneti› (ISMENNT, the gopher of the Icelandic Education Network), the KIDLINK gopher, the New York State Education Department (NYSED) gopher, and Big Sky Telegraph in Montana. A similar range of information services for educators exists on the World Wide Web.

The TARGET->/HIT-> discussion on LM_NET about "K-12 access to the Internet", referred to above, raised some basic concerns about access to equipment and about lack of Internet knowledge and skills in schools. It also indicated some issues that would need to be addressed, including potential problems with challenges from the community over some of the material that students might access, the amount of time it would take to monitor student access throughout a school, and the perceived lack of quality of much of the information on the Internet. However, there was also a perception that people were anticipating problems and sometimes making quite restrictive plans on the assumption that there would be problems. The idea that there would be problems also led, in some cases, to the school library abandoning the idea of Internet access for students, while it was possibly available to students elsewhere. But, as Pamela J. Tinker noted, "some of us, on the other hand, feel that this is another information resource and the library media center needs to be the hub of the access, even if it is also available elsewhere in the school" (Tinker, 1993). The issues associated with student use of the Internet in schools are discussed further in Chapter Eight.

STUDENT PROJECTS BASED ON THE INTERNET

Several different Internet-based projects for schoolchildren and their teachers were mentioned in the responses to the survey of LM_NET members, and more detailed information about most of these can be found on the various education gophers. In addition, projects carried out via the Internet have been described in papers for conferences such as the annual NYSERNet conferences, the annual conferences of Computer Pals Across the World, the Tel*Ed 93 conference, and the annual "Databases in Schools"/"Multimedia in Schools" conferences.

To give an indication of what has been done and what is possible, some of these projects are described below. The examples have been chosen to reflect involvement of schools in different countries and groups at different age levels, as well as to illustrate the wide range of curriculum applications. All can or do involve the school library in some way.

- **Computer Pals Across the World (CPAW)** is an international electronic mail writing project that commenced more than ten years ago as the Australaskan Writing Project, and today involves people in more than 20 countries, including the United States, Australia, the United Kingdom, Canada, New Zealand, Russia, Finland, Japan, Germany, Denmark, and Indonesia. It provides school students of all ages, and their teachers, with opportunities for cultural exchange through reading, writing, exchange of information, and participation in cooperative projects. Projects under way in early 1994 included Environmental Watch, Acid Rain, Drinking Water, a mathematics project, and creative writing projects. Founded by Malcolm Beazley, an Australian, and operated by volunteers in several countries, Computer Pals Across the World is co-ordinated by an international board. Participants receive a newsletter by electronic mail, and support materials are available. The organization also has a World Wide Web server. (For further information, contact Computer Pals Across the World, PO Box 280, Manly, NSW 2095, Australia.)
- **Arctic Drift Stream Expedition 1994**. The Arctic Drift Stream Expedition (15 February to 1 June 1994) set out from England to cross the Arctic Ocean from Siberia via the North Pole to Canada, a journey of 1,400 miles, that had never before been undertaken. Through the Global Youth Communications Network (GYCN) Arctic 94 Conference/Mail exploder, a conference on GreenNet, and in conjunction with the British newspaper, the *Guardian*, schools all over the world could follow the expedition, send messages to the team, and take part in associated environmental projects.
- **NEWSDAY** is an international cross-curriculum project

through which students in each participating school produce a local newspaper based on the news despatches submitted on the NEWSDAY news wire by student correspondents. Students take on the roles of news gatherers, reporters, editors, layout and graphics artists, and publishers. A variety of methods can be used to produce the newspapers, from simple word processing packages to full desktop publishing packages. All school age levels can participate. All participating schools receive a newspaper produced by each of the other schools involved in the project. There are several NEWSDAYs each year, announced well in advance, and often with a special theme. Schools wishing to participate need to register and upload between five and ten news stories on the day. (For further information, contact the Global SchoolNet Foundation, PO Box 243, Bonita, CA 91908, USA.)

- **NASA's FOSTER On-line Project** is a project in the "Sharing NASA With Our Classrooms" series. It focuses on airborne astronomy missions in which researchers fly on NASA's Kuiper Airborne Observatory with an infrared telescope, at 41,000 feet above the earth; the altitude reduces problems associated with atmospheric absorption. The project was based in Hawaii and California in mid-1994, and the astronomers shared information with schools via the Internet, and responded to email questions from schoolchildren and their teachers. There is an online archive of background material about the observatory, the mission, the people involved in the work, lesson plans, images, and email messages available via ftp or gopher. In addition, a listserv has been created to facilitate discussion among teachers who are using the FOSTER Project resources in their classrooms, and NASA has produced a supporting videotape about the Kuiper Airborne Observatory.
- **The Wolf Studies Project** of the International Wolf

Center in Ely, Minnesota, "allows students and teachers around the world to hear, see, and track radio-collared wolves in the Superior National Forest via the Internet". School students and their teachers are able to read reports, see pictures and video images, and follow the wolves' movements and activity, as the information is posted to the Wolf Studies Project Gopher server.

- **The Middle School Math Project**, "Puzzle Now!", is an interdisciplinary project involving grades 6–8 mathematics and language arts students and their teachers, operated via the VA.PEN network in Pennsylvania. The aims are to motivate students to work on mathematics problem solving activities; to encourage a clear, concise, and logical approach to problem solving; to provide students with opportunities to develop their writing skills; and to give students experience with the computer and telecommunications as tools for problem solving. The puzzles presented to students are not just entertaining; working on them helps the young people to develop an understanding of mathematical concepts. In addition, students learn to work together and cooperate to develop a solution to each puzzle, (Network Working Group, 1994)
- **KIDLINK** is an international email network for young people aged 10 to 15. It is based on a series of projects, all of which are intended to get young people involved "in a global dialogue" so that "by hearing a range of opinions and developing familiarity with different ideas, we hope to overcome some communications barriers and increase co-operation, and help people to take a global and more long-term perspective on current issues". The KIDLINK Project was founded in 1990 by Odd de Presno of Norway, with Canadian and United States support. To date, more than 50,000 people in more than 50 countries (including Australia, Peru, Brazil, New Zealand, Denmark, Iceland, Japan, the United Kingdom, and the United States) have taken

Greetings From Buckman

Welcome to the Buckman School World Wide Web Server. This is an experimental site which will highlight the activities and events taking place at our school. It is very much under construction.

To check the current weather conditions in Portland, Oregon, please press here.

For the most current satellite photo of the Pacific Northwest, please press here.

For information on recent earthquake activity in the Pacific Northwest, please press here.

Areas to Explore

Mixed Age Internet Explorer Class (Area under construction)

To download a copy of our **Kindergarten Spanish Counting Book** (Macintosh version only) press here .

To read an **HTML** (Mosaic) version of the **Buckman Kindergarten Spanish Counting Book** please press here .

Camp Hancock Journal
A 4th grade student's reflections on her trip to Camp Hancock .

Special thanks to the folks at Murdock Educational File Server (daVinci.Vancouver.wsu.edu) for allowing us to post here.

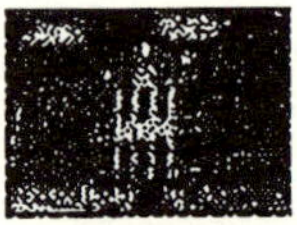

- Buckman School
- 320 SE 16th Avenue
- Portland, Oregon 97214
- 503-280-6230

6.1 The World Wide Web home page of Buckman School, Portland, Oregon, USA.

part. Projects have included "travelling the world", a "virtual vacation", environmental projects, and projects related to the cost of living, native literature, and the South Pole. KIDCAFE provides an environment where children can "chat" online with others around the world. The KIDLINK gopher provides information on how to take part in KIDLINK projects, using KIDLINK in the curriculum (with sample lesson plans), research and reports related to KIDLINK, and some sample materials created through KIDLINK projects.

SCHOOLS AS INFORMATION PROVIDERS

Through the Internet, school students and teachers have access to information from around the world and to resources that can enrich their studies. By searching online, students can learn information skills, and by taking part in Internet-based projects, they can increase their awareness of the world. However, some schools have taken all this a step further: not only are students and teachers in the school consumers of information from the Internet, but they are also information providers, introducing an entirely new dimension into the use of the Internet in educational settings. As the World Wide Web home page of Hillside Elementary School puts it, "our goal is to incorporate use of the resources on the Internet into the curriculum of elementary school students and to have students participate in creating resources that are on the Internet". The announcement of this Web server put it in another way: "our objective is to have students not just look at the Internet and take information from it, but to participate in building and shaping their own small part of the Information Superhighway" (Collins, 1994a).

In 1993, at least two schools established gophers on the Internet. The Bloomfield Hills School District Model High School gopher in Michigan has information about the

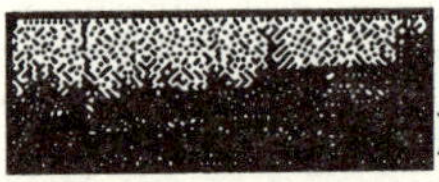

Hillside Elementary School

The pages of information on this World Wide Web server are being created by a classroom of sixth grade students at Hillside Elementary School in Cottage Grove, Minnesota. This is a joint project of Hillside Elementary School and the University of Minnesota College of Education. Our goal is to incorporate use of the resources on the Internet into the curriculum of elementary school students and to have students *participate in creating resources* that are on the Internet.

School is out for the Summer

We will be organizing some teacher projects this summer, but the kids will not be involved again until next September.

We consider this a pilot project which was extremely successful. We will be documenting and sharing our work over the summer and putting the information up on our server. We hope to be able to help other schools duplicate our efforts and build upon them in their own ways.

Comments and suggestions are welcome and may be sent to
`events@hillside.coled.umn.edu`

- Hillside Web Happenings

- Mrs. Collins Sixth Grade
  - Home Pages
  - Internet Research Project
- Mrs. Reid Third Grade
  - Home Pages
- Parent Teacher Association

Some other schools.

6.2 The World Wide Web home page of Hillside Elementary School, Cottage Grove, Minnesota, USA.

school; "What's Happening at MHS"; reference works; electronic art; links to libraries, ftp sites, other gophers, and other resources; and USENET news and weather. In New York City, the Ralph Bunche School gopher is part of this grade 3–6 school's teaching and technology program. Although both gophers are designed to give the members of their school community access to Internet information, neither highlights their own school library.

However, there was strong school library involvement in two more recent school gophers. The gopher, or "electronic information service", of Bemidji Middle School in Bemidji, Minnesota, was a joint project of the school and Bemidji State University's Department of Professional Education, and the project coordinator in the school was the library media specialist, Edee Miller. The gopher has information about the school, sections for each of the school's three grades, information about northern Minnesota, CNN Newsroom project information, and links to other information sources on the Internet. At Lakeside School in Seattle, Washington, the gopher is designed to facilitate "the sharing of information within the Lakeside community, ... collaborations with other schools and organizations, ... the gathering of information from other sites on the Internet" (from the Welcome section of the gopher). There is a library services section on the gopher with its own welcome message, reading lists for summer reading and reading lists on particular topics, information about the school library's print and nonprint resources, information about the school library's automated catalog, and a link to the online catalog of Seattle Public Library.

At the end of 1992, World Wide Web software became generally available, and in 1993 this method of providing information on the Internet became increasingly popular. During the early months of 1994, several schools announced World Wide Web servers, the first apparently being at Grand River Elementary School in Minnesota, USA. More than half of these schools were elementary schools. It is easy to see the appeal that the Web might have for young students, with its capability to handle graphics and color pictures. The server of Grand River Elementary School, for example, incorporated a home page for each of the fifth-grade students taking part in the project. These student pages each had an autobiography and some of the student's own art work (in full color). The students had electronic mail accounts and could receive messages from people who had "visited" their home page. And there is evidence that people *did* visit. The Hillside server had record-keeping facilities, and information about daily connections was posted on the server. During the week of 16–23 May 1994, for instance, the Hillside server was accessed from outside by more than 1,000 people on five of the seven days, and connections were made to it from 19 different countries (including Turkey, Taiwan, Australia, Spain, Singapore) and from 39 states of the United States.

Apart from information about the students themselves and their teachers, and about the school, these Web servers often have samples of student projects, particularly projects based on the Internet. A report of student activity at Hillside Elementary School gives an idea of the level and complexity of some of the research and information coordination work of sixth-grade students who worked on Internet research papers to be mounted on the World Wide Web server. The students wrote their papers on such topics as Antarctica, basketball, dinosaurs, dogsledding, Mars, the Shoemaker-Levy Comet, the Soviet Union, virtual reality, and weather. All of the research was done via the Internet. The papers were developed in the hypertext script that forms the basis of pages on the World Wide Web. They incorporated hypertext links to original sources of information that were used for each research paper. Some of these were quite sophisticated. For instance, the Shoemaker-Levy page included a dynamic link that would automatically search the whole Internet World Wide Web for current Shoemaker information. The Mars page included direct links to incoming photographs so that the newest pictures were downloaded directly to the page when it was displayed on the screen of a person accessing the school's server (Collins, 1994b).

In addition to information about the school and the work of the students, most of the school servers also have local information and links to other Internet resources and sites that will be useful for members of the school community. The Buckman School home page had links to sections provided by a Mixed Age Internet Explorer Class, a version of the Buckman Kindergarten Spanish Counting Book, a fourth-grade student's Camp Hancock Journal, plus current weather for Portland and information about earthquake activity in the Pacific Northwest. The Claremont High School server has "links to academic resources for our high school students, ... and access to our anonymous ftp site" (Muir, 1994) plus access to Internet indexes, catalogs, and resource lists. The home page of Platte Canyon High School in Bailey, Colorado, has links to Platte Canyon School District Lessons, to Colorado State University, and to the NCSA Mosaic Internet home page (and from there to the whole of the Web), while the Mona Vista High School server in Cupertino, California, has links to Educational Online Sources, and thus to freenets, gophers, and other information servers.

The following schools were among those with World Wide Web pages in mid-1994 (the name of the school is followed by the URL of the school's home page):

- Arbor Heights Elementary School, Seattle, Washington, USA.
  URL: `http://www.halcyon.com/arborhts/arborhts.html`
- Buckman School, Portland, Oregon, USA.
  URL: `http://buckman.pps.k12.or.us/buckman.html`
- Grand River Elementary School, Grand River, Minnesota, USA.
  URL: `http://web.cal.msu.edu/GR/grintro.html`

- Hillside Elementary School, Cottage Grove, Minnesota, USA.
  URL: `http://hillside.coled.umn.edu/`
- Murray Elementary School, Ivy, Virginia, USA.
  URL: `http://ourry.edschool.virginia.edu/murray/`
- Ralph Bunche Elementary School, Harlem, New York, USA.
  URL: `http://Mac94.ralphbunche.rbs.edu/`
- Riverside Elementary School, Princeton, New Jersey, USA.
  URL: `http://192.152.5.115`
- Claremont High School, Claremont, California, USA.
  URL: `http://www.cusd.claremont.edu`
- John H. Springman Junior High School, Glenview, Illinois, USA.
  URL: `http://ncook.k12.il.us/sp/sp_home_page.html`
- Los Alamos High School, Los Alamos, New Mexico, USA.
  URL: `http://lahs.losalamos.k12.nm.edu/`
- Mona Vista High School, Cupertino, California, USA.
  URL: `http://www.mvhs.edu/`
- The Peddie School, Hightstown, New Jersey, USA (Web server created by student Daniel Berlin).
  URL: `http://www.peddie.k12.nj.us`
- Platte Canyon High School, Bailey, Colorado, USA.
  URL: `http://k12.colostate.edu/k12resources/ais/platte.html`
- Smoky Hill High School, Aurora, Colorado, USA.
  URL: `http://smokywww.ccsd.k12.co.us/Department/Department11.html`

FUTURE APPLICATIONS

How do school librarians see the future? In the questionnaire survey of LM_NET members, respondents were not only asked what they were using the Internet for, but also what they would *like* to be able to use the Internet for.

This latter question was interpreted by different people in different ways, though the responses tended to fall into five categories: those concerned with the technical aspects (the Internet tools); those who wanted to extend their use across more school subjects; those who wanted access to more resources and services; those who were interested in more activities based on the Internet; and those who were concerned with issues of organization of information on the Internet and access to it.

The respondents who answered in terms of the technical possibilities highlighted the Internet tools that they were not as yet using but would like to be using. The tools most often mentioned were ftp ("to download files"), gopher, IRC, and access to full-text services. None of these is new, of course, and many other respondents had access to, and could use, all of the tools mentioned. Rather, the list reflects the different levels of skills of members and the different levels of access to Internet tools and services at the time of the survey.

The people who were concerned about the use of the Internet in teaching in the future wanted to see its use extended across more subjects in their school, for instance, science, language arts, social studies (all subjects in which Internet resources were being used in some other schools). Access to full-text resources and to online book reviews were seen as being particularly useful for classroom work. People who wanted more or better access to resources on the Internet mentioned access to DIALOG, OCLC, and CARL, and also to the National Geographic Kids Network and FrEdMail. In terms of activities, respondents mentioned electronic mail communication with students overseas, student participation in discussions with other schoolchildren via the Internet, and class participation in research projects via the Internet. Independent research and information skills development were also mentioned in this context. Again, there is nothing here that is essentially new—while these resources and activities were on the "wish list" for some schools, they were already part of the educational program in others.

The final group, those who were concerned about the organization of information on the Internet and access to the net, wanted "more organization" of Internet resources, and they wanted tools that were "easier to use". They also wanted resources organized with the specific needs of schools in mind, interfaces that had been created to assist the occasional and nonexpert user, and finding aids that reflected the needs of schools. While some of the suggestions may be a little unrealistic, given the nature of the Internet, they do provide evidence of the frustration that many teachers and school library personnel feel when attempting to come to terms with this new medium of communication and information access. Other comments showed some appreciation of the complexity of the Internet and its distributed nature. The suggestions made included graphical user interfaces, online tutorials, and a kind of "intelligent personal agent"—a software tool that could be programmed and used to scout for relevant resources.

REFERENCES

ACTEIN, ACT Education Information Network (1994), Pilot Service to Selected Schools, A Collaborative Approach to Networked Information Services and Education Resources Involving the ACT Universities and the ACT Schools, Document available on the ACTEIN gopher on the Internet, April.

American Library Association (1988), *Information Power: Guidelines for School Library Media Programs*, American Library Association, Chicago.

Aversa, Elizabeth Smith and Mancall, Jacqueline C. (1989), *Management of Online Search Services in Schools*, ABC-CLIO, Santa Barbara, California.

Berger, Pam (1991), "Databases for student research", *Information Searcher* 4, no. 1, pp.14–17.

Campbell, Shirley (1992), "Online services for school libraries update", *Access* 6, no. 2, May, pp.36–37.

Cargo, Margaret, Walker, Eugenia, and Reedy, Jackie (1991), "Online at Troy High School", *Information Searcher* 3, no. 2, pp.3–14.

Clyde, Laurel A. and Kirk, Joyce (1987), "Online information in schools", in *Proceedings of the Third National Conference on School Library Automation, Held at the Eden Park Conference Centre, Adelaide, 1986*, The Conference Committee, Adelaide, pp.53–77.

Clyde, Laurel A. and Kirk, Joyce (1989), "The use of electronic information systems in Australian schools: a preliminary survey", *School Library Media Quarterly* 17, no. 4, Summer, pp.193–199.

Collins, Stephen E. (1994a), First Elementary School Web, Message posted to the Net-Happenings listserv on the Internet, 16 March.

Collins, Stephen E. (1994b), Hillside Elementary WWW Events, Message posted to the LM_NET listserv on the Internet, 27 April.

D'Amicantonio, John (1991), "Using online services in the junior high school", *The Computing Teacher* 19, no. 2, October, pp.53–54.

Epler, Doris (1989), *Online Searching Goes to School*, Oryx, Phoenix, Arizona.

Estabrook, Noel (1993), Telecommunications and Education, Keeping Up With the 20th Century, A Compendium of Electronic Resources for Education, Michigan State University, July.

"FirstSearch discounted for school libraries" (1994), *OCLC Newsletter*, January/February, p.27.

Funk, Evie (1994), HIT-> DIALOG Information Services, Message posted to the LM_NET listserv on the Internet, 7 August.

Guthrie, Judy and Crane, Beverley (1992), "Online adds realism to science projects", *The Computing Teacher* 19, no. 5, February, pp.32–33.

Hanson, William R. (1992), International Intellectual Electronic Resources and the Calgary Board of Education, A Terminal Report of Research and Investigation Conducted Between September 1, 1991 and March 30.

Hunter, Beverley and Lodish, Erica K. (1989), *Online Searching in the Curriculum: A Teaching Guide for Library Media Specialists*, ABC-CLIO Santa Barbara, California.

Internet Access Now Available for All Minnesota Teachers (1994), Message posted to the Net-Happenings listserv on the Internet, 27 July.

Irving, Ann (1990), *Wider Horizons: Online Information Services in Schools*, The British Library, London.

Kessler, Jack (1993), Journals, Message posted to the PACS-L listserv on the Internet, 4 March, and reproduced in Rich, Paul (ed.), White House Communication Policy, A Workbook of Internet Documents, Hoover Institution, Stanford, pp.1–2.

Lathrop, Ann (1989), *Online and CD-ROM Databases in School Libraries*,

Libraries Unlimited, Littleton, Colorado.

Mancall, Jacqueline C., Lodish, Erica K., and Springer, Judith (1992), "Searching across the curriculum", *Phi Delta Kappan* 73, no. 7, March, pp.526–528.

Markowitz, Nancy Lourie and Crane, Beverly (1991), "Online goes to elementary school", *Information Searcher* 3, no. 3, pp.1–4.

McClanahan, Gloria (1994a), Internet Use, Electronic mail message, 14 June.

McClanahan, Gloria (1994b), TARGET-> Internet Use, Message posted to the LM_NET listserv on the Internet, 14 June.

Muir, Robs John (1994), Announcing...A New Web Server for Pre-Collegiate Education, Message posted to the Net-Happenings listserv on the Internet, 10 April.

Nelson, Lea (1992), "Online services for school libraries: an interview with Shirley Campbell at Radford College", *Access* 5, no. 4, November, pp.22–24.

Network Working Group (1994), FYI on Questions and Answers, Answers to Commonly Asked "Primary and Secondary School Internet User" Questions, Document available on the World Wide Web, February.

NYSERNet (1993), NYSERNet Conference 93, Access to the World's Information Resources, Conference announcement posted to the NYSERNet gopher on the Internet, September.

Online Information Services for Schools: Implications for School Libraries (1987), Australian Library and Information Association, School Libraries Section (WA Group), Perth, Western Australia.

Pastecki, Ronnie (1994), Student Use of Internet, Message posted to the LM_NET listserv on the Internet, 5 August.

Rice, Craig D. (1993), IECC—International E-Mail Classroom Connections, Message posted to the LM_NET listserv on the Internet, 6 October.

Sapienza, Lee (1992), "Sphinxes, diamonds and werewolves", *Information Searcher* 4, no. 2, pp.14–16.

Schipman, Mavis (1993), "Teens online at Douglas Middle School", *Information Searcher* 5, no. 3, pp.3–4.

Schneider, Karen G. (1993), Twenty-two Internet Reference Success Stories, Document posted to the PUBLIB listserv on the Internet, 24 September.

Sears, Bill (1993), Scholastic Network, Message posted to the LM_NET listserv on the Internet, 3 October.

See, John (1994), Internet Top Five, Document available from the MSTE gopher in the path `/Other Gopher Servers/ USA/ Minnesota/ Minnesota Society for Technology in Education (MSTE)/ Internet Resources K-12/ The "List"`.

Szeliga, Gail M. (1994), Internet Reference Success Stories, HIT-> Message posted to the LM_NET listserv on the Internet, 15 May.

Tenopir, Carol (1994), "Collaboration through networking: the online experience in school libraries in the United States", Paper presented at the SLOC Conference 1994, "Collaboration Creates Vision", Perth, Western Australia, June.

Tinker, Pamela J. (1993), Internet Access for Students, Message posted to the LM_NET listserv on the Internet, 30 October.

Warner, Virginia et al. (1993), "Environment Watch 1992–1993, a teleteaching project of Computer Pals Across the World", Paper presented at the Tenth Anniversary Conference of Computer Pals Across the World '93, Trondheim, Norway, August.

Wee, Jan (1993), Uses of the Internet (Responses From LM_NETters), HIT-> Message posted to the LM_NET listserv on the Internet, 8 October.

CHAPTER SEVEN

BARRIERS

INTRODUCTION

In Chapter Five, the discussion centered on the characteristics of a group of Internet-using educators (members of LM_NET), and their reasons for becoming Internet users. Chapter Six looked at the purposes for which the Internet was being used in school libraries and by school librarians, and at the possibilities that existed for using the Internet in school libraries. While the LM_NET members who provided information for the survey were often very enthusiastic about using the Internet, and generally committed to the idea that it has considerable value in education, it is clear that even these pioneers are not using it as much or in as many ways as they would like. Even a cursory reading of messages on the LM_NET listserv brings an awareness that there are many barriers to the use of the Internet in schools and school libraries, and where the Internet is being used, many barriers to its most effective use. These barriers will be discussed in this chapter. Finding strategies for reducing or overcoming them will be a problem for teachers and school librarians, educational administrators at all levels, policy makers and politicians, and communities themselves.

THE LM_NET SURVEY

One of the questions in the online questionnaire survey

of LM_NET members asked respondents what they saw as being the barriers to the use of the Internet in schools. They were asked to indicate all the factors that they felt were applicable, based on their own experience, and Table 7.1 summarizes the responses to this question from the people who were working in schools. Table 7.2, on the other hand, indicates the barriers that people felt were the most important. Many respondents appear to have found it difficult to nominate the one single barrier from among those on their list that they felt was most critical. In fact, more than 20 percent did not even attempt to do it, perhaps because they felt that all were significant, or that different barriers were important at different times, or that the issue was too complex to be dealt with in this way. Some even wrote a comment beside the question to the effect that the exercise was "too hard", others that "all are important". However, despite the relatively high nonresponse rate to the part of the question that involved ranking, one factor did emerge as being of particular importance as a perceived barrier to the use of the Internet in schools.

Early in 1994, United States Federal Communications Commission chairman Reed Hundt told the *New York Times*, "there are thousands of buildings in this country, with millions of people in them who have no telephones, no cable television, and no reasonable prospect of broadband services. They are called schools" (Stout, 1994). Even the vice president of the United States has noted the problem: in December 1993, Al Gore told the National Press Club that "when it comes to ensuring universal [access to networks]..., our schools are the most impoverished institutions in our society". The reality is that only three percent of United States classrooms had telephone lines (Salvador, 1994, p.35) let alone access to the Internet. The comments of Hundt and Gore are reflected in the results of the survey. Almost four-fifths of the respondents felt that a barrier to the use of the Internet in schools was "insufficient telephone lines". Further, more people cited this as the single most important barrier to the use of the Internet in schools than any other factor.

Table 7.1
Barriers to the Use of the Internet in Schools
(67 School-Based Respondents)

BARRIER	NUMBER	PERCENTAGE
Insufficient telephone lines	53	79.10
Insufficient hardware	48	71.64
Lack of knowledge on the part of the teachers	47	70.15
Lack of time in the school schedule	32	47.76
Poor or difficult access to hardware	31	46.27
Lack of financial support	30	44.78
Cost of Internet access and use	20	29.85
Inadequate information provided through the school system	19	28.36
Lack of administrative support	15	22.39
Lack of interest on the part of the teachers	15	22.39
Inadequate district or school level guidelines	8	11.94
Other	5	7.46
No answer	3	4.48

The telephone has been an important communications technology for more than a century, yet it still has not been accepted as a necessity for schools beyond the front office. Some school librarians are searching the Internet from their home phone lines to provide service to their school community, and teachers in California (and elsewhere) are paying for telephones in their classrooms. If nothing else, at least the current debate about the National Information Infrastructure (NII) in the United States has highlighted the basic need for telephones in classrooms and school libraries, and some North American telephone companies have announced programs for providing schools with access. But even if Al Gore's challenge to the communications industry (made in a speech to the Television Academy on 11 January 1994) to "connect all of our classrooms, all of our libraries ... by the year 2000" (Gore, 1994a) were to be taken up, many of the children in the United States school system today could have left school by the time their classrooms and libraries have access. And further, as a commentary in ALAWON (the American Library Association Washington Office Newsline) indicated, "nothing in the speech or background materials ensures that this will happen, beyond a reference to reduced universal service obligations for providers [who] offer to connect with schools" (National Information Infrastructure ..., 1994).

Table 7.2
Most Important Barriers to the Use of the Internet in Schools
(67 School-Based Respondents)

BARRIER	NUMBER	PERCENTAGE
Insufficient telephone lines	15	22.39
Insufficient hardware	5	7.46
Lack of knowledge on the part of the teachers	8	11.94
Lack of time in the school schedule	9	13.43
Poor or difficult access to hardware	1	1.49
Lack of financial support	3	4.48
Cost of Internet access and use	3	4.48
Inadequate information provided through the school system	1	1.49
Lack of administrative support	1	1.49
Lack of interest on the part of the teachers	5	7.46
Inadequate district or school level guidelines	0	
Other	2	2.98
No answer	14	20.89

While lack of sufficient telephone lines is a real barrier to use of the Internet and online information services (except where those services can be used through a local area network), there are also other hardware or equipment barriers that were noted by respondents. More than 70 percent of respondents who worked in schools indicated that insufficient hardware was a problem, and more than 45 percent cited "poor or difficult access to hardware" as a barrier. Some respondents mentioned an additional factor, "hardware which does not work correctly". One elaborated on this, describing a situation in which 6 out of 19 machines had to have the motherboard replaced, there were long waits for equipment to arrive and for telephone lines to be put in, and software corrections were needed, all of which slowed down the implementation in the school. This type of situation can be very discouraging for people who want to be able to use the Internet to find information, but do not want to become "techies" in order to do so. It is related to another problem that was mentioned often, "lack of technical support", including lack of technical support within the school itself.

Some of the barriers cited were related to personnel, and particularly to teachers and school administration. Just over 70 percent of respondents felt that "lack of knowledge on the part of the teachers" was a barrier to the use of the Internet in schools, though the teachers were not necessarily blamed for this, there were comments about the need for more time and money for staff training and professional development. While just over one-fifth of respondents pointed to "lack of interest on the part of the teachers" as a problem, for five it was the most significant barrier. Clearly, where it is a problem, it is an important one. "Teacher reluctance" was noted by some as a separate issue, and this was more likely to be mentioned in negative terms than teachers' lack of knowledge, as in "reluctant teachers too busy coaching volleyball". "Lack of administrative support" appeared to be less of a barrier than lack of knowledge or interest on the part of the teachers, being cited by a little over one-fifth of respondents (but being listed by only one as the most important barrier). However, "lack of financial support", which often reflects lack of administrative support, was cited by twice that number as a barrier, and "administrative ignorance" was noted as an additional issue by some.

In relation to personnel barriers, a problem mentioned by some respondents was the "difficulty of teaching" the teachers about the Internet, since "there are so many things to learn and they have so little time ... even the interested teachers are strapped for time". The time factor was cited in several different contexts, including time for the school librarian to learn the techniques that were needed, time to teach the teachers and students, time to keep up to date with developments.

There were comments about the "general lack of information" available on Internet access and use and particularly information about school level applications. "The information provided by the school system needs to give curriculum applications for Internet use for ALL areas. The teachers need a REASON to take the time to learn the process. We are working on that at school level. It would help to have district support." Yet only around 28 percent of respondents cited "inadequate information provided through the school system" as a barrier, and only one respondent saw it as the most significant barrier. Evidence was cited in Chapter Five that showed that, except in regions or states (such as Texas) where there was a network for schools, the school district or other wider authority appeared to have little influence in introducing school librarians to the Internet and promoting its use to them. Perhaps people in schools have simply given up on the education authorities and the school systems as sources of information on this topic; perhaps, because use of the Internet appears to have been a "grass roots" development (just as the use of computers was in many places), people have been accustomed to locating information themselves as best they can.

Many of the barriers discussed above were not significant for all respondents, and it is probable that different barriers are significant in any one school at different times. As one respondent noted, initially the most significant barriers were "phone lines and hardware, [but] if they were available, it would be difficult to find time to provide sufficient training; also many teachers would not take advantage of it. However, a number are eager to use it more than they are able to." Another commented that in the early stages the problem was "time to develop a service and get administrators interested enough to support [it] financially", but once the school community had access, then the problems would be lack of interest and/or knowledge on the part of the teachers, and "insufficient hardware".

OTHER RESEARCH

Barriers to the use of information technology in schools and school libraries have been discussed often in the research literature of education and school librarianship over the last decade, even to the extent that there have been comments about this apparently negative focus (Collis and Levin, 1993). However, an emphasis on the problems is natural in the early stages of implementation of any new concept or technology. At a time when only a small number of schools appear to have been successful in establishing a program based on the use of a new technology, and others are struggling to do so, the barriers and the factors that hinder implementation are of great interest, both to the schools and to policy makers. Other studies of the adoption and use of information technology in schools and school libraries shed some light on the barriers noted by LM_NET members, and, in some instances, help to explain them.

Computers can be used in school libraries for many different purposes, including library automation, providing access to CD-ROMs, using online information services and electronic mail, and accessing the Internet. Studies of the introduction of computers in school libraries, at this broader level, provide information about barriers that is relevant to the implementation of Internet services. In 1994, Australian school librarians were surveyed through the regular "Computers in School Libraries" column of the Australian national school library journal *Access* (Clyde, 1994) about their use of computers. In all, 334 computer-using librarians from primary and secondary schools, government and nongovernment schools, in all eight states and territories, responded. The survey showed considerable use of computers (particularly for library automation and CD-ROMs), but nevertheless most respondents were conscious that more could be done, and this is reflected in their comments about barriers to the use of computers in school libraries or factors limiting their use. While the comments were related to the use of computers in school libraries in general, rather than specifically to the use of the Internet in school libraries, they are still relevant in this more specific context. Basically, the barriers that were identified could be grouped under five topics: money, time, physical facilities and equipment, human factors, and policy and planning.

In response to the question, "What do you see as the main barriers to the use of computers and information technology in school libraries generally?", 233 respondents (69.76 percent) mentioned money, or, rather, lack of it. This was sometimes expressed in terms of financial constraints or the difficulty of raising funds. This was as true for those school libraries that had already invested significantly in information technology as for those that were just beginning. It seems that almost all respondents felt that what they had was not enough, and many justified this in terms of the need to teach information skills with appropriate technology. Some of the needs (such as for specific CD-ROMs) were not relevant in the context of the use of the Internet, but the need for hardware, software, a local area network, and online time are all important for Internet use. The start-up costs, in particular, were perceived to be a big barrier for schools that had not yet begun to use information technology in the school library. It was noted that "even though things are getting comparatively cheaper", more and more things were needed as time went on, and so new sources of funding had to be found to make ongoing purchases to keep abreast of new developments. People involved in the survey were aware that any technology becomes outdated very quickly, and they saw this as adding further to the costs of using computers. In the survey of LM_NET members, money was not mentioned as often as a barrier, but financial constraints were an implied barrier, for instance in comments about lack of funding to attend courses, lack of support staff, and the need to seek support for appropriate budget allocations.

A second major barrier to the introduction and effective use of computers and other new technology was time. School library staff felt that neither they nor the teachers had time to learn about the new technology, to demonstrate it effectively, to train others, or to evaluate and select appropriate resources. There was too little time to plan for the integration of information technology into the curriculum or to work cooperatively with teachers to ensure that it was used effectively. The time available to teachers for inservice activities was inadequate, particularly when there were so many new developments. Many respondents, while clearly feeling overwhelmed by the present rate of change, were also aware that they were likely to have even less time in the future, and this was a source of further anxiety. Concerns about the lack of time to explore the Internet, to learn about the resources available through it, and to teach others were also evident in the results of the survey of LM_NET members.

Physical facilities and equipment were another source of concern to Australian school librarians. As often happens in other countries, some Australian school libraries occupy "outdated physical surroundings", old buildings that had not been designed with today's technology in mind. But even in the best-designed libraries, space became a problem when new technologies were added to existing ones and the usage of the facilities changed. Some libraries lacked basic necessities like power points and telephone lines, an echo of the LM_NET survey results. Fears about security (which were sometimes well founded) created further barriers. One school librarian commented that the school had "learnt the hard way of the problems that arise when computers are stolen"; another noted that "kids steal, abuse, muck about with computers". Negative experiences such as these lead to an unwillingness to invest more money in technology.

Some of the barriers to the use of computers and information technology in school libraries were human ones. On the one hand, many of the people responsible for school libraries felt that their own training and skills were inadequate to cope with new developments in technology; in response to a question about the main barriers, one person said, "untrained people like me in charge of school libraries", while another saw "my lack of expertise" as a real problem. In addition, many respondents felt that they had inadequate support in the school, in terms of technical support (particularly for networks) and in terms of library support staff. On the other hand, some felt that a major human resources barrier was one that was outside the school library, in the form of resistance from other school staff members, and even from principals. Some were gentle about this, commenting on the teachers' fear of the unknown, their anxiety when faced with technology, their lack of time, the few opportunities for continuing education. Others were more blunt, referring to "computer illiterates" who opposed new ideas or "buried their heads in the sand" and refused to acknowledge new realities.

A further barrier to the use of new technology in school libraries in Australia was a perception of lack of planning and lack of vision at the management level in schools and beyond. Related problems that were mentioned were a lack of leadership from the state education departments, confusion, and an absence of reliable information. In these times of "devolution" of decision making to schools, school-based funding and management, and "on-site problem solving", strong practical central leadership is not likely, but survey responses indicated a desire for clear policy and for planning at a level wider than the individual school or even the region. These ideas are not restricted to Australia. The widespread adoption of computers and various forms of information technology in school libraries has coincided with the move to school-based or site-based or building-based decision making, and so, at a time when a large investment in hardware and continuing education is necessary, schools often have few sources of help within the wider school system. In addition, the adoption of information technology has tended to be a "bottom up" movement in many places, with some schools and individual teachers within schools wanting to use the technology before the school system administration is even aware of its potential benefits. This same situation has prevailed so far in the early stages of school library use of the Internet.

A more specific 1987 research study that focused just on the use of electronic information systems in Australian schools (Clyde and Kirk, 1989) identified a basically similar list of perceived problems and barriers. In this pilot project, school librarians in 51 schools where online information services were used were surveyed, through a mailed questionnaire. Most responding schools were using more than one online information service; many were using several. While the Internet was not an option for school libraries at this stage, the services used included the Australian SCIS and NEXUS services for schools, newspaper databases such as PressCom and QNIS (the Queensland Newspapers online service), and the international DIALOG and ORBIT (now Questel/Orbit) services. The problem or barrier most often mentioned (in fact, it was mentioned by three-quarters of the respondents) was cost. Other perceived problems included "limited access to equipment within the school", the limited time available for teaching students and teachers about the systems and for teacher librarians and other school library staff to develop facility in using the systems, access to training for staff, limited space, "unreliable and difficult-to-use hardware", "uninterested teachers", and a lack of "education-oriented services". A more general difficulty was perceived to be the overall level of computer literacy in schools.

The researchers who carried out this survey noted that their own perception (based on responses to various questions) was "that lack of knowledge of the options and lack of online search skills were major barriers, which is ironic considering that all schools included were committed to using online services and information" (Clyde Kirk, 1989, p.198). In relation to the latter, the same is true in many ways of the responses to the LM_NET survey: large numbers of LM_NET members were using only a few Internet tools or services, and there were comments that indicated both lack of knowledge of what was available and fairly undeveloped Internet skills. If these are problems for school librarians who are using the Internet, then they must be much greater barriers for nonusers. In discussing the results of the 1987 Australian study, the researchers commented, "Clearly school administrators, classroom teachers, teacher librarians, and parent groups all need more information about what is available, the likely cost, and appropriate educational applications" (p.198). The real problem is who is to provide this, and how it is to be made available to schools.

The 1993 report of the national survey of *Telecommunications and K-12 Educators* in the United States by Margaret Honey and Andrés Henríquez, referred to in Chapter Five, discusses barriers to the effective use of telecommunications. It helps to put the findings of the studies discussed above, and the LM_NET survey, into perspective. Barriers that they identified included lack of time in the school schedule, insufficient information about telecommunications being provided through the school systems, inadequate financial support, and a lack of policy and guidelines, as well as technical barriers associated with hardware, software, and search interfaces or systems. Honey and Henríquez note that many of these barriers would be familiar to teachers and school administrators who were attempting to introduce any new form of information technology into a school, and, indeed, they are evident in the results of the studies cited above. However, they also note that "new barriers appear with the advent of telecommunications technology", with the introduction of online searching, electronic mail, and/or the use of the Internet. The most obvious, and the most critical, of these new barriers is the problem of insufficient telephone lines into school buildings (Honey and Henríquez, 1993, p.32). And so it was that this problem headed the list of barriers identified in the LM_NET survey; even in schools where some forms of information technology were being used, it suddenly became critical when teachers and school librarians wished to implement new programs based on telecommunications. For this, a telephone line is a basic requirement.

In a 1993 doctoral thesis for the Florida Institute of Technology, Michael Anthony Gallo used a case study of a Florida high school to investigate the effects on teachers of "direct and unrestricted access to the Internet" provided via the school network as part of a special project. In the process, he identified problems that the teachers encountered when using their Internet connection, in other words, problems or barriers that arose after an Internet connection was in place, that inhibited its use or effective use. These problems included inadequate computer literacy skills on the part of the teachers (what Gallo calls a "comprehension" problem), technical problems with the computers and the local area network (LAN), and time.

In terms of computer literacy, Gallo observed that teachers often "lacked a basic understanding" of how their computers worked and how to use them. This made it difficult for them to use basic Internet applications that depend on some computer skills. Related to this was the need for good training, and for appropriate, nontechnical manuals. Not only did many teachers have problems in understanding and using their computers, but they also had trouble coming to terms with the Internet, what it is, and how it functions, even though books were available to them. The books were "scary" for some teachers, partly because of "esoteric" language and obscure terminology, though Gallo also noted that other teachers were enthusiastic about "being able to learn a new language and immerse themselves in a new culture".

Technical problems identified by Gallo that affected teachers' use of the Internet included problems with the LAN through which the Internet connection was made, malfunctioning computers, and technical support problems. Local area networks are not simple to set up, and considerable expertise is needed both to develop the LAN and to manage it once all the connections are in place. Many schools do not have, and cannot hire, a person with appropriate knowledge and skills, and where this is the case, problems are almost inevitable. Even with a well set up LAN, there are problems from time to time that require diagnostic skills. Despite all the problems, LANs have many advantages, but there needs to be a wider recognition of the need for skills and expertise in LAN management in schools. In response to an online survey by Doug Johnson (1993), several LM_NET members indicated that they were managing networks in their libraries and/or schools. In many cases, they were doing this "on top of all the other duties and with a few sessions of inservice for training", and Johnson concluded that on the whole, the responses made "a powerful argument for budgeting for training and staff".

The third major problem area identified by Gallo, time, is a barrier at all stages: it can be difficult for people to find enough time to learn enough about the Internet to be convinced of its value and to get connected, but once connected, lack of time can be a barrier to use. Even though teachers in Gallo's study had unrestricted access to the Internet at school, most found that they needed long, uninterrupted blocks of time in which to explore, to learn from the handbooks, and to experiment with Internet tools. Consequently, despite their insistence that their personal time was "precious", most wanted access to the Internet from home so that they could work more effectively with Internet tools and resources. This same need was reflected in some of the responses to the LM_NET survey—some school librarians were using the Internet from home in the evenings, even when they had a school connection, just to get a span of uninterrupted time in which to work at the computer.

In summing up his findings, Gallo commented that the problem of time was a very strong barrier when people began to use the Internet, and it continued to be a problem. However, as they used the Internet more, the teachers in his study tended to "make an Internet-time commitment", even though this may have encroached on their daily schedule and their personal time. He noted that the teachers' "reports of insufficient time were consistent with the current literature on educational technology", but also consistent with other research findings was the teachers' willingness to commit their own time to using the Internet when they began to find it personally gratifying and of benefit in their classroom teaching.

OTHER BARRIERS

The barriers to the use of the Internet in schools and school libraries that are discussed above were identified through the survey of LM_NET members, through other research projects, and through the research literature. Evidence collected by monitoring LM_NET and other listservs, from the general literature about the Internet, and from conference papers and other sources, generally confirms the findings from the more formal sources. However, the informal sources also suggest some further barriers to the use of the Internet. Some of these make it difficult for educators to learn about the Internet, while others affect the use of the Internet in schools and school libraries.

It is clear that people face enormous problems when coming to terms with the Internet, not least of which is finding out what to do and where to look for information. The teachers in Gallo's research study found difficulty with Internet language and skills, but the less formal sources suggest that, for many people, there is a problem at an even more basic level. If someone knows nothing, and has no help through a project, how do they find out even the basics? This explains the enormous popularity of printed guides to the Internet, despite the fact that they are likely to be more outdated than the tools available on the net itself.

There is a perception among some librarians, based partly on the difficulties people find in trying to come to terms with the Internet, that the information resources on the network are a "mess", and often of poor quality. Questions of information organization and information access, as well as information quality, tend to concern librarians more than other people because of the nature of their professional training. Certainly the librarians involved in the study of *Public Libraries and the Internet/NREN*, carried out by Charles McClure and his team from Syracuse University, were suspicious about these factors (1992, p.19). They were not only a barrier to effective Internet use, but they also tended to discourage librarians from becoming involved in using the Internet.

For people in schools and school libraries, particularly in North America, a factor that has discouraged the provision of Internet access for students has been a perception that the Internet is "loaded" with pornography, obscenity, and other "icky stuff", and that "undesirable people stalk the electronic corridors of the net", waiting to pounce on innocent children. It is certainly true that some of the material on the Internet may be unsuitable for young people, just as magazines, films, television programs, and books sometimes are. There is material on the Internet that some people find offensive, obscene, blasphemous, unpleasant, insensitive, embarrassing, silly, or "politically incorrect", or that they believe to be untrue. Unfortunately, all people don't feel the same way about the same things, and it is difficult to get agreement about what might come under each heading. However, there is also an enormous range of resources that can be used to great benefit in education. People using the Internet represent the whole spectrum of humanity, and people's individual aims, attitudes, beliefs, and behavior do not always appeal to others on the net. Just as in the real world, on the Internet there are people who are unpleasant, antisocial, or even criminal, though fortunately these people are in the minority on the net, just as they are in real life. These factors have led some educators and parent groups to oppose children's use of the Internet, or to demand that it be used only under strict supervision. They have also led to many suggestions that material on the Internet be monitored or even censored in some way, so that children see only what is deemed educationally valuable for them. This issue will be discussed further in the next chapter, since it is one that has emerged in many discussions about the use of the Internet in schools.

Although the Internet is international, its origins in the United States, and its rapid development in countries like Canada, the United Kingdom, and Australia, have ensured that the basic language of information and communication on it is English. In recent years, there has been an increase in the number of Internet listservs, newsgroups, gophers, World Wide Web servers, Internet Relay Chat channels, and ftp archives that are based on another language or languages, but still, the major sites in the field of education are in English. This means that many of the resources on the Internet are not accessible to people who do not read English. Even in countries where children are taught English in schools from a relatively early age, young children are still not going to have the English language skills needed to make use of the Internet resources. This has been a major barrier to the educational use of the Internet in countries where the first language of communication and education is not English. In these countries, the cultural values embedded in much of the English-language information and services may also make the material unsuitable for local use even in translation, unless it is also substantially adapted.

Other barriers to the use of the Internet in schools and school libraries that have been noted in the informal sources include lack of local access to an Internet node, (Huberman, 1994) the refusal of some Internet access providers to allow schoolchildren on their systems, the unreliable or poor quality telephone lines in some countries or regions, and the requirement in some countries that people pay not only for electronic mail that they send but also that which they receive (as also happens on some American commercial services). In addition, despite the fact that the number of countries with Internet connections has grown in the last few years, there are still countries where Internet access is not possible.

OVERCOMING BARRIERS

For many of the barriers to the use of the Internet in school libraries, there are no easy solutions, and no solutions that can be guaranteed to work everywhere. Some of the problems, such as space problems or the availability of hardware items like modems, usually need to be addressed at the school level; others, such as the development of policies and guidelines, at the district or wider system level. However, even a broad statement like this is inappropriate in some settings. For example, the provision of telephone lines may be seen simply as an everyday administrative concern in an Australian independent school or a British public school, but it is an issue that has been taken up at the federal level by the United States government. By the same token, while policy and planning for a school system is usually seen as the province of the wider education authority, voluntary groups of school librarians, or professional associations, have been known to take matters into their own hands and develop appropriate guidelines in a situation where none exist and there have been no official moves to create them.

In her 1990 book, *Wider Horizons: Online Information Services in Schools,* Ann Irving presents another perspective on barriers to the implementation of programs based on using the Internet in schools. She writes, not about barriers or problems, but more positively about "management issues" associated with the introduction of information technology in schools. Further, she presents examples from case studies to show how these issues were resolved in some British schools. For Irving, school librarians are managers in their own setting, and management issues that they face include time management, the need for appropriate training for personnel, budgeting, lobbying, seeking support within the school and outside it. All these are important at all times, and especially so when new technology is being introduced.

A positive approach is also taken by Kieth Wright in his book, *The Challenge of Technology: Action Strategies for the School Library Media Specialist,* published by the American Library Association in 1993. He discusses barriers to the "integration of computer-related technologies" in general, including program barriers ("barriers created by the ways in which the programs of the school are carried out") and technical barriers. He then provides a chapter on "overcoming the barriers to computer-related technologies", with strategies for action arranged under ten headings. Some of the strategies imply culturally based assumptions about the ways in which schools are run and the ways in which education is provided, but, nevertheless, school librarians outside the United States may well be able to adapt much of his advice to their local setting, just as the ideas derived from the British case studies of Irving will need to be adapted to other settings.

However, some of the barriers to the use of the Internet in schools and school libraries cannot be resolved (at present at least) through action by people in schools or school systems, though educators may well be able to influence developments through lobbying. The barriers that come into this category are those associated with the Internet itself, the information on it, the interfaces available, and the skills required to use it. It is generally recognized that there are problems associated with the Internet as an information delivery and communications system, problems that have their roots in its early development as a system for academic and defense researchers, and in the technology within which it grew. Changes are under way, driven partly by the needs of the increasing numbers of people who are using the Internet, and their requirements for simpler and more structured access. In fact, developments like gopher and World Wide Web are a response to this situation. School librarians need to be active, through their professional associations, through their school systems, through their representatives in government, and via any other means available to them, to make sure that the needs of schools are taken into account in any future developments.

REFERENCES

Caywood, Carolyn (1994), Re: Why Aren't Public Libraries Stampeding to the Nets?, Message posted to the PUBLIB listserv on the Internet, 24 April.

Clyde, Laurel A. (1994), "Computers in school libraries survey", *Access* 8, no. 3, August, pp.30–35, 29.

Clyde, Laurel A. and Kirk, Joyce (1989), "The use of electronic information systems in Australian schools: a preliminary survey", *School Library Media Quarterly* 17, no. 4, Summer, pp.193–199.

Collis, Betty and Levin, Jim (1993), Research on Telecommunications and Learning: An International Perspective, Paper presented at the Tel*Ed 93 Global Connections International Conference, November. Proceedings available through the CoSN gopher.

Cullen, James G. (1994), Response Statement to Vice President Gore's Speech on the Administration's Telecommunications Initiatives, Document posted to the PUBLIB listserv on the Internet, 12 January.

Gallo, Michael Anthony (1993), Assessing the Effect on High School Teachers of Direct and Unrestricted Access to the Internet: A Case Study of an East Central Florida High School, PhD thesis, Florida Institute of Technology, Melbourne, Florida.

Gore, Albert, *Vice President* (1993), Remarks by Vice President Al Gore at the National Press Club, 21 December 1993. Message distributed by the White House on CompuServe, 21 December.

Gore, Albert, *Vice President* (1994a), Remarks by Vice President Al Gore, Royce Hall, UCLA, Los Angeles, California, 11 January. (Speech to the Television Academy).

Gore, Albert, *Vice President* (1994b), Vice President Proposes National Telecommunications Reform, Message distributed by the White House on CompuServe, 11 January.

Hamilton, Betty Dawn (1993), TARGET-> Technology Training, Message posted to the LM_NET listserv on the Internet, 3 October.

Heath, Scott (1994), Research Project Report, "Schools and Change", Document posted to the EDTECH listserv on the Internet, 9 January.

Honey, Margaret and Henríquez, Andrés (1993), *Telecommunications and K-12 Educators: Findings From a National Survey*, Center for Technology in Education, Bank Street College of Education, New York.

Huberman, Debbie (1994), Re: Why Aren't Public Libraries Stampeding to the Nets?, Message posted to the PUBLIB listserv on the Internet, 24 April.

Irving, Ann (1990), *Wider Horizons: Online Information Services in Schools*, (Library and Information Research Report 80), The British Library, London.

Johnson, Doug (1993), Digest of Who's Managing the Network Responses, Message posted to the LM_NET listserv on the Internet, 10 October.

Maak, Laurie (1993), School Needs Survey, Electronic mail message, 28 June.

McClure, Charles R., Ryan, Joe, Lauterbach, Diana, and Moen, William E. (1992), *Public Libraries and the Internet/NREN: New Challenges, New Opportunities*, School of Information Studies, Syracuse University, New York.

Means, Barbara, et al. (1993), *Using Technology to Support Education Reform*, USGPO, Washington, DC.

(1994), National Information Infrastructure—Gore's January 11 Speech, ALAWON (American Library Association Washington Office Newsline) 3, no. 3, 22 January.

Pacific Bell Announces Vision for Universal Service (1994), Message posted to the Net-Happenings listserv on the Internet, 17 February.

Rabe, Eric (1994), Bell Atlantic, TCI Announce Basic Education Connection to Information Super Highway for K-12 Schools, Message posted to the TELECOMREG listserv on the Internet, 10 January.

Rothman, David (1994a), Gore's Speech and Bell Atlantic Reply, Message posted to the PUBLIB listserv on the Internet, 12 January.

Rothman, David (1994b), Gore and Bell At.: Mr Smith Goes to Washington? Why Not?, Message posted to the PUBLIB listserv on the Internet, 14 January.

Salvador, Roberta (1994), "The emperor's new clothes", *Electronic Learning*, May/June, pp.32–46.

Stout, Connie (1994), NII and Education, An Analysis, EdPOL-D (Education Policy Digest, electronic journal of the Scholastic Network) 1, no. 2, February.

Tenopir, Carol (1994), "Collaboration through networking: the online experience in school libraries in the United States", Paper presented at the SLOC (School Library Organisations Council) Conference 1994, "Collaboration Creates Vision", Perth, Western Australia.

Tornatzky, Louis G. (1994), RFI: Technology in Schools, Message posted to the comp.infosystems newsgroup on USENET, 3 February.

Treagust, David F. and Rennie, Leonie J. (1993), Implementing Technology in the School Curriculum: A Case Study Involving Six Secondary Schools, Journal of Technology Education 5, no. 1, Fall, Downloaded from LISTSERV@VTVM1.CC.VT.EDU

Wright, Kieth (1993), *The Challenge of Technology: Action Strategies for the School Library Media Specialist*, American Library Association, Chicago.

CHAPTER EIGHT

ISSUES AND DEVELOPMENTS

INTRODUCTION

The Internet is both relatively new and rapidly changing. Its availability and use within the community has meant that many people and organizations have had to adapt to the new environment and to review and reassess the ways in which they do things. Both libraries and schools have been affected. However, the use of the Internet raises many questions and issues, which are being discussed in the professional literature and the popular media. Most of these concerns were raised by LM_NET members in their responses to the questionnaire survey, and they surface from time to time in discussions on the listserv itself. There are no easy answers to these questions, and the issues are likely to be discussed on an ongoing basis, since many people have strong feelings about them.

Some of the issues have been mentioned in earlier chapters of this book, in particular Chapter Six ("The Internet in School Libraries") and Chapter Seven ("Barriers"). The issue of equity of access to the Internet for all schools was one that was mentioned often by LM_NET members. For many of the schools that were already connected (and for some schools that were about to be connected), there was concern about the problem of students accessing inappropriate materials through a school Internet account. The need to teach appropriate Internet skills as information skills was an issue that was raised by many respondents to the questionnaire survey, and this was a particular concern where school access to the Internet was very limited. Other issues associated with the use of the Internet in schools and school libraries that are discussed in the literature include censorship of various kinds, copyright and intellectual property issues, security, funding, commercial use of the Internet, and liability issues (these have come into focus with two successful court cases involving slander or defamation charges based on messages posted to the net).

In this chapter, access issues will be discussed, particularly the problem of equity of access in general, and the more specific issue of use of the Internet by women and girls. Other issues to be dealt with include censorship of Internet resources and "protection" of Internet users from materials considered to be harmful, ethics and ethical behavior on the nets, network security and privacy issues, and information skills instruction. Within each section of the chapter, there are pointers to Internet resources that provide further information or shed some light on the issue or problem under discussion. The chapter concludes with a brief discussion of likely future developments.

EQUITY OF ACCESS

In an interview on the PUBLIB listserv in September 1993, author and "net.traveller" Howard Rheingold identified equity of access as one of the key problems associated with the development of the Internet. "If we are not going to continue to evolve toward a two-tiered society of those who are plugged in and those who are not", he said, "we have to come to grips with the problem of universal access" (Rheingold, 1993). This issue was also identified by respondents to the LM_NET survey, several of whom commented that they would like to see access to the Internet available in every classroom, even in every home.

Access has two major components: technological

access, that is, access to the equipment and facilities necessary to connect to the Internet, and intellectual access, the knowledge and skills necessary to locate and use the information and services on the Internet. Though separate issues, both are interrelated, especially in the sense that people must have a certain level of intellectual awareness before they are willing to give priority to making the facilities available, yet without the facilities, the skills cannot be developed.

Many commentators have noted the inequity of access to computers and information technology in the community in general and within and among schools. Alan November is one of these; he has said that in the United States, "the current public school system is incredibly inequitable", citing a ten thousand dollars per pupil difference across the state of Illinois as an example (November and Thornburg, 1994, p.25). While the relationship is not absolute, these differences in funding are reflected in differences in the provision of access to technology in schools. The results of the LM_NET survey provide some evidence for differences in levels of provision even among those schools that have Internet access. Nevertheless, school funding is not necessarily an indicator of commitment to technology; other factors, such as teachers' and school administrators' knowledge of information technology, and community awareness of it, are also important.

The discussion of access issues is sometimes carried on without common points of reference, and this has not always helped. So often, participants mean different things by the same phrases or base their comments on different assumptions. Mitch Kapor has been quoted as saying that "98% of US households have TVs (only 93% have telephones) and all those 98% paid for their TVs—television is important enough that people go out and actually spend money on it" (Kapor, 1994). However, the educational level and the skills needed to watch television and those necessary to use computers and particularly the

Internet, are very different as are the base level costs. People who could not afford a computer or Internet access and who could not use it if they did have access, are more likely to be able to afford a television set—and are certain to be able to use it. It is also worth noting that Kapor is talking about "households"—the truly marginalized members of society do not live in the "households" of the surveys. In a posting to the PUBLIB listserv on the Internet, Karen G. Schneider discussed the issue of poverty and its effects from the point of view of a city public library in the United States:

> Every day we see poor people in this library. Some people are *obviously* poor—their personal appearance speaks for their situations. But many, many more people are impoverished in ways at once subtly apparent yet highly pernicious: they are poorly educated, poorly skilled and poorly prepared for the massive changes in information-sharing behavior our world is now experiencing. These poor are the children growing up without exposure to computers—not at school, not at home, not even, for the most part in our libraries. These poor are the adults with such weak education and limited information-seeking skills that they passively accept the quality, quantity and media of information we provide them, regardless of how limited or antiquated our services. These poor are the people who have never heard of the "information superhighway", who will not purchase computers with modems, who have never touched keyboards, who do not know what the Internet is. Those of you who believe that "everyone" is aware of the upcoming information revolution do not work with the reality of poor inner-city lives.

While some public libraries are providing Internet access for members of the community, there are problems beyond physical access that mean that these initiatives may not help the truly "information poor". As Schneider notes, "one of the quandries of the information revolution is that those who are information-poor are unaware of it, so they are unable to participate".

In a sense, "elitism is inherent in the Internet", (Phillips, 1994, p.50) in that, even with simplified graphical interfaces, literacy is an absolute requirement for its use. People have to be able to read and write well beyond the level of functional literacy; they have to be able to follow instructions and directions, and to take the initiative in accessing services or participating in net-based activities. Further, given the size of the Internet and the amount of information available through it, they have to be able to make evaluative judgments. Not only does this mean that functionally illiterate adults are excluded, but it also means that the extent of participation by young children will be limited.

Within schools, access to the Internet may be affected by another factor. David Thornburg has said that "you can have all the great goodies in the world at your disposal, and [yet] in the absence of a dedicated, committed teaching staff", no effective use will be made of the technology. "The role of the classroom teacher is essential for real equity" (November and Thornburg, 1994, p.25). This can be taken even further—without knowledgeable school administrators who have kept abreast of current developments, the technology is unlikely to be made available in the first place.

However, while lack of teacher awareness is a particular problem, and one which was highlighted in some of the responses to the LM_NET survey, it is not just a problem of teacher attitudes or willingness to learn. Even where teachers have had Internet accounts made available to them, they are being "abandoned at the gates" of the Internet unless they are also given guidance and assistance in using the new tools and resources (Copley, quoting Prescott Smith, 1993). A related issue is convenience of access for teachers: "If the teachers have to leave the classroom to have access or if they run into other problems", then they will not be disposed to use the Internet in classroom work—or even be able to develop the skills to do so (Copley, quoting Kevin Berry, 1993). Inservice education and continuing education opportunities for teachers are critical if students in their classroom are to have access to the Internet in any meaningful way.

The whole issue of equity of access has many facets. Even in the so-called developed countries, Internet access can be affected by poverty, by access to education, by literacy skills. These problems are magnified in some developing countries. Access can also be affected by the language of literacy (regardless of the level of literacy in that language), by geographical location (in relation to an Internet node), by sex (women may have lower levels of education, girls may have fewer opportunities than boys to use the Internet), by age (the elderly may be deprived of opportunities to acquire technological skills), by the philosophical views of those who control the access to information (deliberate censorship or attempts to protect people from what is considered undesirable may result in limited access). Some of these facets, particularly those that are important for school libraries, will be discussed in more detail in later sections of this chapter.

CENSORSHIP OR PROTECTION

When the Internet is used by children, the question sometimes arises of how to manage their access so that they do not see material that the school, their parents, or the community might find inappropriate. This is variously called "protecting children from harm" to "censorship". It is an issue which arouses heated feelings, even among professional school librarians who might be expected, on the basis of the many statements of professional ethics and "freedom to read", to oppose censorship of information. It raises a range of related issues, which are hard to deal with. For example, the school librarian has to answer the question "who is my client?" when providing service to schoolchildren. If the client is the child, then the child has the same right to expect confidentiality that an adult client has. On the other hand, if children have different rights in libraries from those that adults enjoy, then who, and under what circumstances, has the right to say what the child will see or read? Do teachers and school librarians have different legal obligations when a child is at school? In some places, they do, but this is not always the case. Is it, in fact, possible to monitor or restrict children's access to information, in any form, in schools? Are there any circumstances in which censorship, under whatever name, is justified?

In Chapter Seven, barriers to the use of the Internet in schools were discussed. In the United States and some other countries, one barrier has proved to be the fear that school children might use the school facilities to access inappropriate materials, or that they might accidentally find materials that are pornographic, blasphemous, or otherwise undesirable. Given the enormous range of educationally valuable material on the Internet, it seems a pity that the fear that young people might see inappropriate material has meant that they may not get Internet access at all. This is especially so when, as has been pointed out, students are likely to "hear much worse language on the street", get more and "better pornography at the corner newsstand", and see nothing "as bad as the violence they are exposed to at home every night on prime-time television" (Collins, 1994). Yet, "practically speaking, the presence of X-rated material ... is a real threat to the continued support of a program in the public schools" (Cisler, 1993).

An additional factor is that there is no truly effective way to restrict access, except by supervision (which involves time and money) or by making a preselected set of Internet resources available to students on the local area network (a solution that also involves time and personnel resources). In 1994 onwards commercial solutions began to emerge, in the form of Internet screening tools designed to filter out or restrict access to undesirable sites (examples include Cybercop and NetNanny). Supervision in some form is essential if students are to be encouraged to reflect on and learn from their online experiences. On the other hand, the disadvantages of a completely restrictive approach are many. Probably the most serious are that it does not encourage students to develop appropriate Internet skills, nor does it encourage them to take responsibility for their own behavior. As one member of LM_NET has commented, "instead of trying to make the world safe for students", it might be better to spend more time "educating students and making them aware of the world and its dangers, so that they are safe for the world" (Collins, 1994). This approach is supported by Howard Rheingold (1994), who has said that "we are going to have to teach our children well. The locus of control is going to have to be in their heads and hearts, not in the laws or the machines", and they will need "a solid moral grounding and some common sense" to deal not just with the Internet but with life in the information society. At a time when it is "becoming technically impossible" to restrict access to information on the Internet, education may be the best defense against "shock to our moral codes".

In an attempt to deal with these issues, the Minnesota Coalition Against Censorship (MCAC) has developed an Internet discussion statement as a basis for the use of the Internet in elementary and secondary schools as an educational resource. This discussion statement backs up the Minnesota Public School Internet Policy which has been adopted by the Board of Directors of the Minnesota Coalition Against Censorship. The discussion statement reads as follows:

> The Minnesota Coalition Against Censorship believes that access to the Internet should be made available to all teachers and students in the public schools as a source of information and vehicle of communication. Professional school personnel have a responsibility to help students acquire the skills needed to make educational judgements about locating and using information on the Internet. School officials have a responsibility to inform parents and the public about the Internet as an information source and vehicle of commu-

nication and the importance of providing access to and skills of use to prepare students to participate in a global information society.

Making Internet access available to students carries with it the potential that some students might encounter information that some have identified as controversial and of potential harm to students. Because information on the Internet appears, disappears, and changes, it is not possible to predict or control what students may locate. Just as public librarians do not attempt to control the public library environment, school officials should not attempt or promise to control the Internet environment for students. Given the constantly changing information environment, creating what some would call a "safe environment" is impossible and implying that it is being done is a disservice to parents and the public. At the same time, school officials should make sure that parents are aware of the individual student's responsibility to use Internet resources in an ethical and educational manner. The focus should shift from controlling the environment to providing individual users with the understanding and skills needed to use the Internet in ways appropriate to their individual educational needs.

MCAC opposes the use of techniques to prevent student access to information that some have identified as controversial or of potential harm to students. Such schemes include: using coded account identifiers for students, restricting certain databases and sources of information to accounts identified as educational, limiting accounts to teachers, having owners and operators of information services screen access and communication, or having students voluntarily impose restrictions on themselves in exchange for the privilege of having an Internet account. Any of these strategies restrict student access to information or ability to communicate and should not be used by school officials or other agencies responsible for providing Internet access.

Because the Internet is an interactive medium and provides a method of communication for students, school officials must exercise the same concerns for privacy that exist in traditional methods of communication. School officials may not impose restrictions, exercise prior restraint, or otherwise interfere with student communication with other individuals on the Internet, but school officials should expect that students will apply the same privacy, ethical and educational considerations they apply to other communication.

School officials should address issues of access to the Internet in their school board adopted selection policies. While Internet resources are not selected in the sense of selecting a book or video, educators can apply the same selection criteria to electronic resources as they apply to other resources. Likewise, school officials should adopt procedures to handle concerns about Internet information similar to the procedures used for other educational resources.

School officials should also adopt guidelines for student use of their Internet accounts. To protect the due process rights of students, guidelines should define appropriate educational and ethical uses of the Internet, identify individual student responsibilities, and outline procedures for enforcing behavior on the Internet and handling violations.

The Internet Policy document of the Minnesota Coalition Against Censorship indicates that schools should adopt formal policies related to the Internet, and that these policies should include statements affirming the following precepts:

- "Students have the right to examine a broad range of opinions and ideas in the educational process, including the right to locate, use and exchange information and ideas on the Internet."
- "Students have the right to examine and use all information formats, including interactive electronic formats."
- "Students have the right to communicate with other individuals on the Internet without restriction or prior restraint."
- "School officials must respect a student's right to privacy in using Internet resources and using the Internet as a vehicle for communication."
- "School officials, school employees, or other agencies responsible for providing Internet access must not make individual, arbitrary, unreviewed decisions about Internet information sources."
- "School officials must apply the same criterion of educational suitability used for other educational resources to attempts to remove or restrict access to specific databases or other Internet information sources."
- "If restrictions are placed on student access to Internet resources, it is parents and only parents who may place

restrictions on their children, and only their own children. Parents may not tell the school to assume responsibility for imposing restrictions on their children."

- "Students are responsible for the ethical and educational use of their own Internet accounts."
- "Students have a responsibility to respect the privacy of other Internet users."
- "Policies and procedures to handle concerns raised about Internet resources should be similar to those used for other educational resources."

The gopher of the Ontario Institute for Studies in Education (Canada) has a section devoted to the use of Internet resources in elementary and secondary schools, with collections of documents related to censorship, pornography, violence, and other Internet access issues. Other collections of policies and guidelines can be found on the Inspire gopher in the United States, the Texas Armadillo gopher, and the MERIT gopher (also in the United States). Censorship or restriction of access to Internet resources in elementary and secondary schools has been discussed extensively on several Internet listservs, including LM_NET, EDNET, EDTECH, ETHICS-L, and IFREEDOM, and the postings (which represent many different points of view) can be read through the archives of each listserv. In addition, the archives of both LM_NET and EDTECH contain many sample school Internet policy statements, acceptable use policies, student and parent consent forms, and access agreements, which school librarians and others in the school setting will find useful in developing school-level policies, guidelines, and procedures.

ETHICS

At the Tel*Ed 93 conference of the International Society for Technology in Education, a panel session was devoted to a discussion of "Telecommunications and Ethics" in education. A basis for the discussion was the observation that "increased access to information resources in electronic form has created a host of new ethical problems and has changed the context in which a number of ethical issues arise". As an example, it was noted that "although most educators and students understand well the concept of tangible property ownership and rights, such concepts are not well understood as they apply to electronic information resources" (Resta, et al., 1993). Further, the increasing use of online information services and Internet resources, the panelists felt, would provide "even greater challenges to schools" in encouraging students to be ethical and responsible in their use of these new technological tools and resources. Among the ethical issues that were seen to be important in this context were copyright and intellectual property (and the related issue of plagiarism), system security and "hacking", confidentiality and privacy, and "telecommunications courtesy" or appropriate online behavior.

The point has been made that legal rules and ethical standards have been used, in many cases, to overcome shortcomings in the telecommunications systems in use today, and that, with better-designed systems, some of the existing regulations would be unnecessary (Palme, 1993). In any case, it is difficult to apply the legal requirements of any one country in an international setting, and so there has been a considerable reliance on generally accepted conventions or guidelines as a basis for Internet use. "These guidelines are varied and complex, evolving and changing to address specific issues. However, it is fair to assume that whatever these are, they are grounded in and reflect moral and ethical attitudes" (BITNET Network Information Center, 1993b). Regardless of the reasons, it is likely that codes of ethics and "acceptable use policies" will continue to be the basis of Internet standards at least into the immediate future.

Nevertheless, the behavior of small groups of Internet

users, including practices such as propagating massive numbers of unsolicited electronic mail messages across the networks, and marketing tactics of service providers that fail to reveal the actual nature and costs of services rendered, has caused concern at the national and international levels. This prompted a Statement of Policy on the "proper use of resources on the Internet" from the Internet Activities Board in the United States—a statement titled "Ethics and the Internet". This document notes that "the reliable operation of the Internet and the responsible use of its resources is of common interest and concern for its users, operators and sponsors". The Internet Society Board of Trustees, meeting in Prague in June 1994 during the Society's International Networking Conference (INET '94, held in conjunction with the Joint European Network Conference), announced that a set of ethical guidelines would be developed. This was to be done through the Society's Internet Architecture Board (IAB) (as the body which oversees the architecture of the Internet and sets its standards), the Society's Advisory Council (representing companies, foundations, and government agencies), and "the Internet community at large". The Society's Resolution 94, passed in Prague, states that "since the Internet will only function effectively in a spirit of cooperation", the Board of Trustees "recognizes the need for an Internet Code of Ethics and the importance of educating the Internet community about it". A draft code was to be ready for consideration by the Board of Trustees by December 1994. However, while "the Society is the global international organization for the Internet, its technologies, and applications", it has few real powers at the base level, and it depends chiefly on its considerable influence to ensure the adoption of its guidelines and codes of ethics.

In the meantime, in another announcement, the Internet Activities Board endorsed a statement of the Division Advisory Panel of the United States National Science Foundation Division of Network, Communications

Research and Infrastructure. As paraphrased by the Internet Activities Board, this statement characterizes as unethical and unacceptable any activity or use that deliberately:

- attempts to gain unauthorized access to the resources of the Internet;
- disrupts the intended use of the Internet;
- wastes resources (people, capacity, computer) through such actions;
- destroys the integrity of computer-based information; and/or
- compromises the privacy of users.

The principles have been adopted as components of other ethical statements or acceptable use policies, for example the acceptable use policy of the Corporation for Research and Educational Networking (CREN) in the United States, and that of Iceland's ISnet (SURIS) national research and education network.

As more and more schools make use of Internet resources and allow students to use Internet services, the need for school-level acceptable-use policies has become apparent. These are often associated with statements about the ethical use of the Internet in schools, and with access policies for school students. Sometimes students and their parents/guardians are requested to sign a consent form and/or an agreement before the student is permitted to use the Internet from school facilities. This form or agreement may have any of several purposes. It is usually designed to ensure that students are aware of their responsibilities as Internet users and take them seriously. It may also be designed to ensure that parents/guardians understand the services that their children will be using, and the value of these services in their children's education. It may indicate to parents that though the school will supervise students, it does not have any control over the information on the Internet. It may include a statement about costs.

The NuevaNet Acceptable Use Policy and Contract was

developed in the Nueva School in California as a basis for use of the school's NuevaNet, a connection to the Bay Area Regional Research Network (BARRNet), which in turn connects to the Internet (Abilock, 1994). Users of NuevaNet include students of the school (P-8) and their parents/guardians, teachers, school support personnel, administrators, other school staff, and educators and students from other institutions who are working with the Nueva School. The policy, developed through a process of consultation and checked by lawyers, quotes the school's Mission Statement as a basis for the network activity:

> NuevaNet provides open access to ... local, national, and international sources of information and collaboration vital to intellectual inquiry in a democracy. In defining the Internet's resources as an extension of the Library, this network subscribes to the Library Bill of Rights which states that "A person's right to use a library should not be denied or abridged because of origin, age, background, or views". In turn, every NuevaNet user has the responsibility to respect and protect the rights of every user in our community and on the Internet. NuevaNet account holders are expected to act in a responsible, ethical and legal manner, in accordance with the Nueva Code of Conduct, the missions and purposes of the other networks they use on the Internet and the laws of the states and the United States.

The code of conduct for all users of NuevaNet in the school states that the "NuevaNet account holder is responsible for his/her actions and activity within his/her account", and that "unacceptable uses of the network will result in the suspension or revoking of these privileges". The examples given of unacceptable use are as follows (Abilock, 1994):

1. Using the network for any illegal activity, including violation of copyright or other contracts.
2. Using the network for financial or commercial gain.
3. Degrading or disrupting equipment or system performance.
4. Vandalizing the data of another user.
5. Wastefully using finite resources.

6. Gaining unauthorised access to resources or entities.
7. Invading the privacy of individuals.
8. Using an account owned by another user.
9. Posting personal communications without the author's consent.
10. Posting anonymous messages.

When parents/guardians and students sign the consent and waiver form attached to the policy, they agree to abide by these conditions. Further, it is suggested that "the student and his/her parent(s) or guardian(s) should discuss these rights and responsibilities together".

A collection of Internet ethics statements and acceptable use policies from elementary and secondary schools is available on the AskERIC gopher. There are also pointers to this collection from other educational sites on the Internet. There is another collection of statements on the "acceptable and unacceptable use of net resources (K-12)" on the Armadillo educational gopher in Texas. The statements and policy documents will assist teachers, school librarians, and others who are developing codes of ethics or Internet access policies for their own schools or school systems.

NETWORK ETIQUETTE

Despite many arguments and discussions about the need to regulate "cyberspace", the Internet, to a considerable extent, has been kept inhabitable for its many millions of users by a form of self-regulation that appeals as much to self-interest and shared values as to any authority. The point has been made that "the most effective ways of networking, getting help, finding information, gathering people together, making friends, and so forth, are also the most socially responsible ways of doing these things". What has been called "the network's tremendous capacity for self-regulation" (The Internet as Commons, 1994) has so far been the basis of ensuring a reasonably fair deal for everyone, though some attempts have been made to introduce more formal regulatory procedures. User contracts and acceptable use policies for members of particular networks and online services are examples of more formal mechanisms; files of FAQs (Frequently Asked Questions) to assist users of listservs and newsgroups, and codes of "netiquette", are less formal mechanisms.

The need for some generally accepted conventions of electronic communication seems to have arisen because electronic mail offers few visual clues and no auditory clues for the people who interpret the written messages. In today's world, there are comparatively few people who are trained in the art of letter writing, and informal written communication tends to be fairly unsophisticated. Most people today are accustomed to receiving information, not from unadorned text, but in the form of messages from radio and television. Even printed communication, in today's world, normally provides typographical clues and often illustrations that help the reader to make an interpretation. The combination of naive writers, and readers who are deprived of the clues to which they are accustomed, in a context in which cultural and other indicators are absent, sometimes results in highly charged online situations. Attempts at online humor and sarcasm are often misinterpreted, and, in any case, humor does not always cross cultural or national boundaries. In addition, the speed with which an electronic mail message can be fired off sometimes means that messages are sent which would, under other circumstances, have been thought through more carefully. All of these factors have had a part in establishing the need for formal or informal codes of "netiquette".

Network etiquette, or "netiquette", has been described as "the informal set of rules, civilities, and social graces that have evolved in cyberspace, the do's and don'ts of online behavior" (Ross, 1994). Many listservs, USENET newsgroups, electronic bulletin boards, and online services have more or less formal network etiquette or electronic mail etiquette guides for the use of participants; an example is the "LM_NET Network Etiquette" document that is posted on the listserv from time to time (Eisenberg and Milbury, 1994). As well as providing practical information about such things as the correct way to send messages, the use of sensible subjects to describe message content, and formatting a message, these documents usually include information on signatures, smileys, and "flaming", as well as information about any "acceptable use" or "appropriate use" policy.

Basic to the idea of "netiquette" is the admonition to "never forget that the person on the other side is human" (Chuq Von Rospach, 1993). When someone is sitting in front of a computer screen, it is all too easy for them to feel that they are interacting with words and hardware, rather than with people. If the people behind the words are kept in mind, then a savage response to a message is less likely. Other "things to remember" (Chuq Von Rospach, 1993) in electronic communication include the following:

- Be brief (long answers take up bandwidth and the time of readers);
- Be discreet (not only are messages on listservs and newsgroups read by thousands of people around the world, but they may be stored in online archives or on hard discs anywhere);
- Be aware that "your postings reflect on you—be proud of them";
- "Think about your audience";
- "Don't overdo signatures";
- Watch your own spelling, and avoid "spelling flames" when others use strange spellings—apart from the fact that spelling rules are not universal in English, many of the users of international networks do not have English as their first language, and some users have to work with software which makes it difficult for them to correct errors before they send a message.

"Flaming" has been an unfortunate part of Internet culture; although it is considered by many network citizens to be both a network tradition and an art form, it can nevertheless be very destructive. In fact, many newsgroups and listservs have disintegrated in the wake of "flame wars". In part, flaming arises from the failure to observe the admonition to remember that "the person on the other side is human". However, it also demonstrates the Internet's tendency to reflect real life, with its good and bad aspects. Some people on the nets use "great skill" in "making nuisances of themselves", just as people do in the public places of the real world. The Internet has "individuals who fly into abusive, self-righteous tirades ... at the first sign of disagreement ... they blurt out angry vituperation, abandoning the editing process of common courtesy that took us thousands of years to acquire" (Brin, 1994, p.56). Yet these people, in their way, resemble the motorist who cuts off others on the road and roars away with an obscene gesture. The flamer is another by-product of our modern society, just as other unpleasant aspects of life are. The teaching of network etiquette as part of the normal process of using networks is thus necessary in schools, just as schools socialize children in other ways.

In 1994, Virginia Shea published a book called *Netiquette,* designed to bring "etiquette to the bustling frontiers of cyberspace" and to offer "the guidance that all users need to be perfectly polite online". Covering everything from the elements of electronic style to the "art of flaming" to "virtual sex", it entertains and informs. The third chapter, with its ten "core rules of network etiquette", is excellent reading for network "newbies". Equally effective, but in a different way, is Brad Templeton's satirical compendium on "netiquette", called "Emily Postnews Answers Your Questions on Netiquette", a guide to how NOT to behave on the networks. Available by ftp and on many gophers, this provides some excellent, if disguised, advice for the novice, and some fun for the experienced network navigator.

A listserv called Netiquette: the Mailing List has been

established for people who wish to discuss network etiquette. This is an unmoderated list that is open to all net users.

SECURITY

As is the case with network etiquette, security is an ethical (as well as technical) issue on the Internet, and one that involves everyone. To a great extent, all users share the responsibility for ensuring that the Internet functions smoothly; it is in their own interests to do so. However, just as it is almost impossible to set rules for online behavior, so it is almost impossible to force Internet users to take security into account when they use remote services or when they set up their own services. Security has two facets: the responsibility of information service providers to ensure that their systems are as secure as possible to protect their organization and their users; and the responsibility of users of the systems to act in an ethical way in all their Internet activities. Breaches of security are usually deliberate, though the intent may not always be malicious. However, some breaches are accidental, the result of a combination of inept behavior on the part of users coupled with poor security mechanisms on a system or systems.

In his 1992 book, *The Internet Guide for New Users*, Daniel Dern suggests that Internet security can be categorized by the type of threat to the system and the origin of that threat. Among the threats that he identifies are unauthorized access to data; users assuming the identity of another person (usually though not always with the aim of causing harm); users who deny the transmission of messages that were sent from their site or account; and programs such as viruses that are disguised threats to systems.

In terms of access to data, privacy is an important issue. To ensure that users of a system are who they claim they are, many Internet services require some form of authentication, usually a password. Yet when passwords are transmitted across networks in an unencrypted form, they are vulnerable. This is particularly an issue when passwords guarantee some form of payment or when they are used to access services that are restricted in some way. However, the other side of this issue is that passwords can be used (by system managers and others) to keep track of the password holder's activities and to collect information about system users. While strategies such as encryption help to protect passwords from improper use by others, they do not protect system users from improper collection of data through monitoring of password use on the system. In any effort to improve security, in "real life" as well as online, there is a necessary trade-off between respecting the privacy of the individual and giving power to a system monitor to maintain security for all.

The recent debate in the United States about the "Clipper Chip" (a form of encryption for which the keys would be held by government agencies) reflects this dichotomy. As proposed, the Clipper Chip would ensure the privacy of individuals while giving the agencies the power they claimed they needed in order to suppress criminal activity through the nets. However, public acceptance of the Clipper Chip or similar strategies depends on acceptance of the idea that government agencies will always act in the best interests of the legitimate network users, and this is unlikely to be accepted.

As the Internet has become more popular, so it has become fertile ground for fraud and other activities that are designed to mislead and to cause harm. Cases of business fraud have received the most publicity, with newspaper headlines like "Fraud on the Internet—It's I-Way Robbery" appearing in the major newspapers (Gram, 1994). Financial regulators in Vermont and other states issued warnings in 1994 about the "growing number of scams perpetrated via the Internet and the booming computer bulletin board services" (Gram, 1994, p.46), particularly fraudulent stock and securities offers. In addition, there have been cases of misuse of credit card information that was sent over the Internet to pay for goods or services ordered online, usually the result of security breaches. There have also been cases where Internet users have assumed false identities in order to mislead others, sometimes with criminal intent. While the security risks have been identified in a number of reports (Snell, 1994), there is still a general lack of awareness of the need for security, even in businesses linked to the Internet. An overall lack of experience in dealing with Internet fraud and other types of online crime (such as theft of data) has made the situation more complicated. Internet users need to take reasonable precautions online, just as they have learned to take precautions when on the streets of today's cities and towns, and schoolchildren need to be made aware of the need for sensible online behavior, just as they are taught to cross streets in an appropriately cautious way. They should be taught to check on the veracity of information obtained online, just as other information sources would be checked. They should be told not to give personal information to strangers online, just as they are taught to be wary of strangers in the street. They don't need to be frightened, but they do need to be careful. Like "netiquette", these behaviors should be emphasized as a basis for online activities in schools.

Computer viruses are another security-related issue. Like Internet fraud, they have received a great deal of publicity, yet few people really understand what computer viruses are and how they are transmitted. While some computer viruses have been little more than pranks, others have been malicious, and both types have been known to cause damage to infected computer systems. The best-known episode is that of the "Internet Worm". This was a self-replicating program that was loaded onto the ARPANET section of the Internet in the United States by a graduate student in 1988; it traveled from computer to computer across the country in the space of less than 24 hours via a flaw in a version of a UNIX electronic mail program. Before it was stopped, it infected some 2.000 large computers, slowing them down or causing them to crash. In the process, it became a much-hyped media event (Clough and Mungo, 1992). The Internet Worm caused problems on a large scale, but there have been many lesser instances of people finding that unwelcome computer viruses have been downloaded from an electronic bulletin board or other online source, along with legitimate programs. It is, however, almost impossible that a virus would be downloaded as part of a document or information file. As with fraud, sensible behavior and reasonable precautions will go much of the way to ensuring that viruses will not be a great problem in the school setting, though there is, of course, no ultimate deterrent, short of closing down all computers. Any downloaded software should be checked on a standalone machine with a virus checker before being loaded onto a local area network. All computers in the school should have the current version of a good virus detection program. All school data files should be backed up regularly, and two backup copies should exist at any time, in case there are problems with one backup. And finally, as part of their Internet work, students should be made aware of potential problems and taught to act responsibly.

The United States National Computer Security Association has established a forum on CompuServe (a commercial online information service) to provide information about security measures for all types of computer systems and to provide a forum for discussion of the issues associated with computer security. The discussion is moderated by experts in various aspects of computer security.

GENDER ISSUES

In terms of equity of access to the Internet, women are one of the disadvantaged groups. While estimates of women's participation vary, it seems that, "on many systems, women comprise between 10 and 15 percent of the online population". Online services which place an emphasis on the development of a community (such as the WELL and Seniornet) attract higher numbers of women, although the WELL still has only 15 to 20 percent women members (Hoai-An Truong, 1993). On the other hand, their numbers are much lower on electronic bulletin boards and unsupervised, informal services. So it is that overall estimates of the proportion of women users are usually under ten percent of the total. Other figures quoted in Chapter Five support this. Even on some USENET newsgroups established specifically for the discussion of women's concerns (`alt.feminism` and `soc.women`), the majority of participants are men (Shade, 1993). Groups like LM_NET are exceptions in the online environment. Further, not only are women less likely to be Internet users than men, they are also less likely to find the Internet a hospitable place once they are online, and this can influence their level of participation.

Many different reasons have been suggested for the lower levels of Internet use by women. An important one is clearly economics. In the United States, "on average, women's salaries are 40% lower than men's, leaving women with less disposable income for computers, modems, software, online services and any additional phone charges" (Hoai-An Truong, 1993). More men are likely to be in university, technical, management, or other positions where they have subsidized access to the Internet, and they are also more likely to have educational or technical training to allow them to participate online. Women have a different attitude toward computers from that of men (Kantrowitz, 1994), and they have to be convinced that the Internet will be useful before they are willing to spend time experimenting with its sometimes "impenetrable interface" and arcane procedures. Despite advances in education, "computers are still seen to be boy-stuff across the board, [and] many women are still uncomfortable with them" (DeCandido, 1994).

Once online, many women find the Internet an uncomfortable or even hostile place, especially in the early stages of their participation. They are less well equipped than men to deal with traditions of the net, such as flaming. "Since women tend to use language differently" from men, "these highly aggressive language patterns" may be a considerable barrier (Hoai-An Truong, 1993). Differences in communication styles between men and women often further complicate the issue; the mode of communication typically preferred by women is based on an accommodating and less direct style that is designed to avoid confrontation and arguments (Tannen, 1990). At an even more basic level, new research suggests that there are some fundamental differences in the ways men and women think, that is, there are basic cognitive differences between the sexes (Hinkel, 1992). Taking this further, Valerie Frissen (1992) cites male control of the development of technologies and systems, and particularly information systems, as leading to systems that are not in tune with women's cognitive styles and therefore uncomfortable for them to use.

Although the Internet has been promoted as a "great equalizer, where race, class, gender, sexual preference, and physical appearance make no difference, many women are finding otherwise", says Julie Petersen (1994), who described some instances of sexual harrassment on "the Internet's vast, male dominated network" in an article for *Mother Jones* magazine. Much of this occurs in USENET newsgroups and in live "chat" sessions on IRC (Internet Relay Chat) or in MUDs. "Unfortunately, it seems that the way USENET is set up, women are the zebras, and men are the lions, and the Internet is one big Serenghetti. And that's not right" (Zelek, 1994). And so, "fleeing from the wolves", women are "gravitating towards online services designed especially for them like Women's Wire of San

Francisco and Echo of New York" ("Wolves on the Highway", 1994).

All this calls for some further comment. First, it needs to be stressed that not all men are "wolves on the highway"; very few are, but then, as many writers have pointed out, it only takes a few to make the environment less than attractive. Nor can it be said that all women are uncomfortable with the behavior of those who have been categorized as "wolves". Secondly, the issue has often been discussed, in newspapers and popular magazines, under headlines that are inflammatory and designed to raise the level of anxiety about this new communications medium. Headlines like "Wolves on the Highway", "Neanderthals on the Networks", and "Emailers Stalk Blonds on Campus" add little of substance to the debate, and even obscure the issues for many readers.

It needs to be stressed that the services that are being referred to here are not the type of Internet services that would normally be used in schools, though it is possible that, in an unsupervised setting, children could "wander" into inappropriate groups. From the point of view of schools, a major concern is an indirect one. With fewer women on the networks, and with those who are there participating less than the men in public forums, the Internet will continue to be a place that is less hospitable to girls, and girls will have fewer role models of network-using women to relate to during their school years.

In recent years, several groups or organizations have been formed to address or discuss the issue of gender representation in computing and telecommunications, among them USENET newsgroups and listservs. The SYSTERS listserv for women systems administrators and women in computing was one of the earliest, and it has received some publicity in magazines for working women and in other places. BAWiT (Bay Area Women in Telecommunications) was formed in California by a group of women who work in telecommunications, to discuss women's professional and social issues and computer networking, and "by doing so to advance the state of women who use telecommunications to provide a higher profile for women in the industry, and to encourage women and girls in their exploration of computers". The American Library Association's Feminist Task Force has established a listserv called FEMINIST on the Internet, for the discussion of feminist issues and issues related to women on the networks. Library Women and Technology (LIBWAT-L) is a more recent listserv for people interested in the effect of new technologies on sex roles in the library environment.

INFORMATION SKILLS

According to the American national guidelines for library media programs, published in 1988 as *Information Power,* the mission of the school library should be "to ensure that students ... are effective users of ... information". Guidelines from many other countries also highlight the importance of information skills in the educational process and as essential life skills. For instance, the 1993 Australian document, *Learning for the Future,* prepared for the Australian School Library Association and the Australian Library and Information Association, says that "the ability to process and use information effectively is more than a basic tool for the empowerment of school students; it is in fact the basic survival skill for those who wish to be successful in the 1990s and beyond" (p.1).

It is clear that information skills are now increasingly being seen as the critical skills for life in the information age. They may be discussed in terms of the development of "information literacy", the skills needed "to use information purposefully and effectively" (Todd, Lamb, and McNicholas, 1993, p.20). In today's schools, information skills are often taught cooperatively, as a natural part of the different subjects in the school curriculum, so that the skills are reinforced through ongoing use for appropriate tasks. There are many different schemes for information skills development, and each has its supporters. However, regardless of the scheme, students are usually taught to identify or define a problem, to decide what information is needed to deal with the problem, to decide what sources might provide that information, to locate information in those sources, to analyze and evaluate the information in terms of the problem, to organize and apply it in working on the problem, to present the results in a form that can be readily understood, and to evaluate the effectiveness of the whole sequence of activities and tasks. The process is sometimes referred to as the information process or the enquiry process or the research process. It is just as relevant to the use of the Internet as it is to work involving more traditional information sources.

However, important these skills are, other information skills are also becoming important—in fact, the basis for information skills is undergoing a change. Newer information sources, including the Internet and cable television, which provide more information than anyone could ever come to terms with, underlie this trend. As the "information flood" described by Alvin Toffler in his 1980 book *Future Shock* turns into a deluge, more and more writers are discussing a condition called "information overload". This is a condition that was "rare ... just a few years ago but one that is common today" (Mandel, 1993). People are bombarded with information, whether or not they actively seek it out, and when they do seek it out, they find that they are "drinking from a fire hose". Among the skills needed today are the skills of message handling and information filtering. People need skills for dealing with information overload, for organizing information so that it can be found again when it is needed, for selecting the information sources that they will monitor, and for evaluating information as to whether or not they have an immediate need for it.

To support this, tools are already emerging that can be

used for information filtering and for monitoring information sources. However, "these tools will accelerate a trend toward narrow but intensive information and communications that enhance personal identity" and personal productivity (Mandel, 1993), but possibly at the risk of cutting the individual off from others who have different interests and goals. There are implications in this for education, beyond information skills instruction, particularly in terms of educating "the whole person" as a member of the wider society and not just enhancing the skills of the student as information user or consumer.

FUTURE DEVELOPMENTS

This book was written at a time when the Internet was undergoing great change, and it remains unclear just which direction future developments will take. In 1993 and 1994, millions of new users had joined the Internet, and many thousands of new information providers had made databases and services available. Each month, the Internet reaches into more and more countries, though people in those countries may not enjoy access to the full range of tools and services. New software tools like Mosaic and Netscape have made the Internet a more user-friendly environment (Taylor, 1994), but at a cost: users need more sophisticated computers to use this kind of software, and its use consumes more Internet bandwidth. Whereas once the Internet was based on electronic mail and text or data files, it now supports the dissemination of information in multimedia formats, including sound, still and moving images, and broadcast radio and video programming. Undoubtedly, all these trends will continue to influence the development of the net in the immediate future.

In other areas, though, the trends are much less clear, and there is considerable disagreement about the future of the Internet. While some commentators predict a virtual "global village" comprising interlinked communities based on shared interests and concerns, others foresee "a global mall owned and controlled by corporations who are largely unaccountable to the nation-states in which they operate" (Open Magazine..., 1994). Privatization and commercialization of the Internet are viewed by some people with anticipation, as developments that will lead to new opportunities and new services. For others, these ideas represent a threat to current "net culture" and raise questions of control of information and barriers to the free flow of ideas.

It is already obvious, in countries like Australia, Canada, and the United States, that the present situation will not continue, and that at least some change is inevitable. It is clear that congestion on some parts of the network is already a problem in some places and on some links. This congestion is a result of increasing usage of network services, a more diverse range of applications and tools, and multimedia databases and services which make much greater bandwidth demands. Congestion is also due to the increasing presence on the networks of commercial information providers who require fast "turnaround" of messages and data. The wellknown University of Michigan economist Hal Varian has predicted that the Internet is likely to face some kind of usage-based pricing structure in the future (Love, 1994) largely because of the new demands being made on the Internet. It is argued that no government can possibly commit unlimited funds to support a network that continues to grow exponentially and which is used by an increasingly diverse population that has already extended well beyond the academic and research population for whose use the networks were originally funded.

Although only a little more than half of all Internet traffic now passes through the Internet backbone in the United States, the United States Internet structures remain critically important for the development of the Internet worldwide. Thus a document issued by United States

President Bill Clinton's administration late in 1993, *The National Information Infrastructure: Agenda for Action*, has aroused considerable interest in other countries. Already, some proposals outlined in this document have passed into legislation, while other aspects of the document are under consideration in relation to various bills before the United States Congress or Senate.

It is obvious that information services in schools will be affected by the outcome of the current discussions about the future of the Internet and by legislative activity. However, the directions that developments will take remain unclear, and the sometimes superficial presentation of the issues in the popular media has not helped to create an informed climate of opinion. Some of the professional associations in the fields of librarianship and education have been taking steps to ensure that their members are aware of developments and issues, since any developments related to the Internet are likely to affect libraries and information services. The American Library Association's Washington Office Newsletter, ALAWON, distributed electronically on the Internet, has been an important source of up-to-date information on developments related to the National Information Infrastructure. Other organizations, such as the Electronic Frontier Foundation, have been attempting to publicize the issues through the traditional media and through electronic publications on the Internet itself.

REFERENCES

Abilock, Debbie (1994), NuevaNet Acceptable Use Policy and Contract, Document posted to the LM_NET listserv on the Internet, 6 May.

American Library Association (1990), Access to Resources and Services in the School Library Media Program, An Interpretation of the Library Bill of Rights, American Library Association, Chicago.

American Library Association (1991), Free Access to Libraries for Minors, An Interpretation of the Library Bill of Rights, American Library Association, Chicago.

Astbrink, Gunela (1994), "Will people with disabilities be riding the 'information highway' or be left on a side street?", *Link-Up*, September, pp.7–10.

Australian School Library Association and Australian Library and Information Association (1993), *Learning for the Future: Developing Information Services in Australian Schools*, Curriculum Corporation, Melbourne.

Bielfeldt, Talbot (1994), "Towards a manual of online style", *TIE (Telecommunications in Education) News* 5, no. 3, Spring,pp.27–29.

BITNET Network Information Center (1993a), Corporation for Research and Educational Networking (CREN), Acceptable Use Policy, 1 January.

BITNET Network Information Center (1993b), Why the Need for Appropriate Policies on Internet Use, Electronic mail message, 23 February.

Brin, David (1994), "The good and the bad: outlines of tomorrow", *Information Technology and Libraries*, March, pp.53–61.

Brzovic, Alice (1994), Electronic Mail Etiquette, Electronic mail message (article originally published in *Berkeley Computing and Communications* 3, no. 6, September).

Cisler, Steve (1993), Community Computer Networks: Building Electronic Greenbelts, File available from `ftp.apple.com` in the `/ftp /alug/communer` directory.

Chuq Von Rospach (1993), A Primer on How to Work With the USENET Community, Document posted to the EDTECH listserv on the Internet, 18 June.

Clough, Bryan and Mungo, Paul (1992), *Approaching Zero: Data Crime and the Computer Underworld*, Faber and Faber, London.

Collins, Stephen E. (1994), Student Use of Library Modem, Message posted to the LM_NET listserv on the Internet, 14 August.

Copley, Tom (ed.)(1993), In This Issue, in Telelearning Network Synthesizer (electronic journal on the Internet), 2, 16 December.

DeCandido, GraceAnne (1994), PUBLIB Interview, Document posted to the PUBLIB listserv on the Internet, 20 March.

Dern, Daniel (1992), *The Internet Guide for New Users*, McGraw-Hill, New York.

Drinking From a Fire Hose: Managing Networked Information (1993), 7th Biennial VALA Conference and Exhibition, Melbourne Hilton on the Park, 9–11 November, Conference announcement posted to listservs on the Internet, November.

Ebbs, Geoffrey (1994), "A case for censorship", *The Australian*, 21 June, p.33.

Eisenberg, Michael and Milbury, Peter (1994), LM_NET Network Etiquette, Message posted to the LM_NET listserv on the Internet, 18

March.

Frenkel, Karen A. (1990), "Women and computing", *Communications of the ACM* 33, no. 1, November, pp.34–47. (Copy available on the gopher of the Ontario Institute for Studies in Education OISE, 22 February 1994).

Frissen, Valerie (1992), "Trapped in electronic cages? Gender and new information technologies in the public and private domain: an overview of research", *Media, Culture and Society*, January, pp.31–49.

Gendron, Mark (1994), Traffic Control Threatens the Info Highway, Article posted to the Net-Happenings listserv on the Internet, 20 April (originally published in *The Vancouver Sun*, 1 April 1994, p.D17).

Godin, Seth (1993), *The Smiley Dictionary*, Peachpit Press, Berkeley, California.

Gram, David (1994), "Fraud on the Internet—it's I-way robbery", *The Australian*, 5 July, p.46.

Hinkel, Susan R. (1992), Technology and Gender, Document available on the gopher of the Ontario Institute for Studies in Education, 22 February 1994. (Paper excerpted from *New Tech News*, The Council of Wisconsin Libraries, 1992).

Hoai-An Truong (1993), Gender Issues in Online Communications, Document available on the gopher of the Ontario Institute for Studies in Education, February 1994.

The Internet as Commons (1994), in The Network Observer (electronic journal on the Internet) 1, no. 3, March.

Internet Society (1994), ISOC Proceedings on Conduct Code Underway, Media Advisory, Prague, 17 June, Document posted to the Net-Happenings listserv on the Internet, 20 June.

ISnet (1994), ISnet Acceptable Use Policy, Document available on the University of Iceland gopher, [undated].

Johnson, Doug (1994), Signatures, Message posted to the LM_NET listserv on the Internet, 22 February.

Kantrowitz, Barbara (1994), "Men, women, and computers", *Newsweek*, 16 May, pp.36–43.

Kapor, Mitch (1994), Universal Access Compared to What?, in EDUPAGE (electronic newsletter on the Internet), 4 August (quoted from *Technology Review*, August/September 1994, p.42).

LaQuey, Tracey and Ryer, Jeanne C. (1992), The Internet Companion: A Beginner's Guide to Global Networking, The Online Bookstore Edition, Document downloaded from the Internet, 21 June 1993.

Love, James (1994), Notes on Professor Hal Varian's April 21 Talk on Internet Economics, Document posted to the TAP-INFO listserv on the Internet, 3 May.

Mandel, Thomas F. (1993), Surfing the Wild Internet, Scan No. 2109, SRI International Business Intelligence Program, Document available on the Ontario Institute for Studies in Education (OISE) gopher on the Internet.

Minnesota Coalition Against Censorship (1994), Minnesota Public School Internet Policy, Document posted to the LM_NET listserv on the Internet, 25 August.

Minnesota Coalition Against Censorship (1994), Internet Statement, Document posted to the LM_NET listserv on the Internet, 26 August.

The National Information Infrastructure: Agenda for Action (1993), Document available on the NYSERNet gopher on the Internet.

November, Alan and Thornburg, David (1994), "Will the superhighway really change schools?", *Electronic Learning,* May/June, pp.24–25, 94.

Open Magazine Interviews Herbert Schiller, The Information Superhighway: Paving Over the Public (1994), Document posted to the Net-Happenings listserv on the Internet, 30 March (originally published in Z *Magazine,* March 1994).

Palme, Jacob (1993), Legal and Ethical Aspects of Computer-Mediated Communication, in The Electronic Journal of Virtual Culture (electronic journal on the Internet) 1, no. 4, 30 June.

Petersen, Julie (1994), Sex and the Cybergirl, in Mother Jones (electronic journal on the Internet), May/June.

Phillips, Gerald M. (1994), A Nightmare Scenario: Literacy and Technology, in IPCT Interpersonal Computing and Technology: An Electronic Journal for the 21st Century (electronic journal on the Internet) 2, no. 2, April, pp.50–73.

Polly, Jean Armour (1992), Surfing the Internet, Document downloaded from the Empire Schoolhouse gopher on the Internet, 28 November 1993.

Resta, Paul, Bowman, Sally, Hunter, Bill, Stout, Connie, and Weitzner, Daniel (1993), Telecommunications and Ethics Panel, Proceedings of the Tel*Ed'93 Global Connections Conference (available on the CoSN gopher on the Internet).

Reynolds, Dennis J. (ed.)(1991), *Citizen Rights and Access to Electronic Information, A Collection of Background Essays Prepared for the 1991 LITA President's Program,* Library and Information Technology Association, Chicago (an information packet distributed at the 1991 American Library Association Conference in Atlanta, Georgia, and available on the American Library Association gopher on the Internet).

Rheingold, Howard (1993), PUBLIB Interview, Document posted to the

PUBLIB listserv on the Internet, 14 September.

Rheingold, Howard (1994), Internet Censorship, Article reposted to the PUBLIB listserv on the Internet from the WELL, 25 April (published in the *San Francisco Examiner*, 5 April 1994, and in *The Australian*, 21 June 1994, p.32).

Rinaldi, Arlene (1994), The Net: User Guidelines and Etiquette, Florida Atlantic University, Document available via ftp (URL: `ftp://ftp.lib.berkeley.edu/pub/net.training/FAU/netiquette.txt`).

Robotham, Julie (1994), "Code of practice for e-mail users after court case", *The Australian*, 23 August, p.24.

Ross, Seth (1994), NEW: Netiquette—The Network Etiquette Mailing List, Message posted to the Net-Happenings listserv on the Internet, 12 June.

Schneider, Karen G. (1994), The Poor Will Always Be With Us, Message posted to the PUBLIB and Net-Happenings listservs on the Internet, 27 March.

Shade, Leslie Regan (1993), Review, "Women, Information Technology, and Scholarship", in The Electronic Journal on Virtual Culture (electronic journal on the Internet) 1, no. 6, September 27.

Shapiro, Norman, et al.(1985), Towards an Ethics and Etiquette for Electronic Mail, (Publication R-3283-NSF/RC), Rand Corporation, Santa Monica, California.

Shea, Virginia (1994), *Netiquette*, Albion Books, San Francisco.

Snell, Monica (1994), "Security not a big worry for business", *The Australian*, 5 July, p. 22.

Stoll, Clifford (1989), *The Cuckoo's Egg*, Doubleday, New York.

Tannen, Deborah (1990), *You Just Don't Understand*, Ballantine, New York.

Taylor, Jeanie, Kramarae, Cheris, and Ebben, Maureen (ed.) (1993), *Women, Information Technology, and Scholarship*, The Center for Advanced Study, University of Illinois, Urbana, Illinois.

Taylor, Roger (1994), "Brave new Internet", *Internet World*, September, pp.36–42.

Templeton, Brad (1993), Dear Emily Postnews, Emily Postnews Answers Your Questions on Netiquette, Document posted to the EDTECH listserv on the Internet by Noel Estabrook, 18 June.

Todd, Ross, Lamb, Liz, and McNicholas, Celeste (1993), "The power of information literacy: unity of education and resources for the 21st century", in *Towards the 21st Century: Books and Media for the Millenium, Selected Papers from the 21st Annual Conference of the International*

Association of School Librarianship, Belfast, Northern Ireland, 1992, International Association of School Librarianship, Kalamazoo, Michigan, pp.19–34.

Toffler, Alvin (1980), *Future Shock,* Bantam, New York.

Wajcman, J. (1991), *Feminism Confronts Technology,* The Pennsylvania State University Press, University Park, Pennsylvania.

"Wolves on the highway" (1994), EDUPAGE, (electronic newsletter on the Internet), 20 March (extracted from *Wall Street Journal,* 18 March 1994, p.B1).

Zelek, Chris (1994), Paw Prints, in Refractions (weekly electronic magazine on the Internet) 1, no. 6, 15 June.

APPENDIX ONE

GLOSSARY

This glossary provides explanations for basic Internet terminology. It covers most of the Internet-related terms used in this book, or terms that are likely to be needed by school library personnel who use the Internet. It is arranged in alphabetical order, with cross references.

For more detailed information, or for explanations of terms not included in this glossary, readers are advised to consult a specialized Internet glossary, such as the "Glossary of Terms" available on the gopher of the Ontario Institute for Studies in Education (OISE) in Canada or the following:
Malkin, G. and Parker, T. LaQuey (eds)(1993), Internet Users' Glossary. (Available by ftp from `nic.merit.edu` as `/documents/fyi/fyi_18.txt`).

AARNet. Australian Academic and Research Network. A network linking universities and research organizations in Australia and connected to the Internet.
Address. This may mean the unique Internet address of a host computer, or the email address of an Internet user. In either case, the address will be given in a standard format, consisting of a number of "domains" separated by punctuation or symbols. The first part of the address is the user ID; the second is usually the name of the node or host on which the person has his or her Internet account, followed by abbreviations for the name of the institution, the type

of institution, and the state and/or country. Thus, the author's email address, `anne@rhi.hi.is`, indicates that her user ID is simply "anne", her node on the Internet is Reiknistofnun Háskólans (rhi, the Computer Centre of the University of Iceland), at Háskóli Íslands (hi, the University of Iceland), in Iceland (is, the top-level domain abbreviation for Iceland). Many Internet addresses are a great deal more complicated than this, especially when a person has access via a special account on a secondary network connected to the Internet. Always type addresses exactly as they appear, complete with symbols like @, %, {}, and so forth.

American Standard Code for Information Interchange. See ASCII.

Anonymous Ftp. See Ftp.

Archie. An Internet search tool that allows users to search for information located at remote sites where files are made available via anonymous ftp. It is essentially an archive or storage service that keeps a record of the contents of hundreds of ftp sites worldwide. Users may need to telnet or gopher to a computer that has Archie facilities in order to use it.

ARPANET. Advanced Research Projects Agency NETwork. The ARPA network was created by the United States Department of Defense in the late 1960s and early 1970s, and it represents the genesis of the Internet.

ASCII. American Standard Code for Information Interchange. A standard method of representing text, including letters of the alphabet, numbers, and symbols, as a numeric code. This makes it possible for documents to be transferred easily between computer systems.

Backbone. A set of high-speed data connections within a wider network that connects the smaller and slower networks.

Bbs. See Electronic Bulletin Board.

BITNET. The name is said to stand for "Because It's Time Network". BITNET is an educational network based in the

United States, that links universities, research organizations, and other institutions. It began in 1981 as a connection between CUNY (New York) and Yale and expanded rapidly. A BITNET address consists of a username followed by the @ symbol and a host name (the name of the computer through which the user enters the network), for example, LM_NET@SUVM. BITNET users can be reached from the Internet by adding .BITNET to the BITNET address, for instance, LM_NET@SUVM.BITNET.

Bulletin Board System. See Electronic Bulletin Board.

Campus Wide Information System. See CWIS.

CA*NET. The Canadian Academic Network, a national research and education network linked to the Internet.

CANARIE. A project for the development of an advanced national research and education network for Canada.

Cello. Software that allows users of IBM PC computers or compatibles with Windows to browse the Internet through World Wide Web. It was developed at Cornell University.

Chimera. Chimera is a World Wide Web browser for IBM PC and compatible computers running XWindows.

Client. A program on a user's computer that is used to access services on a remote computer. Client/server system "architecture" splits up the functions of accessing remote services into those handled by the "server" (the computer that provides the information) and those handled by the "client" (the computer where the information is being displayed and used). So, for instance, a "gopher server" provides information in a structured format, while a "gopher client" allows the user to search for information in various ways, and to load that information into his or her own computer. **See also Server.**

Community Freenet. See Freenet.

Computer Conferencing. An online "meeting" of a group of people, to discuss a particular topic. Input is usually via the keyboard, and all members of the conference can contribute and respond.

Consortium for School Networking (CoSN). A consortium formed in 1991 by representatives from forty institutions and state education departments in the United States to foster the use of computer networks in elementary and secondary schools. The address is PO Box 65192, Washington, DC 20035, USA.

CoSN. See Consortium for School Networking.

CWIS. Campus Wide Information System. A system for disseminating news, announcements, directories, and other information, including library catalogues and files, to a university or college community. Such systems are often based on gopher software. **See also Gopher.**

Cyberspace. A term popularized by William Gibson in a series of novels that began with *Neuromancer,* it has come to mean the world of the Internet, the electronic universe that parallels the real, physical world.

Domain. A part of an electronic mail address; each address consists of several domains, separated by full stops (periods), and arranged in hierarchical sequence. The top level domain in most addresses is the two-letter country abbreviation; in older United States addresses, the final domain may represent the type of organization.

Downloading. Transferring files or documents from a remote computer to the user's own computer, so that they can be read, or manipulated in a variety of ways (for example, with a word processor or desktop publishing program).

DUM. See MUD.

EARN. European Academic Research Network. The European equivalent of BITNET, a network linking universities and research organisations.

ECHO. European Commission Host Organisation. ECHO is the host through which the databases of the European Commission are made publicly available for searching via the Internet or via modem. ECHO provides the management and computing infrastructure. It is based in Luxembourg.

Electronic Books. The full text of books, available as files on the Internet, for searching, reading, or downloading.

Electronic Bulletin Board. Sometimes called a bbs or bulletin board system. A computer with special bulletin board software and dial-in facilities, set up to provide information and electronic messaging services. Some electronic bulletin boards are very small and set up by hobbyists; others are set up by organizations and companies to provide serious information services. Some electronic bulletin boards can be used only by paying members; others allow public access.

Electronic Journal. Normally a periodical or magazine that is delivered to the subscriber by electronic mail, either as a complete file or as a Table of Contents. If the latter, then the articles themselves are available via email or ftp. Some electronic journals now include graphics, and special client software may be required in order to read them on the screen. Some electronic journals are now made available via gopher or World Wide Web, either in addition to, or in place of, an electronic mail version. See Chapter Two for further information.

Electronic Mail. See Email.

ELM. An electronic mail system, used on UNIX computers, for sending, receiving, and managing electronic mail.

Email (E-mail). Electronic mail; originally messaging between computers but now the basis of many Internet interactions between individuals and organizations or groups. Electronic mail messages can be sent to one person or to a group of people. Specialized electronic mail software provides the basis for messaging, and the many different software packages provide different facilities, though all will cover the basics of Internet mail. See Chapter Two for further information.

Encryption. A method of protecting computer data by "encrypting" or coding it for transfer between computers.

Ethernet. Network hardware and software used for LANs

(local area networks) within and between organizations. Ethernet will support a wide variety of computers, and the components are widely available from many commercial sources internationally.

EUDORA. Electronic mail software for Macintosh and other personal computers. EUDORA provides a graphical user interface for Internet email, with pull-down menus and a range of features, including the capability to transfer different kinds of files as attachments to email messages.

European Academic Research Network. See EARN.

European Commission Host Organisation. See ECHO.

FAQ. Frequently Asked Questions. A file maintained by a USENET newsgroup or members of a listserv and posted regularly to the group. The FAQ contains a list of those questions that are most often asked by new members, along with the answers. This means that established members of the group do not have to answer the same questions again and again as each new member joins, and the ongoing discussion is not interrupted by the same questions. The FAQ document of a group, when compiled with care, can be an important source of current information about the topic of the newsgroup or the listserv; it can come to represent the collective wisdom of a group. Some FAQ documents are carefully produced, with references, and some are even indexed. New members of any group should read the FAQ document if one is available.

Fetch. A program for the Apple Macintosh that provides an easy-to-use front end for file transfer protocol (ftp) and simplifies the downloading of files and programs from remote computers.

FidoNet. An international network of computers that uses the FIDO dial-up protocol, a "store and forward" system. This means that permanent links are not required to maintain a large and geographically dispersed network. Using the telephone lines, the FidoNet computers communicate automatically at set times, transferring the information that has been loaded into the system between connections.

FidoNet provides cheap and effective network access for schools.

File Server. A computer that provides linking services for a network, stores files, and provides network users with access to those files.

File Transfer Protocol. See Ftp.

Finger. This Internet command has several uses. It allows the user to see who is currently logged in on his or her own host. On many systems, it can also be used to see who is logged in on a remote computer. Finger can also be used as a tool for information provision; it can be set up in such a way that people who "finger" a computer using a particular command extension receive current information.

Flame. An electronic mail message, USENET newsgroup posting, or listserv posting that is insulting, unnecessarily argumentative, irrational, obscene, or inflammatory. Where good sense, courtesy, and considerations of "netiquette" prevail, "flame wars" can be avoided, and life on the net is more pleasant for all concerned.

Freenet (Free-Net). Sometimes called community freenets, these are public access computer services, usually established in a city or local area by volunteers, with the support of local groups and organizations, usually including libraries, community centers, colleges, schools, businesses. They provide local and other information, email services, access to other information services, and access to the Internet. See Chapter Two for further information.

Frequently Asked Questions. See FAQ.

Ftp. File Transfer Protocol. This standardized set of rules and procedures allows an Internet user to transfer files, in a variety of formats, from a remote computer (or host) to his or her own computer. This can be done even when the two computers are of different types and have different operating systems. Some hosts provide "anonymous" ftp facilities—that is, anyone can log in, using the username "anonymous", and access the files. See Chapter Two for further information.

Ftpmail. A system that enables Internet users who do not have ftp capability to get files from ftp sites via email. The user sends a standard, four-line request message to an ftpmail service (a computer), and the requested file arrives as an email document. The service may take from a few minutes to a couple of days, depending on the number of jobs being handled by the ftpmail service.

Gateway. A computer connection between two or more computer networks, so that communication across the networks is possible, and files and applications can be used across the networks (even when the computers are of different types, and use different systems and protocols).

.GIF. Graphics Interchange Format. A standard format for storing and transferring graphics files on the Internet. .GIF is the file name extension for files in GIF format.

Gigabyte. Used as a measure of computer storage or the amount of traffic over a network.

GINA. Graphical Interface for Network Access. Designed for educators, and particularly for people in K-12 schools, this software package provides people who have an Internet connection with access to electronic mail, computer conferencing, electronic bulletin boards, library catalogs, and other information resources through a common interface. It is especially useful in settings where a school or individual user has dial-up (modem) access to the Internet through a SLIP connection; the SLIP software is an integral component of the package. GINA is available for both the Macintosh and Windows environments. The California Technology Project offers full support within California. GINA is marketed in California; outside California, GINA is available without support. Contact The California Technology Project, PO Box 1842, Seal Beach, CA 90740-7842, USA.

Gopher. Software that allows information providers to set up menu-based information systems ("gophers") and to link them to other information providers on the Internet. The software was developed on the client/server model, and so a gopher client enables the user to search for information on gophers worldwide, and to transfer that information to his or her own computer. See Chapter Two for further information.

Graphical User Interface (GUI). Screen displays based on icons, images, graphics of any kind rather than just alphabetic and numeric characters.

Graphics Interchange Format. See .GIF.

GUI. See Graphical User Interface.

Hacker. A person who uses his or her knowledge of computers and telecommunications networks to gain access to computers, or sections of computers, that are not normally available for public use. Some authors have made a distinction between "hackers", people who just like the challenge of getting into an unfamiliar computer and who usually do no damage, and "crackers", people who gain entry to computers with criminal intentions or who maliciously cause damage to the computers or the data on them. In many countries now, the activities of both groups are illegal.

Header. The first section of an electronic mail message, containing information about the sender, the receiver, the subject or topic of the message, the date, the delivery path, and other information about the origin or delivery of the message. Much of this information is inserted by the electronic mail system on the host computer or the receiving computer.

Host. The computer through which users access the Internet on which they have their own Internet email address. This may be a computer on a university campus, or a computer service provided by a commercial service, or a service provided by a freenet, or any one of a number of other options. Host computers provide user accounts, files, and resources.

HTML. HyperText Markup Language. A set of commands or "syntax" through which text is "described" or marked up for presentation as a hypertext document on World Wide Web on the Internet. It is used by presenters of information on World Wide Web; an understanding of it is not needed by those who will only be using the information. **See also Hypertext.**

HTTP. HyperText Transfer Protocol. This is a way (but not the only way) of retrieving documents from a World Wide Web server.

Hypertext. A database, usually incorporating a range of information formats, which contains links between all parts of the database, based on key words or other features.

HyperText Markup Language. See HTML.

HyperText Transfer Protocol. See HTTP.

Hytelnet. A hypertext-based program that gives users of IBM PCs or compatibles access to a wide range of resources on the Internet, including library catalogs, freenets, gophers, electronic bulletin boards, WAIS, and others. It can work with a dial-up connection via modem to an account that has telnet access to the Internet, or as a link for users of computers on an Ethernet LAN that has telnet access. The program is available by anonymous ftp from sites on the Internet.

Infobot. An information server that responds to electronic mail messages with information in a return electronic mail message. The information supplied usually depends on the format of the message sent, or the format of the address used. For example, *Wired* magazine has an infobot that provides access information in response to a "help" message sent to `infobot@wired.com`

Interface. The means by which users interact with a computer, and the "front end" that the computer presents to the user.

Internet Protocol. See IP Number and **TCP/IP.**

Internet Relay Chat (IRC). This Internet tool enables two users at locations remote from each other to "talk" via the keyboard when both are logged on at the same time.

InterNIC. InterNIC Information Services is a five-year project sponsored by the United States National Science Foundation with the support of General Atomics, AT&T,

and Network Solutions Incorporated. InterNIC maintains an online database about the Internet that is available via telnet, ftp, gopher, WAIS, and electronic mail. InterNIC can be contacted by email at `info@is.internic.net` or by mail at InterNIC Information Services, PO Box 85608, San Diego, CA 92186-9784, USA.

IP Number. Internet Protocol provides for a system of addresses for computers on the Internet; it provides routing information for mail and other services. The IP number of a computer is a unique number that describes the location of a computer on the network. It consists of digits separated by dots, in a prescribed pattern; for example, the IP number of the LC MARVEL computer is `140.147.2.69` **See also TCP/IP.**

IRC. See Internet Relay Chat.

Jughead. This is an Internet search tool with the same interface as VERONICA. It allows users to search for subdirectories or documents that have the required keywords in their names. It presents the user with a list of directories, from which a choice can then be made. Many gophers now have Jughead search facilities as an option.

Knowbot. A program, or "intelligent agent", that collects information from the Internet according to certain directions from the user.

LAN. Local Area Network. The hardware and software that link computers and peripherals such as printers and scanners, within an organization or between close organizations.

Leased Line. A permanent connection provided by the telephone company to link two or more locations. This is an alternative to a modem connection via the standard telephone lines. Normally, a flat fee per month is paid for the leased line, regardless of the amount of traffic over it. Leased lines are generally used where high-speed data communications are important or where large amounts of data are being transferred.

LISTGopher. This is a program that facilitates searching and retrieval of information from listserv archives that are accessible through gopher. The program is available on the Internet; the URL is `gopher://dewey.lib.ncsu.edu:70/11/library/disciplines/library/listgopher`

Listserv. An Internet or BITNET discussion group based on email. Subscribers to a list send email messages to the computer on which the mailing list of subscribers is maintained, and the messages are distributed to all members of the list. Some listservs have simple structures and involve nothing more than the posting of messages for all members to read and usually to respond to. However, others may have any of a range of added features, including an archive of all messages posted to the listserv, a "digest" feature that collects a number of messages into larger postings, links to other listservs, a newsletter, an orientation for new subscribers. Most listservs are free; a few require the payment of a fee. See Chapter Two for further information.

Local Area Network. See LAN.

Lurker. A person who reads listserv messages, but does not take any part in the discussions.

Lynx. A World Wide Web browser program for UNIX and other computers. Lynx is text-based; it does not provide for display of graphics or other Web features.

MicroMUSE. An interactive environment on a computer on the Internet, where users can build virtual communities.

Minuet. A suite of programs for the IBM PC and compatibles, the Minnesota INternet User's Essential Tool (Minuet) provides for POPmail, gopher, telnet, ftp, newsgroup reader, finger, and other tools. Its precursor was POPmail/PC.

MIME. Multipurpose Internet Mail Extensions. A standard for encoding data in different formats (such as text, sound, images, moving pictures) into an electronic mail message. When information is provided about electronic mail software, there will usually be a statement about whether or not MIME is supported.

Modem. A hardware device that allows anyone with a personal computer to communicate via the telephone lines and to access online databases and services. Communications software is also required.

Moderator. The moderator of a listserv (when there is one) performs a function similar to that of the moderator of a meeting. The moderator scans messages before they are posted to the listserv to ensure that they really do cover matters that are of concern to the listserv members, welcomes new members, introduces topics for discussion, and attempts to focus discussion that has bogged down or strayed from the track. Depending on the listserv, the moderator may have other functions as well.

MOO. MOO is a programming environment that allows operators and users to create virtual worlds for a range of purposes, from fantasy games to professional collaboration. There are public MOOs that anyone can join, and private MOOs that people can join only with the permission of the system administrator.

Mosaic. Software that allows users of IBM PC or compatible computers with Windows to browse the Internet through a graphical user interface. There is also a version of Mosaic for the Macintosh. Strictly speaking, Mosaic is a World Wide Web browser; it enables users to move through information on World Wide Web servers on the Internet, to search the information in a variety of ways, and to retrieve the information easily. Information retrieved can be in many forms, including text, graphics, and sound. **See also Netscape.**

MUD. "Multiple-User Dialogue" or "Multi-User Dungeon" or "Multi User Dimension" or what you will. A MUD usually allows a user to assume an identity and enter into a fantasy world as part of an ongoing story or simulation. Many people (even hundreds), from different geographical locations, may be participating at any one time. Sometimes the MUD is based on a book, such as the classic children's series about Narnia, or *The Wizard of Oz,* or *Hitchhiker's Guide to the Galaxy.* Some are based on the Dungeons and Dragons fantasy role playing games. The fact that a MUD has a name that appears to resemble the title of a children's book does not necessarily make it suitable for children, and some MUDs, especially those with violent and/or explicit sexual content, are not suitable for children. There are MUDs that are forums for conversation rather than for fantasy/role playing; some MUDs are educational; there are even MUDs that are social experiments, developed with the aim of creating a better world. **See also MOO** and **MUSE.**

Multipurpose Electronic Mail Extensions. See MIME.

MUSE. Multi User Simulation Environment. These are similar to, and often indistinguishable from, MUDs and MOO. **See also MUD** and **MOO.**

MUSH. See MUD.

National Information Infrastructure. See NII.

National Research and Education Network. See NREN.

National Science Foundation Network. See NSFNet.

Netiquette. Appropriate behavior (etiquette) for network users. Guides to "netiquette" have been compiled, but netiquette really amounts to having consideration for other users and behaving in such a way that other users are not insulted and do not have their rights infringed. "Netiquette" is made more necessary because of the international scale of the Internet and the different cultural and linguistic backgrounds from which "netters" come.

Netscape. A later version of the Mosaic software for Macintosh and IBM PC or compatible computers. Netscape is an Internet browser that provides access to the World Wide Web. It incorporates facilities for accessing sound files and still and moving images as well as text. **See also Mosaic.**

Network. Computers that are linked to provide communications facilities between them, and to share resources, such as software and printers. There are two main types of networks: LANs (Local Area Networks) that link computers and peripherals within an organization or between close organizations; and WANs (Wide Area Networks) that link machines a long way apart—even in different countries.

Network News. See USENET.

Newbie. The Internet term for a person who is new to the networks. When that person flounders around cyberspace making mistakes and asking "stupid questions" that have been asked many times before, then he or she is a "clueless newbie". On listservs and newsgroups, clueless newbies are often told, by irate net citizens, to "read the FAQ" or to "RTFM" (read the, er, manual). Thus do newbies gain their net.experience and learn the conventions of cyberspace.

Newsgroup Reader. A program for reading (and replying to) the messages posted to USENET newsgroups. **See also USENET.**

Newsgroups. See USENET.

NII (National Information Infrastructure). The name adopted to describe a range of policy, legislation, and other developments in the United States related to telecommunications and information networks, including the Internet.

NREN (National Research and Education Network). A term adopted in the United States for initiatives in information networking that incorporate the existing Internet. The NREN was still being discussed and defined as this book went to press.

NSFNet (National Science Foundation Network). A network established in the United States in 1986, based on five super-computer centers. This enabled an enormous growth in the number of network connections, especially from universities, and was partly responsible for the growth of the Internet at that time.

Ping. Ping is a command that allows the user of one system on the Internet to check to see if another system is currently operational.

Point to Point Protocol. See PPP.

POPMail. An electronic mail standard; an abbreviation for "Post Office Protocol Mail".

PPP. Point to Point Protocol. Like SLIP, this serial connection allows a computer on a dial-up line (using a modem) to connect with an Internet host computer using TCP/IP via a server on the host.

Protocol. A set of rules that govern the transmission of data between computers; a set of rules or procedures that must be followed to carry out a particular operation.

Read News. See RN.

RN (Read News). Software that allows users to access the USENET newsgroups on the Internet.

Router. A computer that controls the forwarding of traffic from network to network.

Samba. A World Wide Web browser for users of Apple Macintosh computers.

Serial Line Interface Protocol. See SLIP.

Server. A program that is the basis for providing information from databases or files; a "server" provides the information, while a "client" on the user's computer allows the user to request information and to use it. The "client" and the "server" are both necessary parts of the system for making information available to users. **See also Client.**

Signature. Many electronic mail software packages allow the user to create a "signature" that will appear automatically on every email message sent by that user. Signatures usually include the person's name, address, email address, and perhaps other contact information like telephone number and fax number. Some signatures incorporate graphics and/or a quotation or wise saying of some kind. "Netiquette" suggests that signatures should be kept brief (they take up space in the receiver's mailbox), while including any necessary contact information.

SLIP. Serial Line Interface Protocol. This allows computers on a dial-up line (using a modem) to connect with Internet host computers using TCP/IP, via a SLIP server on the host computer. Not all host sites support this. If a site does allow it, the user's name and password must be added to the SLIP server database of the host, and the user must run SLIP software on the microcomputer as well. Once these tools are operational, the user can run Mosaic, Cello, Fetch, gopher, or other Internet software, as long as the modem can support transmission at reasonable speeds (around 9600 baud and up).

Smiley. In the text-based environment of Internet email, it is difficult to convey emotions and feelings, without typing a lot of words. To get around this, the "smiley" has come into use, as a shorthand way of representing the sender's feelings or mood. The standard smiley :-) is now wellknown, but there are many others.

Sysop. System operator. The person who sets up and manages an electronic bulletin board or online information service.

TCP/IP. Transmission Control Protocol/Internet Protocol. This is the standard protocol or set of rules for transmitting data on the Internet. Computers connected to the Internet need to be able to use this protocol. It will be transparent to Internet users.

Telnet. This "terminal emulation" software allows Internet users to connect to remote computers, and to log in and use files and facilities. Telnet has also become a verb: Internet users "telnet" to remote sites to find information or use services.

Terabyte. Used as a measure of the amount of traffic over a network. A terabyte is the equivalent of 1,000 gigabytes of data.

TurboGopher. Gopher "client" software for Macintosh computers. TurboGopher provides a graphical interface for those accessing the Internet via gopher.

Uniform Resource Locator. See URL.

UNIX. The operating system used by many of the computers on the Internet. The chances are that any host computer that a user links to from their microcomputer to access the Internet will have a UNIX operating system. UNIX is not very user-friendly—hence, in part, the growing number of books that attempt to explain the Internet to new users.

Upload. Transferring files from a local computer to another computer, either via a network, or via a modem and the telephone lines.

URL (Uniform Resource Locator). This is a draft standard for identifying "objects" on the Internet; these objects could include documents, files, computer programs, computers, gophers, USENET newsgroups, electronic bulletin boards, or any other resources. A URL is the equivalent of an address for resources and documents on the World Wide Web. It is always presented in a standard form, and includes the address of the computer on which the information or document is stored. See the discussion of World Wide Web in Chapter Two for further information.

USENET. A UNIX based international network, linked to the Internet, that supports the distribution of messages and newsgroups worldwide. Started in 1979, by December 1993 it had around two million users worldwide, with thousands of different newsgroups. Not all Internet users have access to USENET. When they do have access, the commands that they use are different from the usual Internet UNIX commands. There are USENET newsgroups related to many aspects of librarianship and education.

VERONICA. "Very Easy Rodent-Oriented Net-wide Index to Computerized Archives". This software provides keyword access to information stored on gopher servers worldwide. A VERONICA search yields, not the information itself, but a list of menu choices that will lead to the information. VERONICA facilities are made available on many gophers.

VT100. The VT100 was an early and very common computer terminal developed by Digital Equipment Corporation (DEC); it could be used to work on a computer in the same building or in a remote location. Today, most communications software allows a microcomputer to emulate a VT100 terminal, and thus to interact with larger computers. Many host computers on the Internet require remote users to specify the type of terminal they are using, and in these cases, provision is almost always made for VT100 terminals (or for microcomputers that emulate VT100 terminals—to the host, they are the same thing).

W3. See World Wide Web.

WAIS. Wide Area Information Server. Software that allows users to search remote databases and to download information to their own computers. WAIS operates on the client/server model, and is based on the Z39.50 standard for exchanging information between computer systems that are not similar. WAIS can carry out searches of several databases simultaneously, and can retrieve text, pictures, and computer programs.

WAN. Wide Area Network. A network that links computers over hundreds or thousands of miles.

The Web. See World Wide Web.

WHOIS. This Internet command enables users to search for information about Internet addresses and registered users. It can also be implemented on a local host to provide information about users.

Wide Area Information Server. See WAIS.

Wide Area Network. See WAN.

Windows. Software that provides a graphical user interface and operating environment for computers running the MS-DOS operating system.

WinGopher. Gopher "client" software for IBM PC or compatible computers with Windows. It provides a graphical interface for Internet gopher users.

World Wide Web (WWW). This is a hypertext-based information retrieval system for browsing and searching the Internet. It became available late in 1992 and has since become very popular as a means of accessing the Internet.

Other "client" software packages have been developed to work with World Wide Web; these include Mosaic and Xmosaic. See Chapter Two for further information.

WSGopher. Gopher "client" software for IBM PC or compatible computers with Windows. It provides a graphical interface for Internet gopher users.

WWW. See World Wide Web.

Xmosaic. This is World Wide Web browser software for users of IBM PC or compatible computers with XWindows.

XWindows. See Windows.

APPENDIX TWO

SOME USEFUL JOURNALS AND NEWSLETTERS

This Appendix contains a brief list of printed journals and newsletters related to the Internet. Some are also available online, via gopher, the World Wide Web, or ftp. Some are specifically related to education or libraries, though others have more general appeal, while still being useful in the school or library setting. Subscription addresses have been provided.

• ***Boardwatch Magazine*** is a monthly magazine, established in 1987. Topics covered include online databases, commercial online services, electronic bulletin board systems, and other networking systems worldwide. Each issue has listings of bulletin boards, articles on hardware and software, developments in information technology and telecommunications, modem technology, local area networks, and ISDN. The magazine can be purchased from newsagents. It is also available by subscription; contact Boardwatch Magazine, 8500 West Bowles Avenue, Suite 210, Littleton, CO 80123, USA.

• ***Classroom Connect*** is published nine times a year as "the K-12 educator's practical guide to using the Internet and commercial online services". Articles cover current developments on the Internet and provide information about how Internet resources and services are being used in schools; in addition, each issue contains lesson plans that can be copied and used. The magazine has a World

Wide Web page. It is also available by subscription: contact Wentworth Worldwide Media, PO Box 10488, Lancaster, PA 17605-0488, USA.

• *Information Searcher,* a quarterly newsletter for teachers, teacher librarians, and others interested in applications of online searching, CD-ROM, and the Internet in elementary and secondary schools. It is published by Datasearch Group, 14 Hadden Road, Scarsdale, NY 10583, USA.

• *The Internet Letter,* a monthly newsletter published by Net Week Inc., PO Box 33024, Washington, DC 20033-0024, USA, has the banner subtitle "On Corporate Users, Internetworking, and Information Services". The subscription is probably too expensive for schools, but there is useful information about new Internet services, Internet growth, and commercial interests.

• *Internet Research* is a quarterly journal edited by Charles McClure of the School of Information Studies at Syracuse University. It publishes essays on a wide range of topics related to the Internet, including the development of the National Information Infrastructure, experiments in community information systems, work on the "virtual library", electronic publishing, locating resources on the net, and scholarly networking. The journal is published by Meckler Corporation, 11 Ferry Lane West, Westport, CT 06880, USA.

• *Internet World,* a glossy monthly magazine, is published by Meckler Corporation, 11 Ferry Lane West, Westport, CT 06880, USA. Feature articles discuss different types off Internet resources, resources related to particular topics, and Internet search techniques. In addition, there are shorter articles, announcements about new services and publications, selected news items, information about new products. The journal is available from some newsagents and by subscription, and there is also a World Wide Web version.

• *Matrix News* is a monthly journal that is published in online and paper editions by Matrix Information and

Directory Services (with John Quartermain at the helm). The electronic mail address for inquiries is `mids@tic.com`

• ***Multimedia Schools.*** This new journal was announced in March 1994; the first issue was to be published in May 1994. Aimed at school librarians, media specialists, curriculum coordinators, and teachers, the journal's stated coverage is multimedia, CD-ROM, online information services, the Internet, and educational software. An Internet version and a print version were to be available. The publisher is Online Incorporated, of Wilton, Connecticut. Subscription information is available by telephone at 1-800-248-8466 or 1-203-761-1466 and by fax at 1-203-761-1444.

• ***NetTEACH News,*** a "newsletter for pioneer networking K-12 teachers", is published ten times each year. It is available in a print version and an online version. The address is NetTEACH News, 13102 Weather Vane Way, Herndon, VA 22071, USA.

• ***Online Access*** is published eight times each year by Chicago Fine Print Inc., 920 North Franklin, Suite 203, Chicago, IL 60610, USA. It has articles about online information services, the Internet, electronic bulletin boards, search techniques, and industry developments. It also publishes lists of resources, reviews, and information about new products and services.

• ***Wired*** is published monthly by Wired, 544 2nd Street, San Francisco, CA 94107, USA. It covers all aspects of the Internet and online communications in its own inimitable style. It is available from newsagents in North America and by subscription. *Wired* has a World Wide Web page, with information about the magazine, articles, and subscription forms.

• ***3W*** carries the subtitle "a global networking newsletter". It is published six times a year in the United Kingdom and is available by subscription. Contact `3W@ukartnet.demon.co.uk` by electronic mail for further information.

BIBLIOGRAPHY

This bibliography lists published books, articles, and conference papers related to the Internet, and particularly to the use of the Internet in schools and school libraries. Only English-language publications have been included, and preference has been given to more recent material, to 1994.

Aboba, Bernard (1994), *The Online User's Encyclopedia: Bulletin Boards and Beyond,* Addison-Wesley, Reading, Massachusetts.

Angell, David and Heslop, Brent (1994), *The Elements of E-Mail Style,* Addison-Wesley, New York.

Badgett, Tom and Sandler, Corey (1993), *Welcome to...Internet: From Mystery to Mastery,* MIS Press, New York.

Bailey, Charles W. jnr (1991), "Electronic serials on BITNET", *Computers in Libraries* 11, no. 4, April, pp.50–51.

Bailey, Charles W. jnr (1992), "Network-based electronic serials", *Information Technology and Libraries* 11, no. 1, March, pp.29–35.

Baker, Frank M. (1994), "Navigating the network with NCSA Mosaic", *EDUCOM Review* 29, no. 1, January/February, pp.46–51.

Balas, Janet L. (1993), "OPACs and much more", *Computers in Libraries* 13, no. 1, January, pp.28–29. (The Cleveland Free-Net).

Bauwens, Michel (1993), "The poor man's Internet: reaching the networks with e-mail only", *ASLIB Proceedings* 45, no. 7/8, July/August, pp.201–206.

Blau, Andrew (1993), "K-12 access to Internet: securing the legal framework", *Journal of Science Education and Technology* 2, no. 3, pp.497–503.

Bosley, Anuerin (1993), "Internet soup", *Online Access* 8, no. 6, October.

Branscum, Deborah (1993), "Swap tips around the world", *MacWorld*, April, pp.63–67.

Braun, Eric (1994), *The Complete Internet Directory*, Fawcett Columbine, New York.

Breeden, Laura and Bouman, Lawrence (1993), "Demythologizing the Internet: lessons from the real world", *EDUCOM Review* 28, no. 5, September/October, pp.29–35.

Bridges, Karl (1993), "Gopher your library", *Wilson Library Bulletin* 68, no. 3, November, pp.36–38.

Brunell, David H. (1991), "Internetworking services and the electronic library", *Journal of Library Administration* 15, no. 3–4, pp.21–36.

Bull, Glen, Hill, Ida, Guyre, Ken, and Sigmon, Tim (1991), "Building an electronic academic village: Virginia's public education network", *Educational Technology*, April, pp.30–36.

Burgess, John (1993), "Data highways: complex problems of funding, standards, rules remain unresolved as grid's construction begins", *Washington Post*, 2 May.

Burleigh, Mike and Weeg, Patti (1993), "KIDLINK: a challenging and safe place for children across the world", *Information Development* 9, no. 3, September, pp.147–157.

Burrall, Bill (1994), "The electronic teachers' lounge", *The Computing Teacher* 21, no. 6, March, p.41.

Calcari, Susan (1994), "A snapshot of the Internet", *Internet World*, September, pp.54–58.

Carlitz, R. (1992), Internet Connectivity for the K-12 Community: Stages of Implementation. Report to the Internet Engineering Task Force Working Group on School Networking.

Carlitz, R. D. (1991), "Common knowledge: networks for kindergarten through college", *EDUCOM Review* 26, no. 2, pp.25–28.

Carroll, Jim and Broadhead, Rick (1994), *Canadian Internet Handbook*, Prentice-Hall, Ottawa.

Cisler, Steve (1993), "Cool tools: Macintosh software for the Internet", *Apple Library Users Group Newsletter*, Summer, pp.85–89.

Cisler, Steve (1993), "Protection and the Internet", *Apple Library Users Group Newsletter* 11, no. 4, Fall, pp.88–92.

Clark, Allen (1994), "NASA in cyberspace", *Internet World*, September, pp.44–47.

Clarke, Renfrey (1994), "E-mail helps win release of political prisoners", *Institute for Global Communications—NetNews*, January/February.

Clausen, Helge (1991), "Electronic mail as a tool for the information professional", *The Electronic Library* 9, no. 2, pp.73–83.

Clement, Gail P. (1994), "Library without walls", *Internet World*, September, pp.60–64.

Clement, John (1992), "Network based collaborations: how universities can support K-12 reform efforts", *Educom Review* 27, no. 1, pp.8–12.

Clement, John (1992), "Statewide network connections for K-12 educators", *EDUCOM Review* 27, pp.17–20.

Clement, John (1992), "Surveying K-12 and postsecondary school networking partnerships", *EDUCOM Review* 27, no. 4, July-August, pp.44–46.

Clyde, Laurel A. (1993), "The Internet", *Access* 7, no. 2, May, pp.26–29.

Clyde, Laurel A. (1993), "The Internet: a bibliography for teacher librarians", *The Bookmark* (British Columbia Teacher Librarians Association) 34, no. 4, June, pp.46–48.

Clyde, Laurel A. (1994), "Electronic journals on the Internet", *Emergency Librarian* 21, no. 5, May-June, pp.52–54.

Clyde, Laurel A. (1994), "The Internet: a bibliography for teacher librarians, part 2", *The Bookmark* (British Columbia Teacher Librarians Association, 35, 3, March, pp.36-41.

Clyde, Laurel A. (1994), "Internet resources", *Emergency Librarian* 21, no. 4, March-April, pp.52–54.

Clyde, Laurel A. (1994), "Internet resources for school libraries", *Access* 8, no. 2, May.

Coates, James (1993), "The network of networks beckons to determined on-line explorers", *Chicago Tribune*, 4 April, pp.7, 4.

Cohen, M. and Riel, M. (1986), *Computer Networks: Creating Real Audiences for Students' Writing*, (Technical Report 15), Interactive Technology Laboratory, University of California, San Diego.

Collis, Betty and Heeren, Elske (1993), "Tele-collaboration and groupware", *The Computing Teacher*, August/September, pp.36–38.

Cook, Gordon (1993), "Affordable access is the key to NREN's success", *Network World,* 1 March, p.26.

Cooke, Kevin and Lehrer, Dan (1993), "The Internet: the whole world is talking", *The Nation* 257, no. 2, 12 July, pp.60–66.

Corbin, Roberta A. (1991), "The development of the National Research and Education Network", *Information Technology and Libraries* 10, no. 3, September, pp.212–220.

Crowe, Elizabeth Powell (1994), *The Electronic Traveller: Exploring Alternative Online Systems,* Windcrest/McGraw-Hill, n.p.

Dalton, Marian L. (1991), "Does anybody have a map? Accessing information in the Internet's virtual library", *Electronic Networking: Research, Applications, and Policy* 1, no. 1, Fall, pp.31–39.

Decandido, Graceanne A. (1993), "School librarians on the Internet: an online story", *School Library Journal* 39, January, pp.10–11.

Delfino, Erik (1993), "The Internet toolkit: file compression and archive utilities", *Online* 17, no. 6, November, pp.90–92.

Denton, B. (1992), "E-mail delivery of search results via the Internet", *Online,* March, pp.50–53.

Dern, Daniel P. (1992), "Plugging into the Internet", *Byte* 17, no. 10, October, pp.149–152.

Dern, Daniel P. (1993), "Big Sky Telegraph—a low cost approach to bringing the value of telecommunications, teleliteracy, and the Internet to communities", *Internet World* 4, no. 9, November/December, pp.50–61.

Dern, Daniel (1993), "Start here: how and why to join the Internet and get going", *Internet World,* September/October, pp.67–77.

Dern, Daniel (1994), *The Internet Guide for New Users,* McGraw-Hill, New York.

Dern, Daniel P. (1994), "Net profile: interview with Scott Yanoff, creator of the Internet Services List", *Internet World,* January/February, pp.68–78.

Descy, Don E. (1993), "All aboard the Internet", *Tech Trends,* 38, 1, January/February, pp.29–34.

Deutsch, Peter (1994), "Preserving and promoting the 'Internet culture'", *Internet World* 5, no. 2, March/April, pp.52–55.

Deutschman, Alan (1994), "Scramble on the information highway", *Fortune* 129, no. 3, 7 February, pp.73–75.

Dillon, Martin, et al. (1993), *Assessing Information on the Internet: Toward Providing Library Services for Computer Mediated Communications*, OCLC, Dublin, Ohio.

Directory of Electronic Journals, Newsletters, and Academic Discussion Lists (1994), 4th edn, Association of Research Libraries, Chicago.

Dunston, Stuart (1994), "Internet: network of networks", *21C*, 12, Autumn, pp.76–77.

Eagan, Ann (1993), "Order out of chaos: science databases on the Internet", *Database* 16, no. 6, December, pp.62–67.

Eberlee, John (1993), "Backers of FreeNet hope to promote IS literacy", *Computing Canada*, 18 January, p.38. (Canadian FreeNets in Ottawa and elsewhere).

Eisenberg, Michael and Milbury, Peter (1993), "LM_NET: the school library media electronic community", *Information Searcher* 5, no. 2, pp.1, 6–9, 30.

Eisenberg, Michael B. and Ely, Donald P. (1993), "Plugging into the 'net", *Emergency Librarian* 21, no. 2, November-December, pp.8–16.

"Electronic communication at the White House" (1994), *EDUCOM Review* 29, no. 1, January/February, pp.16–18.

Ellsworth, Jill H. (1994), *Education on the Internet: A Hands-On Book of Ideas, Resources, Projects, and Advice*, SAMS Publishing, Carmel, Indiana.

Elmer-Dewitt, Philip (1993), "First nation in cyberspace", *Time*, 6 December, pp.62–64.

Engle, Mary E. (1991), "Electronic paths to resource sharing: widening opportunities through the Internet", *Reference Services Review* 19, no. 4, Winter, pp.7–12.

Engle, Mary E., Lutz, Marilyn, Jones, William W., and Engel, Genevieve (1993), *Internet Connections: A Librarian's Guide to Dial-Up Access and Use*, American Library Association, Chicago.

Engst, Adam C. (1993), *The Internet Starter Kit for Macintosh*, Hayden Books, Indianapolis.

Estrada, Susan (1993), *Connecting to the Internet: An O'Reilly Buyer's Guide*, O'Reilly, Sebastopol, California.

Fahey, Tom (1994), *Net-speak—The Internet Dictionary*, Hayden, New York.

Falk, Bennett (1994), *The Internet Roadmap*, Sybex, San Francisco.

Farley, Laine (ed.)(1992), *Library Resources on the Internet: Strategies for Selection and Use*, Reference and Adult Services Division, American Library Association, Chicago.

Fisher, Sharon (1993), *Riding the Internet Highway*, New Riders, Carmel, Indiana.

Fraase, Michael (1993), *The Mac Internet Tour Guide: Cruising the Internet the Easy Way,* Ventana, Chapel Hill, North Carolina.

Fraase, Michael (1994), *Windows Internet Tour Guide,* Ventana, Chapel Hill, North Carolina.

Gaffin, Adam (1994), "Visiting museums on the Internet", *Internet World* 5, no. 2, March/April, pp.24–29.

Gainor, Larry and Foster, Erin (1993), "Usenet and the library", *Reference Services Review,* Fall.

Gardner, James (1993), *A DOS User's Guide to the Internet,* Mortice Kern Systems, Waterloo, Ontario.

Garton, Andrew (1994), "The net—promise or threat?", *21C,* 12, Autumn, pp.74–76.

Gates, Rick (1993), "Internet cruising with the Internet Hunt", *The Electronic Library* 11, no. 1, February, pp.19–24.

Geffert, Bryn (1993), "Community networks in libraries: a case study of the Freenet P.A.T.H.", *Public Libraries,* March/April, pp.91–99.

Gerber, Cheryl (1993), "Booming commercial use changes the face of Internet: security, legal issues, come up", *Infoworld,* 12 April.

Gerrand, Peter (1994), "Telecommunications trends", *21C,* 12, Autumn, pp.50–54.

Giagnocavo, Gregory, McLain, Timothy, and DiStefano, Vince (1994), *Educator's Internet Companion: Classroom Connect's Complete Guide to Educational Resources on the Internet,* Classroom Connect, Lancaster, Pennsylvania.

Gibbs, Mark and Smith, Richard (1993), *Navigating the Internet,* SAMS Publishing, Carmel, Indiana.

Gibbs, Mark (1994), *Curious About the Internet,* Kantor, New York.

Giguère, Marlene (1992), "An introduction to services accessible on the Internet", *Education Libraries* 16, no. 2, Summer, pp.5–9.

Giguère, Marlene (1993), "The Internet: a selective annotated bibliography of print material", *Education Libraries* 17, no. 2, Summer, pp. 13–20.

Gilster, Paul A. (1993), *The Internet Navigator: A Guide to Network Exploration for the Individual Dial-Up User,* John Wiley, New York.

Godin, Seth (1993), *The Smiley Dictionary,* Peachpit Press, Berkeley, California.

Godin, Seth and McBride, James S. (1994), *1994 Internet White Pages,* IDG Books, San Mateo, California.

Goldberg, F. (1988), "Telecommunications and the classroom: where we've been and where we should be going", *The Computing Teacher* 15, no. 8, pp.26–30.

Goldsmith, John (1993), "Plugging in to the Internet", *The Bookmark* (British Columbia Teacher Librarians Association) 35, no. 2, December, pp.133–138.

Goldsmith, John (1994), "E-mail introduction: your window on the world of Internet", *The Bookmark* (British Columbia Teacher Librarians Association) 35, no. 3, March, pp.141–148.

Goldsmith, John (1994), "Internet interest groups: using e-mail 'lists' with 'listserv'", *The Bookmark* (British Columbia Teacher Librarians Association) 35, no. 4, June, pp.189–198.

Grundner, Tom (1991), "Free-Nets: community information networks and the Internet", *Research and Education Networking* 2, April, p.14.

Grundner, Tom (1992), "Community access—the National Public Telecomputing Network", paper presented at the Merit Networking Seminars, Making Your NSFNET Connection Count, 1–2 June 1992, Las Vegas, Nevada.

Grundner, Tom (1992), "Whose Internet is it anyway?—a challenge", *Online*, July, pp.6–7.

Gumprecht, Blake (1994), "Internet sources of government information", *College and Research Libraries News* 55, no. 1, January, pp.19–22.

Hahn, Harley and Stout, Rick (1993), *The Internet Complete Reference*, McGraw-Hill, New York.

Hahn, Harley and Stout, Rick (1994), *The Internet Yellow Pages*, Osborne, New York.

Harasim, Linda M. (1993), *Global Networks: Computers and International Communication*, MIT Press, Cambridge, Massachusetts.

Harasim, Linda (1993), "Learning to teach online", *TIE (Telecommunications in Education) News* 5, no. 1, Fall, pp.22–27.

Hardie, Edward T. L. and Neou, Vivian (eds)(1993), *INTERNET: Mailing Lists 1993*, (SRI Internet Information Series), Prentice-Hall, Englewood Cliffs, New Jersey.

Harris, Judi (1992), "Mining the Internet: files for free! FTP file transfers on the Internet", *The Computing Teacher* 20, no. 4, December/January, pp.50–52.

Harris, Judi (1992), "Mining the Internet: telnet cornucopia, interactive access to information resources collections", *The Computing Teacher* 20, no. 3, November, pp.38–40.

Harris, Judi (1992), "Mining the Internet: telnet sessions on the Internet", *The Computing Teacher* 20, no. 2, October, pp.40–43.

Harris, Judi (1993), "Mining the Internet: electronic 'packaging' – file types for file transfer", *The Computing Teacher* 21, no. 2, October, pp.33–35.

Harris, Judi (1993–1994), "Mining the Internet: finding folks on the Internet", *The Computing Teacher* 21, no. 4, December/January, pp.49–52.

Harris, Judi (1993), "Mining the Internet: freedom of the (key)press, Internet-based discussion groups", *The Computing Teacher* 20, no. 6, March, pp.52–55.

Harris, Judi (1993), "Mining the Internet: information by (electronic) mail order—FTP gateways and gophers", *The Computing Teacher* 20, no. 7, April, pp.29–32.

Harris, Judi (1993), "Mining the Internet: networked information location tools: gophers, VERONICA, Archie, Jughead", *The Computing Teacher*, August/September, 21, 1 pp.16–19.

Harris, Judi (1993), "Mining the Internet: software searches, gratis graphics, and other FTP treasures", *The Computing Teacher* 20, no. 5, February, pp.33–35.

Harris, Judi (1993), "Mining the Internet: unpacking data after Internet travel, file compression and decrypting", *The Computing Teacher* 21, no. 3, November, pp.47–49.

Harris, Judi (1993), "Mining the Internet: using Internet know-how to plan how students will know", *The Computing Teacher* 20, no. 8, May, pp.35–40.

Harris, Judi (1994), "Mining the Internet: file location and transfer the easy way, Internet-based client software", *The Computing Teacher* 21, no. 8, May, pp.30–33.

Harris, Judi (1994), "Mining the Internet: information collection activities", *The Computing Teacher* 21, no. 6, March, pp.32–36.

Harris, Judi (1994), "Mining the Internet: Mosaic, exploring cyberspace hypertextually", *The Computing Teacher* 22, no. 3, November, pp. 69–71.

Harris, Judi (1994), "Mining the Internet: 'opportunities in work clothes': online problem-solving project structures", *The Computing Teacher* 21, no. 7, April, pp.52–55.

Harris, Judi (1994), "Mining the Internet: people-to-people projects on the Internet", *The Computing Teacher* 21, no. 5, February, pp.48–52.

Harris, Judi (1994), *The Way of the Ferret*, International Society for Technology in Education, Eugene, Oregon.

Haynes, Elizabeth (1993), "Using the Internet in the K-12 environment", *School Library Media Quarterly* 21, no. 3, Spring, pp.187–189.

Herrington, Jim (1993), "Marketing uncontrolled mayhem", *BCLA Reporter*, June, pp.47–49.

Heslop, Brent and Angell, David (1994), *The Instant Internet Guide*, Addison-Wesley, New York.

Higgens, Steve (1993), "Data highway hits political potholes", *PC Week*, 19 April.

Hoffman, Paul E. (1994), *Internet Instant Reference*, Sybex, San Francisco.

Honey, Margaret and Henríquez, Andrés (1993), *Telecommunications and K-12 Educators: Findings From a National Survey*, Center for Technology in Education, Bank Street College of Education, New York.

Howard, Philip M. (1993/94), "Touring the Internet, Macintosh style: a review essay", *CARF (Computer-Assisted Research Forum)* 2, no. 1, Fall/Winter, pp.1–4.

Howley, Craig (1993), "Of ubiquity and the Internet", *Emergency Librarian* 20, no. 4, p.34.

Hughes, Phil (1994), *Internet Public Access Guide,* SSC Publications, New York.

(1994), "Information highway of hypeway?—sceptics question 'gee whiz' claims for the future during conference"(1994), *Globe and Mail,* 2 February.

The Internet in K-12 Education (1993), Department of Engineering and Public Policy, H. John Heinz III School of Public Policy and Management, Carnegie Mellon University, Pittsburgh.

The Internet Unleashed (1994), SAMS Publishing, Carmel, Indiana. (The book comes with a sampler of software on disc.)

Jackson, May E. (1993), "Document delivery over the Internet", *Online,* March, pp.14–21.

Jaffe, Lee (1993), *Introducing the Internet: A Trainer's Workshop,* Library Solutions Press, n.p.

Janis, Jane Klausmeier (1994), "Getting access to the Internet", *Information Searcher* 6, no. 2, pp.19–22, 28.

John, Nancy Regina and Valauskas, Edward J. (1994), *The Internet Troubleshooter: Help for the Logged-On and Lost,* American Library Association, Chicago.

Jordan, John and Brintle, Lee (1993), "Coalition for communication: developing a public communication system", *Computers in Libraries* 13, no. 2, February, pp.29–33.

Joseph, Linda (1994), *World Link: An Internet Guide for Educators, Parents and Students,* Greyden, Columbus, Ohio.

Kantor, Andrew (1994), "Getting on the net", *Internet World,* July/August, pp.26–28.

Kantrowitz, Barbara (1994), "The information gap", *Newsweek,* 21 March, p.78.

Kantrowitz, Barbara (1994), "Men, women, and computers", *Newsweek,* 16 May, pp.36–43.

Kapor, Mitch (1993), "Where is the digital highway really heading?", *Wired* 1, no. 3, July/August, pp.53–59.

Kapor, Mitch (1994), "Song of the open road" (The EL Interview), *Electronic Learning* 13, no. 6, March, p.66.

Kapor, Mitch and Berman, Jerry (1993), "A super highway through the wasteland", *New York Times,* 24 November, p.A25.

Keays, Thomas (1993), "Searching online database services over the Internet", *Online* 17, no. 1, January, pp.30–33.

Kehoe, Brendan (1993), *Zen and the Art of the Internet: A Beginner's Guide to the Internet,* 3rd edn, Prentice-Hall, Englewood Cliffs, New Jersey.

Kehoe, Louise (1993), "Casting the net worldwide", *Financial Times* 30 November, p.11.

Kelly, K. and Rheingold, H. (1993), "The dragon ate my homework", *Wired*, July/August, pp.68–73.

Kelly, M. G. and Webb, James (1994), "Telecommunications, data gathering, and problem solving", *The Computing Teacher* 21, no. 7, April, pp.23–26.

Kent, Peter (1994), *The Complete Idiot's Guide to the Internet*, Alpha Books, New York.

Kesselman, Martin (1992), "The Internet", *Wilson Library Bulletin*, March, pp.76–78.

Kesselman, Martin (1993), "Beyond BITNET: Telneting to the United Kingdom", *College and Research Libraries News* 54, no. 3, March, pp.134–136.

Klensin, John and Bush, Randy (1993), "Expanding international email connectivity: another look", *ConneXions* 7, no. 8, August, pp.25–29.

Kochmer, Jonathan and NorthWestNet (1993), *The Internet Passport: NorthWestNet's Guide to Our World Online*, 4th edn, NorthWestNet, Bellevue, Washington.

Kollasch, M. (1993), "School media matters: modem operandi", *Wilson Library Bulletin*, May, pp.65–66.

Krol, Ed (1993), "How to find resources on the Internet", *Network World*, 15 February, pp.75–76.

Krol, Ed (1993), "Internet's web is doing just fine, thank you", *Network World*, 19 April.

Krol, Ed (1993), *The Whole Internet: User's Guide and Catalog*, O'Reilly and Associates, Sebastopol, California.

Krumenaker, Larry (1993), "BIX: new windows to the Internet", *Online Access* 8, no. 6, October.

Krumenaker, Larry (1994), "When your library card must be a credit card: telnetting to fee-based databanks", *Internet World*, July/August, pp.84–90.

Kuo, Franklin F. (1993), *Internet: Mailing Lists 1993 Edition*, SRI Internet Information Services, New York.

Kurshan, Barbara (1991), "Creating the global classroom for the 21st century", *Educational Technology*, April, pp.47–50.

Ladner, Sharyn J. and Tillman, Hope N. (1993), "Using the Internet for reference", *Online* 17, no. 1, January, pp.45–51.

Lago, Karen Nadder (1993), "The Internet and the public library: practical and political realities", *Computers in Libraries*, October, pp.65ff.

Lambert, Steve and Howe, Walt (1993), *Internet Basics: Your Online Access to the Global Electronic Superhighway*, Random House, New York.

Lane, Elizabeth and Summerhill, Craig (1992), *An Internet Primer for*

Information Professionals: A Basic Guide to Internet Networking Technology, Meckler, Westport, Connecticut.

Langer, Sonia, Ragnarsson, Baldur, Sheridan, Terry, Pugh, Brenda L., Edwald, Birgir, and Kassam, Salimah (1994), "Calling Iceland, are you online?", *TIE (Telecommunications in Education) News* 5, no. 2, pp.20–21.

LaQuey, Tracy and Ryer, Jeanne C. (1992), *The Internet Companion: A Beginner's Guide to Global Networking*, Addison-Wesley, Reading, Massachusetts.

Lára Stefánsdóttir (1993), "Computer communication in Icelandic schools", *TIE (Telecommunications in Education) News* 5, no. 1, Fall, pp.5–7.

Lee, Mal (1994), "The information hhighway and Australia's schools", *Scan* 13, no. 4, October, pp.36–39.

Leslie, Jacques (1993), "Kids connecting: you've heard it before, but this time it's true: online technology can reform our schools" *Wired*, 1,no. 5, November, pp.90–93.

Levine, John R. and Baroudi, Carol (1993), *The Internet for Dummies*, IDG Books, San Mateo, California.

Li, Xia and Crane, Nancy B. (1993), *Electronic Style: A Guide to Citing Electronic Information*, Meckler, Westport, Connecticut.

Lieberman, Dan B. (1994), "Teens for telnet: K-12 and the Internet", *Internet World* 5, no. 1, January/February, pp.38–42.

Littlefield, Sophie (1994), "Connect to the Internet via SLIP or PPP", *Online Access*, November, pp.16–18.

Littlefield, Sophie (1994), "A visit to eworld", *Online Access*, November,pp.44–47.

Lochhead, Shelley (1994), "The Internet: its impact and possibilities", *Information Searcher* 6, no. 2, pp.1, 10–12.

Lukanuski, Mary (1992), "Help is on the WAIS", *American Libraries* 23, no. 9, October, pp.742–744.

MacDougall, Susan (1993), "Internet prospects for Australian public libraries", *Australian Library Journal* 42, no. 3, August, pp.228–233.

MacDougall, Susan (1994), "Internet and public libraries: a challenge or a threat?", *New Librarian*, June, pp.29–33.

Machovec, George S. (1993), *Telecommunications, Networking, and Internet Glossary*, (LITA Monographs, Number 3), American Library Association, Chicago.

Maciuszko, Kathleen (1990), "A quiet revolution: community online systems", *Online*, November, pp.24–32.

MacPhee, Carl (1993), "Driving down the information highway: what's it all about, anyway?", *Feliciter*, April, pp.24–27.

Malamud, Carl (1993), *Exploring the Internet: A Technical Travelogue*, Prentice-Hall, Englewood Cliffs, New Jersey.

Manger, Jason J. (1994), *The Essential Internet Information Guide*, McGraw-Hill, Maidenhead, Berkshire.

Manger, Jason J. (1994), *The World-Wide Web, Mosaic, and More*, McGraw-Hill, Maidenhead, Berkshire.

Marine, April, Kirkpatric, Susan, Neal, Vivian, and Ward, Carol (1992), *Internet: Getting Started*, SRI International, Menlo Park, California.

Markoff, John (1993), "Keeping things safe and orderly in the neighbourhoods of cyberspace", *New York Times* 143, 24 October, p.E7.

Markoff, John (1993), "Traffic jams already on the information highway", *New York Times* 143, 3 November, pp.A1, D9.

Marshall, David L. (1993), "The Internet connection for electronic ordering", *Computers in Libraries* 13, no. 3, March, pp.26–29.

Mattison, David (1992), "Connecting on the net: a virtuall introduction to the global Internet", *The Reporter* (British Columbia Library Association) 36, no. 2, April, pp.33–38.

Mattison, David (1993), "The Victoria Free-Net: A report from Canada's first free-net", *The Reporter* (British Columbia Library Association) 36, no. 3, pp.37–38.

Mattison, David (1994), "Victoria Freenet: year two of Canada's oldest free-net", *The Reporter* (British Columbia Library Association) 38, no. 3, June, pp.19–20.

McClure, Charles (1992), "A user perspective on developing Internet services", *Computers in Libraries* 12, no. 4, April, pp.53–55.

McClure, Charles R., Bertot, John Carlo, and Zweizig, Douglas L. (1994), *Public Libraries and the Internet: Study Results, Policy Issues, and Recommendations*, National Commission on Libraries and Information Science, Washington, DC.

McClure, Charles, Bishop, Ann, Doty, Philip, and Rosenbaum, Howard (1991), *The National Research and Education Network (NREN): Research and Policy Perspectives*, Ablex, Norwood, New Jersey.

McClure, Charles R., Moen, William E., and Ryan, Joe (1994), *Libraries and the Internet/NREN: Perspectives, Issues, and Challenges*, Meckler, Westport, Connecticut.

McClure, Charles et al. (1992), "The role of the public library in the use of the Internet/NREN information services: preliminary findings", in *Proceedings of the ASIS Mid-Year Meeting*, Albuquerque, New Mexico, 27–30 May 1992, pp.46–62.

McKay, Hugh (1994), "Learning to live with technology", *21C*, 12, Autumn, pp.40–41.

Messmer, Ellen (1993), "Internet retrieval tools go on the market", *Network World*, 15 February, pp.29, 77.

Meyer, Michael (1994), "The on-line war heats up", *Newsweek*, 28 March, pp.32–33.

Miller, Elizabeth B. (1994), *The Internet Resource Directory for K-12 Teachers and Librarians*, Libraries Unlimited, Littleton, Colorado.

Morgan, Eric Lease (1993), *WAIS and Gopher Servers: A Guide for Librarians and Internet End-Users*, Meckler, Westport, Connecticut.

"Mosaic: the killer Internet application" (1994), *Internet Business Journal* 1, no. 9, March (special issue).

Murray, Janet (1993), "K12 network: global education through telecommunications", *Communications of the ACM* 36, no. 8, August, pp.36–41.

Naukam, Larry (1993), "Who ya gonna call?", *Apple Library users Group Newsletter* 11, no. 4, Fall, pp.100–105.

Newby, George (1993), *Directory of Directories on the Internet: A Guide to Information Sources*, Meckler, Westport, Connecticut.

Nickerson, Gord (1991), "File transfer protocol", *Computers in Libraries* 11, no. 9, pp.51–53.

Nickerson, Gord (1991), "Networked resources: the Internet", *Computers in Libraries* 11, no. 8, pp.25–29.

Nickerson, Gord (1992), "The Internet gopher", *Computers in Libraries* 12, no. 8, September, pp.53–56.

Nickerson, Gord (1992), "LIBSOFT: the library software archive", *Computers in Libraries* 12, no. 10, November, pp.56–57.

Nickerson, Gord (1992), "WorldWideWeb: Hypertext from CERN", *Computers in Libraries* 12, no. 11, December, pp.75–76.

Nickerson, Gord (1992), "Networked resources: Usenet", *Computers in Libraries* 12, no. 4, pp.31–34.

Nickerson, Gord (1993), "Connecting to the Internet", *Computers in Libraries* 13, no. 3, March, pp.21–25.

Nielsen, Brian (1990), "Finding it on the Internet: the next challenge for librarianship", *Database* 13, no. 5, October, pp.105–107.

Notess, Greg R. (1992), "Gaining access to the Internet", *Online* 16, no. 5, September, pp.27–34.

Notess, Greg R. (1993), "The Internet meets online", *Online* 17, no. 5, September, pp.84–86.

Notess, Greg R. (1993), "Using gophers to burrow through the Internet", *Online* 17, pp.100–102.

Notess, Greg R. (1994), *Internet Access Providers: An International Resource Directory*, Meckler, Westport, Connecticut.

Oakley, Howard (1994), "Highway code", *MacUser*, 4 February, pp.62–66.

On Internet 94: An International Title and Subject Guide to Electronic Journals, Newsletters, Books, and Discussion Lists on the Internet (1994), Meckler, Westport, Connecticut.

OPAC Directory 1994, An Annual Guide to Online Public Access Catalogs and Databases (1994), Meckler, Westport, Connecticut.

Page, Mary (1993), "A personal view of the Internet", *College and Research Libraries News* 54, no. 3, March, pp.127–132.

Patrick, Doyle (1992), "K-12: linking to the national networks", *Computers in Libraries* 12, no. 5, May, pp.61–62.

Perez, Ernest (1992), "PSILink: Internet connection with just a PC and modem", *Library Software Review* 11, May, pp.6–11.

Persson, Eric (1993), *NetPower: Resource Guide to Online Computer Sources*, Fox Chapel, Lancaster, Pennsylvania.

Peterson, Billie (1993), "Tech talk",*LIRT News*, June, pp.12–13.

Pike, Mary Ann and Pike, Tod G. (1994), *The Internet Quickstart*, Que, Inddianapolis.

"Pioneering the electronic frontier" (1993), *US News and World Report*, 6 December. pp.56–62.

Plunkett, Sandy (1994), "The superhighway to a see-through society", *21C*, 12, Autumn, pp.36–39.

Polly, Jean Armour (1992), "Surfing the Internet: an introduction", *Wilson Library Bulletin*, June, pp.38–42, 155.

Polly, Jean Armour (1993), "ALUG online", *Apple Library Users Group Newsletter*, Spring, pp.33–35.

Polly, Jean Armour (1993), "NREN for all: insurmountable opportunity", *Library Journal* 118, no. 2, 1 February, pp.38–42.

Portersfield, Keith W. (1994), "WWWW (What's a World Wide Web?)", *Internet World*, May, pp.20–22.

Quartermain, John S. (1990), *The Matrix: Computer Networks and Conferencing Systems Worldwide*, Digital Press, Bedford, Massachusetts.

Quartermain, John S. (1993), "Internet misconceptions", *Computerworld*, 22 February, p.83.

Quartermain, John S. and Carl-Mitchell, Smoot (1994), *The Internet Connection: Systems Connectivity and Configuration*, Addison-Wesley, New York.

Quint, Barbara (1992), "Online meets the Internet", *Wilson Library Bulletin*, 66, March, pp.78–80.

Randall, Neil (1994), *Teach Yourself the Internet: Around the World in 21 Days*, SAMS Publishing, Carmel, Indiana.

Ratzan, L. (1993), "The Internet cafe", *Wilson Library Bulletin*, 66, May, pp.79–81.

Reinhardt, Andy (1994), "Building the data highway", *Byte* 19, no. 3, March, pp.46–74.

Ressnick, Rosalind (1994), "Newspapers on the net", *Internet World*, July/August, pp.68–73.

"Revolutionizing the way we do things" (1993), *New York Times*, 24 January, pp.3, 6.

Reynolds, Dennis (1993), "Evaluating dial-up Internet access options", *Computers in Libraries* 13, no. 8, September, pp.86–93.

Rheingold, Howard (1993), *The Virtual Community, Homesteading on the Electronic Frontier*, Addison-Wesley, Reading, Massachusetts.

Riel, M. and Levin, J. A. (1990), "Building electronic communities: success and failure in computer networking", *Instructional Science* 19, no. 2, pp.145–169.

Riel, M. (1992/1993), "Telecommunications: avoiding the black hole", *The Computing Teacher*, December/January, pp.16–17.

Riendeau, Mary (1993), "Flames and punishment: Is there justice on the Internet? And if so, where?", *Internet World* 4, no. 9, November/December, pp.72–75.

Ritter, Don (1993), *The Whole Earth Almanac*, Brady, New York.

Roberts, Michael (1992), "A political perspective on the Internet and NREN", *Computers in Libraries* 12, no. 5, May, pp.58–60.

Robison, David F.W. (1993), *All About Internet FTP: Learning and Teaching to Transfer Files on the Internet*, Library Solutions Press, New York.

Rogers, Al (1994), "Living in the global village", *Electronic Learning* 13, no. 8, May/June, pp.28–29.

Rose, M. (1992), "Are you plugged into the global classroom", *American Teacher* 76, no. 6, pp.8–9.

Rose, M. (1993), "Plugging in to the global classroom", *The Education Digest*, January, pp.36–38.

Rose, Marshall T. (1993), *The Internet Message: Closing the Book With Electronic Mail*, Prentice-Hall, Englewood Cliffs, New Jersey.

Rutkowski, Kathy (1994), "The Internet: beyond e-mail", *Information Searcher* 6, no. 2, pp.14–16, 28.

Rutten, Peter, Bayers, Albert, and Moloni, Kelly (1993), *netguide*, Random House, New York.

Sachs, David and Stair, Henry (1994), *Hands-on Internet: A Beginning Guide for PC Users*, Prentice-Hall, Englewood Cliffs, New Jersey.

Saffo, Paul (1994), "The soul of a social machine" (The EL Interview), *Electronic Learning*, February, pp.16–17.

St. Pierre, Margaret (1994), "Wide area information servers (WAIS) over Z39.50-1988 and beyond", *ConneXions* 8, no. 2, February, pp.15–19.

Salvador, Roberta (1994), "The emperor's new clothes", *Electronic Learning* 13, no. 8, May/June, pp.32–44.

Sanderson, David W. and Dougherty, Dale (1993), *Smileys*, O'Reilly and Associates, Sebastopol, California.

Saunders, Laverna (1993), "Exploring library resources on the Internet", *Internet World* 4, no. 9, November/December, pp.44–49.

Savetz, Kevin M. (1994), "Internet games", *Internet World*, May, pp.28–33.

Savetz, Kevin M. (1994), "MUDs, MUDs, glorious MUDs", *Internet World* 5, no. 2, March/April, pp.46–51.

Savetz, Kevin (1994), *Your Internet Consultant: The FAQs of Life Online*, SAMS Publishing, Carmel, Indiana.

"SchoolNet – Canada's national educational networking initiative" (1994), *TIE (Telecommunications in Education) News* 5, no. 2, p.17.

Schrum, Lynne (1994), "What can you get professionally online?", *TIE (Telecommunications in Education) News* 5, no. 2, pp.8–12.

Schwartz, Dave (1992), "The Internet: pushing the envelope of current knowledge", *Information Searcher* 4, no. 4, pp.15–17.

Scott, Michael (1992), "Patching into the Internet", *Vancouver Sun*, 11 December, p.D11.

Shannon, L.R. (1993), "Getting your feet wet in a sea called Internet", *New York Times*, 26 October.

Shea, Virginia (1994), *Netiquette*, Albion Books, San Francisco.

Silva, Marcos and Cartwright, Glenn F. (1993), "The Internet as a medium for education and educational research", *Education Libraries* 17, no. 2, Summer, pp.7–12.

Simmonds, C. (1993), "Searching Internet archive sites with ARCHIE: why, what, where, and how", *Online* 17, March, pp.50ff.

Simms, Jan and Simms, Bruce (1994), "The electronic generation connection: elementary students and senior citizens meet as partners online", *The Computing Teacher* 21, no. 7, April, pp.9–11.

Singh, Jagtar and Meadows, Jack (1993), "Electronic serials for library and information specialists on Internet", *ASLIB Proceedings* 45, no. 9, September, pp.234–241.

Skrzycki, Cindy (1993), "Dark side of the data age", *Washington Post*, 3 May, p.19. (A discussion of privacy on the Internet and other information "highways").

Smith, Jane (1994), "Hypatia screamed", *Internet World* 5, no. 1, January/February, pp.86–89.

Smith, Richard and Gibbs, Mark (1993), *Navigating the Internet*, SAMS Publishing, Carmel, Indiana.

Sneesby, Guy (1994), "A brave new eworld", *MacUser*, 4 February, pp.68–69.

Snyder, Joel (1994), "Diving into the Internet: the trouble with gopher", *Internet World* 5, no. 2, March/April, pp.30–35.

Stapleton, Ross (1993), "What's NREN", *Online Access* 8, no. 6, October.

Stewart, Tom (1994), "The Netplex: it's a new Silicon Valley", *Fortune*, 7 March.

Still, Julie and Alexander, Jan (1993), "Integrating Internet into reference: policy issues", *College and Research Libraries News* 54, no. 3, March, pp.139–140.

Still, Julie (ed.)(1994), *The Internet Library: Case Studies of Library Internet Management and Use*, Meckler, Westport, Connecticut.

Stix, Gary (1993), "Domesticating cyberspace", *Scientific American* 269, no. 2, August, pp.100–110.

Stout, Connie (1991), TENET: Texas Education Network. ERIC Document ED 350 992.

Strangelove, Michael (1993), "The essential Internet", *Online Access* 8, no. 6, October.

Strangelove, Michael (1993), "Free-Nets: community computing and the rise of the electronic citizen", *Online Access,* Spring, pp.46–47.

Strangelove, Natalie (1993), "Free Internet tips and tools", *Online Access* 8, no. 6, October.

Tannen, Deborah (1994), "Gender gap in cyberspace", *Newsweek,* 16 May, pp.40–41.

Taylor, Dave (1994), "Commercial services on the Internet", *Internet World,* July/August, pp.74–79.

Teles, L. and Duxbury, N. (1991), *The Networked Classroom: An Assessment of the Southern Interior Telecommunications Project (SITP) Phase 1,* Faculty of Education, Simon Fraser University, Burnaby, British Columbia.

Tennant, Roy, Ober, John, and Lipow, Anne G. (1993), *Crossing the Internet Threshold: An Instructional Handbook,* Library Solutions Institute, Berkeley, California.

Tenopir, Carol (1992), "Online searching with Internet", *Library Journal* 117, December, pp.102ff.

Tenopir, Carol (1993), "Hot topics for the new year", *Library Journal,* December, pp.94–96.

Todino, Grade and Dougherty, Dale (1991), *Using UUCP and Usenet,* O'Reilly and Associates, Sebastopol, California.

Truett, Carol (1994), "The Internet: what's in it for me?", *The Computing Teacher* 22, no. 3, November, pp.66–68.

Trujillo, Gary S. (1993), "NativeNet: electronic communications from the Arctic to Amazonia and beyond", *TIE (Telecommunications in Education) News* 4, no. 3–4, pp.9–10.

Tuss, Joan (1994), "Roadmaps to the Internet: finding the best guidebook for your needs", *Online,* January, pp.14–26.

"US President and Vice President announce electronic mail addresses" (1993), *TIE (telecommunications in Education) News* 4, no. 3/4, p.5.

Valauskas, Edward J. (1993), "TurboGopher: Internet access with ease on the Macintosh", *Online* 17, no. 2, March, pp.87–89.

Valauskas, Edward J. (1993), "Using the Internet in libraries", Paper presented at the 59th IFLA General Conference, Barcelona, Spain, August. (184-GUEST-E).

Veljkov, Mark and Hartnell, George (1994), *Pocket Guides to the Internet, Volume 1—Telnetting,* Meckler, Westport, Connecticut.

Veljkov, Mark and Hartnell, George (1994), *Pocket Guides to the Internet,*

Volume 2—Transferring Files With File Transfer Protocol, Meckler, Westport, Connecticut.

Veljkov, Mark and Hartnell, George (1994), *Pocket Guides to the Internet, Volume 3—Using and Navigating Usenet,* Meckler, Westport, Connecticut.

Veljkov, Mark and Hartnell, George (1994), *Pocket Guides to the Internet, Volume 4—The Internet E-Mail System,* Meckler, Westport, Connecticut.

Veljkov, Mark and Hartnell, George (1994), *Pocket Guides to the Internet, Volume 5—Basic Internet Utilities,* Meckler, Westport, Connecticut.

Veljkov, Mark and Hartnell, George (1994), *Pocket Guides to the Internet, Volume 6—Terminal Connections,* Meckler, Westport, Connecticut.

Ward, Lynn (1993), "Exploring the power of the Internet gopher", *Library Technology News* 8, June/July, pp.1–3.

Wasman, Wendy (1993), "Ask Dr Dino, or, my life as an electronic reptile", *American Libraries,* February, pp.122–123. (The Cleveland Free-Net, a community network for children and adults on the Internet).

Watson, Ian (1993), "The great electronic information bazaar—a rough guide to exploring the Internet", *ASLIB Proceedings* 45, no. 6, June, pp.153–159.

"A web of networks, an abundance of services" (1993), *New York Times,* 28 February, p.3, 8.

Wibe, Jan (1994), "Nordic network in data communication", *TIE (Telecommunications in Education) News* 5, no. 2, pp.18–19.

Wighton, David J. (1993), "Telementoring: examining the potential for an educational network", *TIE (Telecommunications in Education) News* 4, no. 3–4, pp.13–16.

Williams, Brian (1992), "Libraries, listservs, and LITA", *Computers in Libraries* 12, no. 5, May, pp.45–57.

Wyatt, Brett (1992), "Bringing Internet to Nevada schools", in Warner, Virginia R. (ed.), *Hands Across the World—Linking Today With Tomorrow, 5th International Conference of Computer Pals Across the World, Reno, Nevada, 9–12 July 1992,* Computer Pals Across the World, Reno, pp.52–54.

INDEX

ABOUT THE AUTHOR

Laurel A. Clyde (BA, DipEd, MA, Sydney University; PhD, James Cook University of North Queensland) is currently a Professor in the Faculty of Social Science at the University of Iceland in Reykjavik. An Australian, Anne began her career as a teacher and teacher librarian in schools in New South Wales, before moving into research and university teaching. Since then, she has taught at four universities and colleges in her home country, and at the University of British Columbia in Vancouver, Canada, as well as in Iceland. Her teaching subjects include online searching, library automation, and school librarianship. She is also an Internet trainer, and has produced a series of Internet manuals for librarians, teachers, lawyers, journalists, and healthcare workers) to support her workshops and courses. She set up the IASL-LINK listserv on the Internet for the International Association of School Librarianship (IASL) early in 1995, and she is also the Internet Webmaster for the Association. For the last five years, she has written a regular column called "InfoTech" for the North American school library journal *Emergency Librarian*, and from 1988 to 1995 she wrote a regular section on "Computers in School Libraries" for the Australian national school library journal *Access*. Among her books *are Computer Applications in School Libraries* (1993*), Computer Software for School Libraries: A Directory* (1989), and (with Robert Sharman) *Western Perspectives: Library and Information Services in Western Australia* (1990). In 1995/1996 she edited *Sustaining the Vision: A Collection of Articles and Papers on Research in School Librarianship, in Honor of Jean E. Lowrie*, for IASL. *School Libraries and the Electronic Community: The Internet Connection* is her first book for Scarecrow Press.